WORKRIGHTS

WORKRIGHTS

Robert Ellis Smith

E.P. Dutton, Inc.   New York

Published in the United States by E.P. Dutton, Inc.,
2 Park Avenue, New York, N.Y. 10016

Library of Congress Catalog Card Number: 83-70192

ISBN: 0-525-24179-5 cl
          0-525-48047-1 pa

Published simultaneously in Canada by Clarke, Irwin & Company Limited,
Toronto and Vancouver

10 9 8 7 6 5 4 3 2 1

First Edition

To Katya

"Every time I passed through those plant gates to go to work, I left America, and my rights as a free man. I spent nine hours in there, in prison, and then came out into my country again."

—a General Motors worker at Lordstown, Ohio

CONTENTS

PART I

The Tyranny of the Workplace

PART II

Fourteen Freedoms in the Workplace

PART III

Self-Determination in the Workplace

Why Workrights:
A Personal Checklist

What in the world does a self-employed writer know about the world of the corporate workplace? What am I doing writing a book about employers when I myself don't have an employer?

Instead of providing the usual biographic laurels at the end of this book, I decided to begin with a chronicle of my own work history. My first experiences in the organized workplace were pleasant enough; it took me a while to understand the plight of employees in America.

I began my career as a reporter for a major newspaper in the Midwest. I was eager and motivated. The people there seemed to like my work and I enjoyed the place. But I now recall that my original interview for the job was rather stiff. Prior to that, I had been subjected to interviews only by college admissions officers, each of whom seemed interested in me, receptive to having me show them my best (even though they had seen hundreds more like me before). In the job interview with the president of the newspaper company, there was a certain uncomfortable rigidity. The president was probing for something *wrong* with me. Or so I felt. For the first time I was a supplicant, *an employee*.

On my second day on the job, I submitted to an inane and intrusive psychological test. The whole exercise seemed senseless to me. I had already been hired by the head of the company and by the editor of the newspaper, and I had even begun work. If I didn't work out, I could be terminated before the end of my probationary period. But apparently the personnel director liked to give tests and no one dared stop him. That newspaper company is still a leader in administering Orwellian tests. Only a few of us stop to ask what those questions have to do with performing jobs. I was not one of those who raised the question.

Like most people, I was somewhat flattered to be asked questions about myself. More important, in the first week on the job, I was eager to please.

It was not long before I discovered cynicism around the office. In fact it was pervasive. Most of my middle-aged colleagues couldn't join in my enthusiasm for the job. They couldn't even encourage me to stay in the newspaper business. They were, many of them, simply beaten down. Much of their free time at work was spent fantasizing about owning their own newspapers. Most of all, my coworkers couldn't stand my willingness to work extra hours. I was happy to do it as long as I was productive.

Of course, I was single then and had plenty of free time. I became an officer of the local unit of the Newspaper Guild, the reporters' union, mainly because only a handful of my colleagues were interested in running. I became involved not because I disliked my work but because I enjoyed it so much and wanted to keep it enjoyable. I had read about inflexible work rules written into labor contracts and I wanted to do what I could to keep the office rules flexible. At the same time, I sensed that without constant monitoring by employees, management would take short cuts and erode established employee benefits.

After a year on the job, I had an opportunity to travel to Europe with friends. I figured that I would not have the chance again to take such a trip and that the travel would broaden my perspective as a news reporter. Without hesitation, I planned to ask for a leave of absence for a month and was prepared to quit if it was not granted. The editor of the paper didn't see the trip my way. He regarded my request for a leave as highly irregular. He could not see how my travel would benefit the company. But he reluctantly agreed to my request.

Just a month after my return, it was necessary for me to take another leave, this one a compulsory leave for military service. I was drafted into the U.S. Army for two years. There I learned many of the negative work habits I came to write about in this book, especially trying to get by with as little work as possible. There was strong peer pressure to do this in the army. You couldn't admit that you were even slightly conscientious about your job. (It occurred to me that this widespread military goldbricking had shaped the attitudes of a lot of my coworkers at the newspaper, most of them recent veterans. These people weren't necessarily lazy—and they weren't limited to the lower ranks of employment; there were plenty in management positions—but they were ashamed to admit that they cared about their work. Their attitudes had a great influence on the workplace, at least in my experience.)

To relieve the tedium and low self-esteem in enlisted military life, I took an evening job at a nearby newspaper. Although my schedule was demanding, I learned the value of moonlighting as a way of varying my work experience so that no single job was debilitating. Ever since then I have worked at more than one job at a time.

I felt a revival of job enthusiasm in 1965 when, out of the service, I became the editor of a small weekly newspaper covering the civil rights movement in the South. The staff was full of idealistic young people united in their common purpose. They made me think of John F. Kennedy's response, two years earlier, when asked whether he enjoyed his job as president. He answered affirmatively, recalling Aristotle's definition of happiness as the full use of one's faculties along lines of excellence. The newspaper did not pay much, but even the older staff members enjoyed coming to work because our goal was worthwhile and we were busy enough not to have time for intraoffice fighting.

Eventually I returned to the Midwest paper where I had begun my career. I was married now, and immediately I sensed a conflict between my work life and my home life. I came to feel guilty about the amount of time I spent at work. I objected to working a night shift that as a single person I would not have minded. It became difficult to reconcile my home life and my work life. Was it impossible to enjoy both?

Because the newspaper could not accommodate my request for a shift that was more compatible with my home life, I left. I joined a newspaper in New York, where the corporate rigidity was even greater. For the first time, I knew the misery of working for supervisors whom I did not respect or like. As hard as I tried, I could not fit in and get along. Nothing worked.

The pay was good, however. Twice a year, in June and at Christmas, the payroll department would distribute generous bonus checks. Each time the bonus seemed a surprise, and each time I would forgive the company its transgressions for another six months.

Still, the bonus checks did not prevent the daily frustrations of the job. I developed a terrible knot in my stomach when it came time to go to work each day. I was rescued by a friend who had a top management position at the newspaper. At first he did no more than sympathize with my complaints (and reveal to me that he was powerless to change the bureaucracy), and this was helpful, but soon he assigned me to a pleasant position in a remote division of the organization. This was the first of several positions in which I worked for bosses who were also friends. These fortunate arrangements shielded me from the utter despair that many people feel in an unhappy work environment. I could still sense these feelings in others, even though I did not experience them firsthand.

I knew that it was not the *size* of the bureaucracy that was creating the unpleasantness, but its rigidity and impersonality. So, when I moved to Washington to work for a huge government agency, I was not apprehensive. In fact, I became exhilarated by the responsibilities, the influence, the intellectual challenge of my new job as press officer in the Department of Health, Education and Welfare. I discovered that there were fewer taboos in government work than in the private sector. My coworkers seemed receptive to new ideas. I think this was true because government employees performed with a sense of security that their jobs would not be snatched away from them because of a single unorthodoxy. Managers in the corporate world belittle this civil-service protection because it creates lots of deadwood around the office. That is true, but it also permits creative employees to take creative risks that benefit the organization.

The drawback of a huge bureaucracy, on the other hand, was that a scandalous proportion of time was consumed by bureaucratic infighting, not all of it related to the mission of the organization. Personality conflicts, prerogatives of entrenched employees, paperwork, approvals, regulations, individual sensitivities, allocation of space and perquisites—all of them occupied a lot of my time and gnawed at my insides. There was hardly time to devote to the substance of our work. There was always a trivial obstacle.

I could not avoid carrying the office tensions home with me. It was difficult to "shift gears" from the complexity and intensity of the workplace to the different demands at home. I wished for a decompression chamber that would ease the daily transition from work to home. Perhaps that is what many working people find in neighborhood taverns on their way home and what others find in the solitude of commuting home by automobile.

In contrast to the huge bureaucracy, my next job was for a small public-interest organization with a half-dozen employees in Washington. Once again I was working for a friend and the office environment was stimulating (although I missed the influence of government work). For the first time, I saw the constant conflicts between the Washington office and the national headquarters of the organization. This is a phenomenon I think exists in many companies and government agencies. Workers around the country think the home office is always dispatching stupid directives from people who don't know what's going on in the real world. Headquarters staff think that people "in the field" are ignorant and unresponsive.

As part of this job I developed a newsletter on the right to privacy. At this point I discovered what I had really wanted to do all along—work as a journalist without the encumbrances of an organization. Before long, I figured that I could produce a newsletter better on my own and have the added gratification of working for myself, not someone else.

Thus, in 1974, I began my own newsletter and called it *Privacy Journal.* I reveled in the freedom of making my own decisions, and living with the consequences. I could not blame some other person or entity when things went wrong. I did not have to share my accomplishments with others who had not contributed to them, or worse, with a faceless organization. *My* name and reputation were at stake.

I came to appreciate that while self-employed persons don't necessarily do things better—surely they don't produce more than large organizations—they do have the satisfaction of knowing that they did it *their* way. In an age of eight-lane highways, they take the meandering country roads. In an age of supermarkets, they remain the corner grocery stores.

In the course of editing my newsletter, I compiled enough information to write a book on the right to privacy. In the book, *Privacy: How to Protect What's Left of It,* I asked readers to write to me with their experiences with regard to invasions of privacy. And they did. Most of the complaints involved employment—access to personal files, pre-employment inquiries, searches of desks and lockers, an employer's interference with one's home life or sex life, obnoxious questionnaires. It became clear that privacy—an issue that is commonly thought to involve personal affairs —actually raises more employment concerns than personal concerns.

People were concerned about privacy largely because of its importance to their status as employees: They wanted medical information to remain confidential not so much because it might be embarrassing among their friends but because the information might affect them adversely at work, might cost them a promotion. They were concerned about intrusive searches and seizures not so much by law enforcement officers but by their superiors at work. People worried about damaging credit files because the records could affect their jobs as well as their ability to make purchases.

The responses to the privacy book led to this book. I looked into the legal status of all individual rights in the workplace, not just privacy rights. I set out to compile a book that for the first time would tell employees and managers alike just what individual rights and obligations exist in today's workplace and which would be recognized in the future.

In attending conventions and conferences of professional people, I became aware of discontent in the workplace at all levels, from top to bottom. Sometimes those at the top were more victimized than those at the bottom. Although these men and women were motivated by the substance of their chosen work, each time the conversation turned to their individual job situations there would be groans, sighs of resignation, or cynical wisecracks.

That dissatisfaction in the workplace of the 1980s and the nascent legal recognition of it are what this book is about. Once again, I invite readers who have personal experiences involving the issues in this book to write to me. The address is *Privacy Journal,* P.O. Box 8844, Washington, D.C. 20003.

Robert Ellis Smith

PART I
THE TYRANNY
OF THE WORKPLACE

1

Introduction

Since the New Deal, it's been fashionable to marvel at the extent of government involvement in what used to be our private decisions. This is true enough. But in the economy of the 1980s, it is the private corporation, not the government, that has the life-and-death power to hire and fire, to transfer to an isolated site, to cut off family health benefits, to curtail freedom of expression, to alter family activities, and to leave psychological as well as physical scars.

It's not the government that forces us to combat the traffic-clogged freeway for an hour each morning and an hour each evening. It's our employer. It's not the government that forces us to choose between a crucial meeting at work and our child's school play. It's our employer. It's not the government that ties our stomachs in knots with bureaucratic hassles. It's our employer.

Yet, we would sooner confront a police officer, who represents the power of the government, than to incur the wrath of our supervisor, who represents the power of our employer.

The reason we are tyrannized by our employers is, of course, that employers are the source of our paychecks—our livelihood. But our jobs represent much more. They are now the source of insurance coverage for ourselves and our families, of paid leisure time, and much of our socialization. Our work is also the source of our dignity. For most Americans, our professions *are* our identities. "What do you do?" is the first question asked at a cocktail party or in an airport waiting area, not "Who are you?" or "What interests you?" Our work holds the key to our dignity. Without it, our self-esteem crumbles. With it, there is always the possibility of realizing our aspirations. We *are* our work.

In order to hold on to this source of our identities, many Americans have had to swallow hard and accept the unacceptable at work. They find themselves putting up with arbitrary policies and rules, bureaucratic bickering, intransigent supervision, and an environment that is demoralizing.

In the past century and before, the work of Americans was most likely even less tolerable, but at least the organizations for whom they worked were not quite so intimidating. Many Americans worked for themselves. Many more worked for small enterprises in which the boss worked right along with his employees. If the situation got bad, the employee could at least find a way to "Go West" and start anew. In the previous century, even those who worked for what were then powerful corporations were employed by relatively small organizations. On the eve of the Civil War, the McCormick tractor plant in Chicago, for example, then the largest of its kind in the world, employed only 123 people, including those in the front office.[1]

As we approach the end of the twentieth century, most

of us are employed by large corporations. The Fortune 500 alone (the largest industrial corporations in the nation) employ 15 percent of the nation's work force, and the smallest of the Fortune 500 companies employs more than 1,000 persons. Sixty-five percent of us are beholden to a private employer (not the government) for the essentials of the good life. And most of those 65 percent working in private employment are employed by huge corporations, where there has never been a premium on individuality or autonomy. No longer is it a viable alternative to "Go West, young man." A person will likely encounter identical conditions at the competing company across town or across the nation, where union restrictions or corporate bureaucracies are equally dehumanizing.

This life-and-death reliance on our employment comes at a time when the individual's leverage vis-à-vis the large private organization is significantly less than his leverage vis-à-vis his government. This is true because our large body of constitutional protections applies *only to actions by the government,* not to actions by private organizations. We have no constitutionally guaranteed right of free speech as an employee, although we do as a citizen. We have no protection against unreasonable searches by a private corporation, even though we do have constitutional protection against such searches by the government. The constitution also protects us from going to jail without an opportunity to confront our accusers. The constitution does not protect us from losing our employment without such an opportunity.

Ironically, the actions of our government agencies are more closely scrutinized by ourselves as voters and by the press as our proxies than are the actions of large businesses. Businesses undoubtedly have a greater effect on our well-being, and therefore on the morale of the nation as a whole, than does our government, but the press does not show the same interest. Most newspapers and television stations have a full-time representative covering Washington, but how many assign someone even part-time to cover the community's largest employer? It is harder for reporters to cover private corporations, because their rights of access are less and the possibilities of retaliation are greater than with regard to the government. And so news people overload us with news about government, when in the 1980s what private businesses are doing is much more relevant to most of our lives.

There is another reason why Americans' leverage with private business is less than it is with government. That is the nature of contemporary capitalism itself. The premium in our economic system, as it has evolved, is in protecting one's own turf, not maximizing profits. The premium is in expanding facilities, not maximizing profits. The premium is on enhancing one's reputation as a professional in one's chosen field, not in working with one's colleagues to produce a better product or service. In such an environment, should it be any surprise that everybody in the organization, whether in the front office or the plant, is demoralized about the possibilities of cooperative action? Even the persons responsible for improving personnel policies are victims of this environment. They say *their* hands are tied, too. The individual employee fighting to preserve his self-respect is left to battle a faceless bureaucracy. At least in dealing with government bureaucracies, the citizen can resort to political pressure.

This negative feeling about our workdays intensified at a time in the late 1970s when general prosperity and new employment opportunities brought salaries and wages to all-time highs. In fact, the pressure by employees for larger and larger paychecks came in part because employees felt they didn't given a damn about the company.

By 1980 and 1981, all the indicators of employee dissatisfaction reached new highs. Opinion Research Corp., which has studied changing attitudes about work for the past twenty-nine years, reported in 1981 that:

American workers at all levels are more dissatisfied in their jobs than at any time in the past twenty-eight years. Middle managers are more unhappy and feel less secure in their jobs than ever before. Clerical workers, blue-collar workers, and managers especially are becoming increasingly critical of the abilities of top management.[2]

Part of the reason for this is that the work force itself had changed. In the 1970s, it became younger, much better educated. It was scattered with new faces—women, blacks, other minorities, the handicapped, members of "two-paycheck families." These new people on the scene were not overly grateful for this new access. On the contrary, they were well practiced in exerting their rights. They had fought discriminatory hiring and promotion policies to get their jobs; they were not about to stop there. They had not lived through the Depression, an experience that had made its survivors feel satisfied just to have a regular paycheck. Joined by other discontented employees already at the company, these new employees pressed for increased recognition of their rights on the job. They tried to loosen the stiff, confining structure of the workplace. They demanded more prerogatives. Employees felt they should be compensated for "all the grief" they got at work—and the grief they found themselves bringing home from work.

A succession of experts have addressed the problem of worker discontent as one of "scientific management," "work welfare," "industrial democracy," "quality of work," and "productivity." Thus, the issue has been seen essentially as a management problem confined to the workplace. In the 1980s, it must be seen as a broader social problem. Worker discontent has spilled over into family life, community life, and political life.

Let there be no doubt that this discontent on the job

takes its toll—outside the workplace. One study showed that men who feel they have little autonomy at work take out their hostilities on their sons at home. Blue-collar workers unhappy at work are less progressive in their politics and use their leisure time less well than employees with better work situations.[3]

"At the plant, the worker's name is 'Hey you,'" says industrial engineer Mitchell Fein. "At home, he's a father, a husband, a community worker." But it's harder and harder for a man to stand tall in those roles if he's treated like a child or a criminal for nearly half of his waking hours, when he is at work.

Dr. Elliott Liebow of the Center for Work and Mental Health at the National Institute of Mental Health, explained the connection: "Job stress may be a very personal experience, but it is by no means a private one. It's crucial to realize that the stresses experienced by the worker and his or her reaction to them—depression, anxiety, anger, boredom, shame—or respiratory, blood pressure, or stomach problems—that these things do not stay in the workplace. The worker takes them home, where they shape his or her relationship with his or her family and friends. These stresses are diffused throughout the community."[4]

An Arizona woman was driven to neurotic depression and an overdose of pills because of pressure at work. A truck driver in New Jersey lost fifty pounds, attempted suicide twice, moved away from home, and was unable to find work again, all because of a traumatic experience at his place of employment.

Barbara Garson, in her 1975 account of work drudgery, *All the Livelong Day,* wrote that after a day in the typing pool she didn't feel like enhancing her knowledge or shopping for just the right item. She was mentally and physically exhausted, even though she did more physical work when she stayed home. "But of course the work I do for myself involves physical strains that tax me, satisfactions that revive me, and repetitious work that actually soothes me,"[5]

Garson wrote. She was not the first person to discover that after a day in the American workplace, whether in an office, shop, or truck, one is not suited to be an adequate spouse, parent, intellectual companion, or lover.

"Working with a computer eight hours a day is the worst possible prologue I can think of to going home and trying to have an interpersonal relationship," says Fernando Bartolome, a professor of organizational behavior who has studied the family lives of busy professionals. Bartolome's observation is particularly important because a larger and larger share of the work of the 1980s involves computers and other automated devices.

Even the on-camera personalities on NBC's "Today Show," who know the glamor and rewards of high-powered television jobs in New York City, showed discontent. After a film report that portrayed bickering, one of them cracked, "Looks like one of our staff meetings." The show is full of ad libs about the frustration of working at NBC. In 1980, Tom Brokaw, Jane Pauley, and Gene Shalit showed great delight in substituting another song for their usual "Today Show" theme. The song struck a chord among the American people. It was a popular hit that year. The song was "Take This Job and Shove It" by Johnny Paycheck.

And that was the way millions of Americans started the day. Everywhere they turned (even then, in a period of relative prosperity), Americans found evidence of unhappiness at work.

Clearly this demoralization of the work force is responsible in large part for the decline in American productivity in recent years. Even the most oblivous executives seem to sense that. But it is rare that this discontent is identified as a factor in the major societal trends of our times: stress, divorce, mental illness, alcoholism and drug abuse, physical illnesses like cancer and heart failure, auto accidents, teenage delinquency, a general distrust of all our institutions, a decline in respect for our fellow citizens, friction between the races.

As a nation, we have even taken to electing as our presidents vibrant men with great ideas and intentions who soon get swamped in the quagmire of their job. Editorial cartoonists, Washington columnists, and the rest of us seem to delight in portraying our presidents as overwhelmed by their jobs. Since John F. Kennedy, the portrait of our president has been that of a man beleaguered by his work, rendered powerless by the surrounding bureaucracy. We see our presidents enjoying themselves only when they are away from their work, or retired from it. And that seems to be the only time we like them.

This portrait of our presidents simply mirrors what many Americans feel about themselves—happy in the leisure activities that higher salaries have made possible and desperately unhappy on the job. People who are unhappy are people who are angry. Angry people eventually react with confrontation.

To reclaim their identities, many workers reasserted themselves in the previous decade in the best way they knew how. They tried to bring to the workplace the individual rights they had gained in their personal and political lives. To secure these rights in the workplace, they went to the same places where they had won their political and personal rights—to the courts, to Congress, and to state legislatures. In the 1970s, in a time of employment for just about everyone, discontented employees filed lawsuits and lobbied legislatures for changes in the way employees were treated. In a time of relative economic stability and prosperity, courts and legislatures were willing to grant these new rights. But the lawsuits took three or four years to develop and to bring to the highest courts in the nation, then an additional three or four years to have an effect in the workplace. The lobbying took a similarly lengthy period and afterward it took additional years for the executive branch to set up enforcement mechanisms.

Thus, the *effects* of the lawsuits and the legislation of the 1970s were just being fully felt in the American workplace in the early 1980s. In the 1970s individual workers claimed in the workplace the rights just previously won outside of the workplace—freedom to participate, an opportunity to change the environment, rights to due process. Now, even in a time of economic retrenchment, these efforts are having their effect. Even though job opportunities have been reduced, important new employment rights are on the books. They affect health and safety, pensions, sex harassment, equal opportunity, freedom of speech, fringe benefits, privacy at work, and abusive firings.

American courts and legislatures have virtually eliminated the traditional view of the American workplace as a master-servant relationship. And they are moving closer to eliminating the traditional view that private organizations in the United States are relatively free of constitutional restrictions.

2

Shaping the Tradition

Workers have always been at the mercy of their employers. Employees in the 1980s can at least take heart that the trend in the last 100 years has been inexorably toward increased recognition of individual rights in the workplace.

The relationship has been one of "master-servant" since the earliest days. And the authority of the master included the ultimate weapon—"the right to terminate at will." One of the first legal codes known to man, the Code of Hammurabi, who was king of ancient Babylon until 1750 B.C., recognized the right of the master to employ whomever he wished and to use his servant in whatever way he wished. The Roman legal code, which recognized essentially the same master-servant relationship, served as a model for our Anglo-Saxon legal heritage. When English law was transferred to the young American nation, courts here accepted the master-servant analogy as appropriate to the employer-employee relationship. At least this meant that the employer, as master, bore a paternalistic responsibility for the servant's welfare. Toward the middle of the nineteenth century, this obligation disappeared as American courts began to view the employer-employee relationship as no more than a contract between equals.

The employer owed nothing to the worker aside from what he had promised, and vice versa.

In 1908, the U.S. Supreme Court described the employment relationship:

The right of a person to sell his labor upon such terms as he deems proper is, in its essence, the same as the right of the purchaser of labor to prescribe the conditions upon which he will accept such labor from the person offering to sell it. So the right of the employee to quit the service of the employer, for whatever reason, is the same as the right of the employer, for whatever reason, to dispense with the services of such employee.[6]

And so the tradition developed—with the support of the courts—that an employer owned the body and soul of a person at work, and even after work. In the 1830s, for example, the thriving textile mills of New England provided their own boardinghouses for employees as a way of controlling their lives. One mill in Lowell, Massachusetts, had the following regulations:

> All persons in the employ of the APPLETON COMPANY are required to observe the regulations of the overseer of the room where they are employed. They are not to be absent from their work, without his consent, except in case of sickness, and then they are to send him word of the cause of their absence.
>
> They are to board in one of the boarding houses belonging to the Company, and conform to the regulations of the house where they board.
>
> A regular attendance on public worship on the Sabbath is necessary for the preservation of good order. The Company will not employ any person who is habitually absent.
>
> All persons entering into the employment of the Company are considered as engaging to work twelve months, and those who leave sooner will

not receive a discharge unless they had sufficient experience when they commensed, to enable them to do full work.[7]

Another mill had these regulations:

The tenants of the Boarding Houses are not to board, or permit any part of their houses to be occupied by any person except those in the employ of the Company.

They will be considered answerable for any improper conduct in their houses, and are not to permit their boarders to have company at unseasonable hours.

The doors must be closed at ten o'clock in the evening, and no one admitted after that time without some reasonable excuse.

The keepers of the Boarding Houses must give an account of the number, names, and employment of their boarders, when required; and report the names of such as are guilty of any improper conduct, or are not in the regular habit of attending public worship.

The buildings and yards about them must be kept clean and in good order, and if they are injured otherwise than from ordinary use, all necessary repairs will be made, and charged to the occupant.

It is indispensable that all persons in the employ of the Middlesex Company should be vaccinated who have not been, as also the families with whom they board: which will be done at the expense of the Company.[8]

Hundreds of young women left their families in the countryside to live in the boardinghouses, six to a room and usually two to a bed. The women were required to live in, unless they had special permission from the mill agent. Most men had no alternative, and so they too lived in. If a worker was fired for violation of the rules, he or she would not get a "discharge" paper, and without it none of the other mills in the area would hire the person. Alcoholic beverages were prohibited, and so was "intemperance," whether on the job or off. One mill advised workers to "report, if requested, the names and occupations" of their visitors. Another said that management expected the boarding-houses to be "tranquil scenes of moral deportment."

And so they were. There were few complaints, especially from the young women away from home for the first time. Having a job was paramount, even if it meant sacrificing human dignity twenty-four hours a day. Besides, if you got fired for violation of the rules, where would you find a place to live? "Company homes, in fact, tied workers to their jobs more effectively than good salaries alone would have done," according to Thomas Dublin in *Women at Work*. This was not the last time that employers would keep employees on the job by exploiting the workers' fears that essential fringe benefits would be lost.

One song of the period went like this:

Oh, isn't it such a pity, such a pretty girl as I—
Should be sent to the factory to pine away and
    die?[9]

At this time, just twelve miles away in Concord, Henry David Thoreau retreated to Walden Pond to find solitude. There, in *Walden* he wrote, "Consider the girls in a factory, never alone, hardly in their dreams."[10]

During much of the nineteenth century, even the largest of American companies employed no more than 100 or so workers. They were owned, managed, and usually held together by one individual or family who set the tone for the whole plant. If sometimes ruthless, at least these charismatic capitalists were visible for the workers to see. The owners' efforts for their own enterprises were evident. After the Civil War, the situation changed, with the gradual expansion of manufacturing plants. The forerunner of Pabst Brewing Co. went from a mere 100 employees in 1870 to 700 in the 1890s. McCormick Tractor Co. in Chicago went from a work force of 123 before the Civil War to 1,400 in 1884. By the 1880s the railroads and textile mills employed a thousand or more employees each. It had become impossible for the individual owner to oversee all of his workers, to keep an eye on all the persons in his employ. The individual leadership of the owner had to be replaced—by delegating supervision to foremen.

By the second half of the nineteenth century the all-powerful foreman ran the workplace. Line workers could focus all of their misery on that one individual, who ruthlessly turned out the work for the owner. "Constant harassment by foreman" became a prime complaint, leading to strikes in the 1890s, like the one at the Pullman train car plant. At the time, a chaplain to the workers said, "Other things being equal, the men could have borne with more grace the reduction of wages. But there was personal abuse and tyrannical dealing in the shops." One female worker wrote to the same pastor:

> It was very hard to have to work for such small wages, which would afford a person a mere existence. But the tyrannical and abusive treatment we received from our forewoman made our daily cares so much harder to bear. . . . She [was one of us but] she seemed to delight in showing her power in hurting the girls in every possible way. At times her conduct was almost unbearable. She was so abusive to certain girls that she disliked, that they could not stand it. . . . When a girl was sick and asked to go home during the day, she

would tell them to their face they were not sick, the cars had to be got out, and they could not go home.[11]

The change to foreman control did not lessen the regimentation of shop rules. Here are the rules in a carriage shop in New York City in 1878:

Working hours shall be 7:00 A.M. to 8:00 P.M. every evening but the Sabbath. On the Sabbath, everyone is expected to be in the Lord's House.

It is expected that each employee shall participate in the activities of the church and contribute liberally to the Lord's work.

All employees must show themselves worthy of their hire.

All employees are expected to be in bed by 10:00 P.M. Except:

Each male employee may be given one evening a week for courting purposes and two evenings a week in the Lord's House.

It is the bounden duty of each employee to put away at least 10% of his wages for his declining years, so that he will not become a burden upon the charity of his betters.[12]

In the same decade an editorial in the *New York Times* called for increased surveillance of government employees and gave the following reasons:

In his private business, every careful citizen investigates a man's character before he trusts him. He often investigates a great many things likely to throw light on character which it is unpleasant for the employee to have looked into. He does not hesitate to inquire as to a clerk's associates, or a cashier's habits of expenditure, or the places in which a book-keeper passes his leisure time.[13]

At the end of the nineteenth century, "there came into existence a number of hitherto unfamiliar agents acting on behalf of the private, commercial, and industrial order. These were the industrial police, the coal and iron police, the railway police, and a host of private operatives. A man could retreat to the privacy of his home, but during working hours he was to discover that he had to surrender more and more of his own individuality."[14]

In 1914, Henry Ford established the "Sociological Department" at Ford Motor Co. to make sure that each of his workers earned the $5 a day Ford was paying them. The department sent fifty investigators out to the homes of Ford employees. "Naturally each worker was expected to furnish information on his marital status, the number and ages of his dependents, and his nationality, religion, and (if alien) prospects of citizenship," wrote Allan Nevins, Ford's biographer. "In addition, light was sought on his economic position. Did he own his home? If so, how large was the mortgage? If he rented a domicile, what did he pay? Was he in debt, and to whom? How much money had he saved, and where did he keep it? Did he carry life insurance, and at what premiums? His social outlook and mode of living also came under scrutiny. His health? His doctor? His recreations? The investigator meanwhile looked about sharply, if unobtrusively, so that he could report on 'habits,' 'home condition,' and 'neighborhood.' . . . All this information and more was placed on blue and white forms."[15]

Work—or at least the work environment—had become bureaucratized. The tyrant was no longer an enterprising entrepreneur building a small business nor a headstrong foreman; it was a faceless, impersonal, impenetrable hierarchy. As companies multiplied in size at the turn of the century and World War I brought demands of increased production, efficiency was the name of the game in American industry. Companies were impressed with the ideas of Frederick Winslow Taylor, whose goal was to make every factory operate with the precision of a finely tuned machine. Taylorism, known also as scientific management, was an attempt to use the methods of engineering on human beings to adapt them to the needs of the production plant. Like just about every other new proposal in the workplace, scientific management was never fully applied over an adequate period of time to see whether it really worked. But variations of it, and partial applications of it by assorted Taylor disciples, left their marks on the American workplace.

Scientific management techniques did not eliminate the foreman, of course. Under scientific management, his job was to make sure all the workers on the assembly line kept pace with the machinery. "The actual power to control work is thus vested in the line itself, rather than in the person of the foreman. Instead of control appearing to flow from boss to workers, control emerges from the much more impersonal 'technology,'" reported Richard E. Edwards in his book *Contested Terrain*.[16] That could just as well be said of the stenographic pool in the automated offices of the 1980s.

In fact, it was said, in 1975, by Barbara Garson. "Word Processing and related new systems are designed to wrest . . . control away from secretarial workers. Letters will be dictated on tape and messengered or tubed to the typing pool. Each typist then receives a constant flow of work and can be held responsible for a specific number of lines a day. She will no longer be expected, or allowed, to schedule her own time. . . . Word Processing systems are actually aimed at controlling the output and reducing the skills of both secretaries and middle management."[17]

With the coming of a more bureaucratized and automated structure in the factories of the early part of the twentieth century, management had to find a way to motivate workers and to keep them loyal to a company that provided a repetitious task day after day. Management turned to the carrot-and-stick approach. It was called "welfare work." Companies began to provide health and welfare benefits that were not even required by the primitive employment laws then in effect—first-aid facilities, ice water, rest rooms, rest periods, paid holidays and (to a limited extent) paid vacations, insurance and pension plans, and profit sharing. This vast array of benefits, then, was the invention of management, not labor, even though unions gradually took them over as vested rights.

This combination of surveillance and fringe benefits in the American workplace in the early part of this century led one contemporary writer to say of U.S. Steel, "The trouble is that the corporation's labor policy is still in the stage of detectives and toilets."[18]

Changes did not come easily to all workplaces. Only the threat of a strike at International Harvester (which by 1900 had absorbed McCormick) brought the installation of pure drinking water and flush toilets to a plant in Chicago. Nor were the benefits anything more than gestures that the company could retract at any time. The rule at International Harvester in the first decade of the century was:

> A pension may be suspended or terminated by the Pension Board for gross misconduct or other causes.[19]

The meaning was clear: workers who lead union organizing efforts would lose their pensions. In fact, twenty workers who had been active organizers at International were not given stock bonuses that went to every other employee in 1903. Sixteen years later the president of the company reiterated the point in a letter to employees:

As you know, our Pension Plan is a purely voluntary expression of the company's desire to stand by the men who have stood by it.

There is no better example of the fragility of fringe benefits for employees—and the self-interest of corporations that inspired them—than the story of paid vacations in the United States.

Vacations were unheard of until the mid-nineteenth century in this country, when a few top executives began to get them. Later, a few clerical workers were awarded paid vacations as owners realized that a break from work actually helped workers reach higher production levels when they returned rested and refreshed. GIVE ALL WORKERS VACATIONS WITH PAY—IT PAYS, said a headline in *Forbes,* the magazine for business, in 1927. By then about a third of all salaried employees were given vacations (even though vacations were required by law at the time by most European countries). In 1920, one company described its rationale for paid leisure time:

> Our plan of vacations serves as a reward for continuous service and prepares the individual for another year of strenuous work. We hope someday to extend the privilege down the line to hourly rated men who have ten or more years of service.

The feeling was not unanimous, as another employer demonstrated:

> I believe that vacations for individual workers have no good effect since they add nothing to their industry, efficiency or loyalty, but might have directly the opposite effect.[20]

Owners who believed in the vacation concept were such strong believers that they usually prohibited any outside work during vacations and built camps where company employees and their families could enjoy their rationed rest and recuperation.

About half of these vacation plans were wiped out in the Depression, and in the 1930s organized labor began insisting on them in work contracts. By the end of World War II, what had begun as a management-sponsored gratuity to increase production had been taken over by labor unions as an unalienable right, just as important as wages in a labor agreement.

Meanwhile, during the early twentieth century, management was insisting more and more on "the right stuff" in the workers it hired. This meant more prying into applicants' backgrounds and more insistance on conformity. The Bell Telephone System elevated this to an art form. A candidate for a telephone operator's position needed at least two superlative letters of recommendation from businessmen and had to survive an obstacle course of tests and interviews. There were a number of restrictions. "She could not be too old, too young, too small, Jewish, or black. Any hearing or sight defects, a slovenly appearance or an unpleasant-sounding voice meant automatic rejection. To be seriously considered for telephone operating the applicant usually had to be a native-born white woman between the ages of fifteen and eighteen with at least six years of grammar school education." According to 1910 guidelines:

> An individual who . . . is perfect physically, that is, not crippled, and who has (1) a calm, clear eye and steady gaze, (2) steady hand and firm set jaws, (3) weight proportional to height, (4) good appetite, [and] (5) healthy, rosy complexion . . . can usually withstand the wear and tear of . . . exhausting work, such as telephone . . . operating successfully.[21]

It is hard to imagine the 1910 guidelines passing muster under Title VII of the Civil Rights Act of 1964, or the section of the Rehabilitation Act of 1973 governing employment of handicapped persons, or the Age Discrimination in Employment Act of 1967.

But what of these requirements from the American Airlines *Uniform Regulations* and *Appearance Regulations,* which run to twenty-four pages and which were in force in 1975? "Foundation, rouge, powder, lipstick and mascara or false eyelashes," said the regulations, "must be worn and maintained at all times." More than three pages were devoted solely to hair, which "must have a set when worn loose or tied back in a peruke; it may not be worn straight." Combs and pins in the hair were not permitted unless "covered with a regulation barrette or ribbons." The supervisor had the prerogative to recommend eye shadow and eyeliner. The regulations also included specifications with regard to maximum weight in proportion to height and hip circumference.[22]

After the coming of collective bargaining in the 1930s, the passage of the National Labor Relations Act of 1935, and the wartime boom, working conditions improved in the United States. The emphasis was now on productivity. "Work, work, and work some more" was the demand from employers. The respect for workers did not increase accordingly.

John Kenneth Galbraith recalls taking a tour of an airplane engine plant in Williamsport, Pa., in 1942. He was taken to the executive offices but was asked not to visit the factory itself because to do so would disrupt production.

"Any labor trouble?" asked Galbraith's escort, "Babe" Meigs, a Chicago publisher who was then in charge of aircraft production for the War Production Board.

"No, none at all," responded an executive of the company.

"You aren't treating the bastards too good, are you?" asked Babe.[23]

Babe's attitude persists today, but after the war the nature of the workplace—or at least the work force—changed. Unions were a fact of life in major industries by now, and management accepted that reality. But it stiffened its stance on what it considered management prerogatives—production schedules and conversion to automation, for instance. As America moved from a manufacturing economy to a service-oriented economy, more jobs became managerial or clerical. By 1955, for the first time in any society, white-collar workers outnumbered blue-collar workers.

World War II changed the workplace in another way. It produced a vast army of returning veterans, now eager for college education and able to get it with government benefits. They were soon well prepared to fill the positions created by the service economy, which was coming to rely increasingly on electronic data processing devices to do the routine work. These returning veterans brought to the American workplace a vocabulary, an outlook, and a perception of organizations shaped by their wartime experience. The postwar period began "the militarization of the corporation."

World War II represented the most notable experience of their lives for the millions of American men who served and survived. A predominantly stag environment, the military showed that men could run the show by themselves. Most likely, the war years brought these young men's first sexual experience, their first taste of beer and liquor, their first chance to drive a vehicle.

These men fought for a noble, patriotic purpose. It was acceptable to express racist sentiments—against Germans and Japanese. They came back to an appreciative nation— there were low-interest loans and insurance, the GI bill for college, plenty of job opportunities. For most, these were truly "The Best Years of Our Lives," in the words of the 1946 film about returning veterans.

Fresh from this maturing experience, the returning veterans applied the traditions and mores of the military to their employment in the private sector, whether as managers or laborers.

One of the strongest traditions brought from the armed services was "goldbricking." Young men discovered in the war years that there was peer pressure to get away with as little work as possible. Ask anyone about his military experience and (except for those on the front), he'll tell you what a good deal he had. He'll tell you that he hardly ever had to work because he knew the colonel or because he tricked the system or because he got himself transferred to a "cushy" spot. When these men became civilian employees, this same attitude pervaded the workplace at all levels, especially in large organizations. There were plenty of employees who were diligent and honest, but they almost had to hide these traits from their colleagues.

The new corporate class used the language of the military—*promotions, discharges, missions, efficiency, strategies, temporary duty, trainees, suitability.*

"I'll tell you what it's like," said a worker in a General Motors assembly plant in the 1970s. "It's like the army. They even use the same words, like *direct order*. Supposedly you have a contract, so there's some things they just can't make you do. Except, if the foreman gives you a direct order, you do it, or you're out. . . . Fired, or else they give you a DLO—disciplinary layoff. . . . [In the army] if your CO [commanding officer] is harassing you, you can file a complaint with the IG [inspector general]. Only thing is, you gotta go up to your CO and say, 'Sir, request permission to see the inspector general to tell him my commanding officer is a shit.' Same thing here. Before you can get your committeeman, you got to tell the foreman exactly what your grievance is in detail. So meantime he's working out ways to tell the story different."[24]

Not surprisingly, individuality was suppressed in the

postwar workplace, just as it had to be in the military. Individual risks were discouraged. Loyalty became important, more important than individual expression. There was an attempt at consensus. "Run it up the flagpole and see who salutes it," became the theme.

The army had placed great reliance on testing, and so did this generation of American managers. They elected a paternalistic general as their president. They treated their corporate wives like military wives. (A guide to *What Every Army Wife Should Know* advised women of that period, "Like wives of many professional men, government officials, and some businessmen, she stands behind, as part of a 'team.' This is not to share in any part of his job but to give solid support in the home and socially." Listed as a negative attribute of the military wife was "complaining when he has to work late.")

The car one drives, the location and size of the home, membership in the country club—all became determined by one's position in the hierarchy. If the hierarchy says, "Move to Kansas City," then move without complaint. If the hierarchy says, "We do it this way because we have always done it this way," then do it this way.

In 1956 came a book that was to provide the new American managerial class with a rare mirror to show what corporate life was doing to its faithful servants. The book was *The Organization Man* by William H. Whyte, Jr.

The organization men profiled in the book not only work for the organization, but also *belong* to it:

> They are the ones of our middle class who have left home, spiritually as well as physically, to take the vows of organization life, and it is they who are the mind and soul of our great self-perpetuating institutions. . . . The word *collective* most of them can't bring themselves to use—except to describe foreign countries or organiza-

tions they don't work for—but they are keenly aware of how much more deeply beholden they are to organization than were their elders. They are wry about it, to be sure; they talk of the 'treadmill,' the 'rat race,' of the inability to control one's direction. But they have no great sense of plight; between themselves and organization they believe they see an ultimate harmony.[25]

Much of Whyte's warning got lost, however, in the quest for prestige in glass towers and in the good life of suburbia. Many executives went no further than Whyte's apparent message that corporate America was producing conformity in dress and life style. And so corporate America co-opted the surface aspects of the new life-styles of the 1960s—longer hair and beards, sideburns and mustaches, deviance and informality in dress, "hip" language. It even came to believe that war—or at least this particular war of the 1960s—was bad for business. Far from being a threat, the protestors of the decade turned out to be a new market for American business. Corporations even found a way to build into their structures outlets for modest levels of dissent and employee participation. When Henry Ford II appeared in sideburns down to his earlobes at the end of the sixties, the incipient revolution had been absorbed by the American business establishment.

It seems to be the nature of American business to exploit and popularize any attempt at serious social reform in the nation. Young people are rebelling in their dress and hair styles? Then start marketing "designer" blue jeans and a Broadway show based on long hair. A new generation is concerned about food additives and environmental pollution? Then market "natural" cereals in "natural" packaging and offer "ecologically sound" products.

In the 1960s, also, American business had no choice but to recruit among the dissenters. Just about all of the young generation, after all, was involved and clearly those who were involved represented the best educated and the most motivated of America's young people. The "best and the brightest" of the World War II generation may have conducted the war in Vietnam, but it was the "best and the brightest" of the "baby-boom" generation that opposed it. Companies that refused to hire persons who could not pass rigid tests of old-fashioned patriotism and obedience to the organization would simply find themselves without the skilled professionals and semiprofessionals they needed in the coming era of high technology. Large corporations, then, found themselves recruiting from a pool of college and high-school graduates who were a discontented lot. These new young employees turned out to be not at all reluctant to question authority, either on campus or in the office. They were solidly against the military way of doing things. This was even true—probably more so—of the army of veterans that returned from Southeast Asia.

There was a symbiotic effect at work here. Discontent in communities throughout the nation naturally created discontent at work. And discontent at work created discontent in communities outside the workplace.

By then one in five employees was a member of a union, including 10 percent of the white-collar work force. One of nine employees was covered by major collective bargaining agreements, many of them offering the benefits that had been battled for seventy years earlier—respectable wages, rest periods, paid vacations and holidays, insurance coverage, medical and dental care, retirement payments, and even paid education. And still workers were unhappy. And many of them were unhappy with their union as well as their employer. The union, after all, was just another hierarchy with which they had to deal to preserve their dignity.

The work force of the 1970s seemed markedly different from that of two decades earlier—there was a declining confidence in all institutions, a tendency to question authority, less loyalty to one's work organization, less willingness to subordinate personal lives, less dedication to work, a search for alternatives to large and traditional bureaucracies, increased importance attached to leisure time, and intolerance for routine jobs and for jobs whose contribution to society at large did not jibe with the individual's view of morality and propriety. At the same time, the American system of tax withholding had created a significant gap between one's salary—as announced by the employer—and one's actual take-home pay. Management and labor were actually talking now about two different things. The former spoke in terms of wages and fringe benefits (including withholding taxes and contributions to Social Security, workman's compensation, and unemployment insurance) and the latter was talking about take-home pay (after deductions). Often the figure varied by as much as 50 percent.

The Republican administration of Richard Nixon commissioned a study of this growing worker discontent that resulted in the publication of *Work in America* in 1973 by the Department of Health, Education, and Welfare. Its conclusion:

> The United States must resolve a contradiction in our nation—between democracy in society and authoritarianism in the work-place.

A member of the group that developed the report, Daniel Yankelovich, a public opinion researcher, found that the college students he queried had the following present priorities in their minds:

> "participation in the decisions that affect one's
>   own work" (57 percent);
> "a secure retirement" (37 percent);
> "the right to work" (27 percent);
> "a minimum income" (26 percent);
> "an interesting job" (17 percent).

George Gallup, the opinion pollster, identified the trend a year earlier in a presentation to the American Management Associations. He reported that 19 percent of American workers were then unhappy in their jobs. Not too threatening, thought the managers. But Gallup went on. In the 18-to-29 age group, 33 percent thought their jobs unsatisfactory. This group admitted loafing on the job; seven out of ten admitted they were not producing to full capacity.

Older workers had different troubles. The *Wall Street Journal* reported in May 1972 that absenteeism and inefficiency were increasing in managerial ranks because of stress at work and problems at home.

And so persons at both ends of the corporate ladder had become victims. Young people, eager for challenging and meaningful work, found only a phalanx of rules and obstacles along with a demoralized collection of fellow workers. They blamed their supervisors for the morass, but more likely they came to see that "the system," the organization itself, was the enemy. The supervisors and the executives above them felt impotent themselves; the rank-and-file workers didn't give a damn and a complex of government regulations, economic realities, and bureaucratic sensitivities made it impossible to get anything worthwhile done during the workday. These people received the most gratification from their professional associations, from private projects at work (those who could, used personal desk-top computers of their own), from hearing about the work of others, from their hobbies, or from the sports page.

David Sirota, an industrial psychologist, said in 1981 that disrespect of employees was greatest in the lower ranks and at the very top of the organization. "Brutalization of people is probably greatest at the top," he said.[26]

An article in 1978 by Irving Bluestone of the United Auto Workers said it best. "Human Dignity Is What It's All About" was the title. In another article, Bluestone wrote:

Surely, then, the time has come for a society anchored in democratic principles to ensure that each individual at his place of work enjoys a measure of the dignity, self-respect, and freedom which are his as a citizen. In his capacity as a worker, he should be afforded an opportunity for self-expression and participation in the decisions that shape the quality of his working life.[27]

Whether that change will come voluntarily or involuntarily to American employers will be answered in the decade of the 1980s. But if the past is a guide, that change will have to be imposed by the courts.

3

The Limits of
the Constitution

There's a strong reason why American courts have intruded into the affairs of private corporations only to a limited degree. It has to do with a fact of life in American law that interests constitutional lawyers but rarely occurs to the rest of us: the U.S. Constitution is a limitation upon government, not private parties. The Bill of Rights—the first ten amendments to the Constitution and the source of our individual liberties—states what government may not do; it does not speak to what one private citizen or one private organization may or may not do to another.

In 1875, just seven years after passage of the Fourteenth Amendment prohibiting states from denying individual rights, the U.S. Supreme Court said, "The fourteenth amendment prohibits a State from depriving any person of life, liberty, or property, without due process of law; *but this adds nothing to the rights of one citizen as against another.*"[28] Eight years later, it said, "It is State action of a particular character that is prohibited. *Individual invasion of individual rights is not the subject-matter of the amendment.* . . . The wrongful act of an individual [or corporation—a 'legal person'] is simply a private wrong, or a crime of that individual."[29]

This doctrine of "state action" is extremely important to understanding constitutional rights. For a private person or organization to stifle your freedom of speech, or unreasonably to search your belongings, or to deny you the right to vote does not violate your *constitutional* rights (although it may offer you the opportunity to sue for assault or breach of contract or personal injury).

A representative of the state—whether a police officer or a school principal—couldn't punish you for going off to religious services, or force you to go. That would be state action that clearly violates the First Amendment protection of free religious expression. But a private individual or organization does not violate the Constitution by doing so because this does not involve any action by state authorities. A private company does not violate your constitutional rights by making you work on election day and thereby making it difficult for you to vote. Nor does it violate the Constitution by insisting that your locker or desk be searched without a warrant or even without a cause for suspicion. A representative of the government couldn't get away with that.

Supreme Court decisions since the 1880s have modified this doctrine to be sure (but not enough to provide any hope that the individual generally enjoys constitutional protections within a private organization). This liberalizing view of the Fourteenth Amendment has come, not surprisingly, as Supreme Court justices began to show more enlightened views on the status of black Americans in the society. Thus, in 1944, the Court could no longer hide behind the "state action" argument to continue to permit the major political parties—which are in fact no more than private organizations—to conduct their crucial political procedures (including the holding of primaries) as if they were the Elks Club or the Rotary. The Democratic and Republican parties may be private organizations, but they happen to nominate the only two viable choices we have in elections; and so, the Court said, they can't continue to deny some

Americans an equal opportunity to participate. In short, no more primary elections for whites only.

The same year, the Court ruled that a labor union, although also a private organization, came under the Fourteenth Amendment when it practiced racial discrimination because the Railway Labor Act, a federal law, set the union up as exclusive bargaining agent.[30]

In 1946 the Court said, "Ownership does not always mean absolute dominion." If a private entrepreneur opens his property for the use of the public in general, then he—or it—will have to recognize that users of the facility enjoy certain constitutional rights. "Thus, the owners of privately held bridges, ferries, turnpikes, and railroads may not operate them as freely as a farmer does his farm." The decision in 1946 meant that company representatives could not prevent visitors to a company-owned town from distributing religious literature. The company was running something akin to a municipality there, said the Court; it has to permit the same sorts of individual rights as an arm of the state does.[31] The Supreme Court in the late 1960s extended this reasoning to a shopping center that had sought to ban peaceful picketing.

But by 1972, the makeup of the Court had changed significantly, and the justices in effect overruled the shopping center decision. Now the court was saying that a privately owned shopping center *could* limit distribution of antiwar handbills. In the same year, the Court limited other attempts to expand the "state action" doctrine to bring private organizations licensed by the state under the umbrella of the Constitution because the private organization was practicing racial discrimination. One case involved a private club licensed by the state to sell liquor.[32]

The main point of all of this is that currently most activities by an employer, however restrictive of individual rights, do not violate the U.S. Constitution. But another point to recognize is that whenever the justices of the Supreme Court perceive a serious injustice over a period of years—as in the case of racial discrimination against blacks—they can, if they want to, find a way to extend constitutional protections even to victims of private, not state, action. This could happen if the justices decide that oppression in the workplace is so acute as to affect adversely the body politic. When the Supreme Court in 1954, under Chief Justice Earl Warren, decided that the Fourteenth Amendment prohibited racially segregated schools, the evidence it used to bolster its conclusion was precisely the kind of evidence that Opinion Research Corp., George Gallup, Daniel Yankelovich, and the National Institute of Mental Health have produced about the workplace, namely that oppression on the job is having significant adverse psychological effects on a large segment of the American population.

Possibilities for the Supreme Court

There are at least seven ways the courts could eventually be persuaded to extend constitutional protection to the workplace.

First, a Supreme Court that becomes sensitive to deprivation of rights in the modern corporation would simply choose to expand the "state action" doctrine as it did in the 1940s. After all, it is not a large jump at all from concluding that a *labor union* may not violate individual constitutional rights to concluding that a *major corporation* may not do so either. A corporation, after all, is created with the permission of the state. Nor is it a large jump from concluding that a company owning and managing a private village must recognize the First Amendment to concluding that a company owning and managing a facility that includes parking, medical facilities, eating facilities, day-care centers, educational programs, and recreational areas must do the same. The first is called a company-owned town and the second is called a company headquarters, but is there any reason to make a legal distinction?

Back in 1952, Adolph A. Berle, Jr., a prominent lawyer and statesman, argued:

> On logical analysis, a corporation, being a creature of the state . . . could not give undue favors to a group it wished to foster at the expense of the rest of the public. This would be true despite the fact that, as owner, it could theoretically do what it pleased with its own property. And this legal restraint would apply . . . to its regulations, practices and day-to-day dealings. The Bill of Rights and the Fourteenth Amendment would thus have direct application to, and also throughout, any corporation whose position gave it power. The preconditions of application [of this legal theory] are two: the undeniable fact that the corporation was created by the state and the existence of sufficient economic power concentrated in this vehicle to invade the constitutional right of an individual to a material degree.[34]

This is only Berle's argument; courts have not gone this far.

Second, a Supreme Court of the future could interpret the *Ninth Amendment* to the Constitution as prohibiting corporate activity that diminishes individual rights guaranteed in the rest of the Constitution. The Ninth Amendment states:

> The enumeration in the Constitution, of certain rights, shall not be construed to deny or disparage others retained by the people.

This amendment has rarely been invoked in arguments before the Supreme Court because of its lack of specificity. But it has been used in lower courts to support the right to an abortion and the right to wear one's hair as one wishes. In fact, the Ninth Amendment offers a fertile ground for an imaginative lawyer. It is not unreasonable to argue that the amendment protects the right of an individual to private employment free of censorship, intrusions, arbitrary actions, stressful or unhealthful conditions, or denial of due process.

Third, perhaps a creative lawyer could persuade the Court that the First Amendment protection of freedom *of* association ("the right . . . peaceably to assemble") implies a freedom *in* an association.

Fourth, the Court could rule that, at least in limited cases, when a private organization infringes on *fundamental rights*—free speech, freedom from unreasonable searches, the right to travel, the right to vote, the right to privacy, equal opportunity—the Constitution does cover corporate action. Such an argument would draw on the arguments presented to the Court in the 1940s.

Fifth, an argument could remind the Supreme Court how all courts have traditionally viewed libel suits against a news publication. The reasoning goes like this: A libel suit is a controversy between one private party—the victim— and another private party—the publisher. But constitutional issues are involved, because if a federal or state court were to enforce a truly restrictive libel judgment on a publisher this would constitute "state action" infringing on the publisher's First Amendment freedom of press. If this is so, why couldn't an argument be made that for a federal or state court to enforce a judgment against an employee fired by a private company for "whistle-blowing" or complaining on the job or involving himself in controversy off-hours *also* constitutes "state action" infringing on the individual's First Amendment freedom of speech?

Sixth, there is a middle road suggested by Yale Law Professor Julius G. Getman and others that courts *give special weight* to complaints against employers when substantive constitutional rights are involved. For instance, he writes, "Freedom of expression at work should be limited only when a strong showing can be made that the expression of ideas or the use of words is likely to cause serious disruption."[35] That is similar to the standard the courts use when ruling on curtailment of free speech by arms of the government. (Free speech may be limited by the government when the speech creates a "clear and present danger.") Labor arbitrators, Getman argues, should be especially "suspicious" when hearing claims that a company has abridged constitutional rights. In such cases, he says, their obligation goes beyond merely deciding whether the strict text of a labor agreement was violated.

Seventh, Article I, Section 8 of the Constitution states, "The Congress shall have Power . . . To regulate Commerce . . . among the several States." This "Commerce Clause" has been used through the years by federal courts to invalidate *state laws and regulations* that retard, burden, or constrict interstate commerce. A novel legal approach could argue that identical and simultaneous actions by *large corporations*—in diminishing free expression by employees, for instance, or their abilities to change jobs as they wish—could have the same result. In other words, it could be argued that this corporate action burdens interstate commerce and usurps a function reserved for Congress.

Whatever the legal argument used, the need to extend the "state action" doctrine to the private sector will become even more acute if the European trend toward "privatization" of municipal services takes hold in this country. The idea of turning over such public services to private companies has been adopted in the past eighty years in selected parts of Europe. For instance, a private company provides fire protection and emergency ambulance service in 271 of the 279 municipalities in Denmark. In France, private companies conduct virtually all of the functions of city building inspectors. The Conservative government in England, desperate to control government spending, is intrigued with "privatization." It is possible that a conservative administration in the U.S., along with financially pinched localities, will also turn to "privatization." This would mean that an increasing number of "public" jobs, where there is now constitutional protection of employees because they are tax-supported, would become private-sector positions without such protection.

None of these legal arguments has been fully developed, to be sure, and the necessary groundwork has not been prepared to get a winning case before the U.S. Supreme Court. But the problem is not *the lack of a legal theory*. As we have seen, there are many theories. The problem is persuading lawyers and judges that appropriate *economic and social policy* requires this new legal doctrine.

No one should expect immediate change, but change will come. After all, in 1905, just twenty-five years before the coming of the New Deal, the Supreme Court was saying, "The freedom of master and employee to contract with each other in relation to their employment, and in defining the same, cannot be prohibited or interfered with, without violating the Federal Constitution." In the decades that followed that now discredited decision, we have had the Social Security Act, the Fair Labor Standards Act, the National Labor Relations Act, the Equal Employment Opportunity Act, the Occupational Safety and Health Act, the Employment Retirement Income Security Act, plus state laws prohibiting polygraph tests of employees, setting minimum wages, establishing unemployment compensation, and requiring employers to grant workers access to personnel records. In the 1980s, we regularly accept governmental intrusions into the old "master/servant" relationship.

Where Are the Civil Libertarians?

In spite of the clear need for a new constitutional approach in the world of private employment, public interest and civil liberties organizations have virtually ignored legal abuses in corporate employment.

Ira Glasser, executive director of the American Civil Liberties Union, said in 1979 that employee rights complaints outnumber all other kinds of complaints now received by the civil liberties organization. But a look at the ACLU's docket of current legal cases will show few if any active challenges to private organizations. Unfortunately, the preeminent civil liberties organization in the U.S. recognizes mainly abuses by government as abuses of civil liberties. After serving as Southern director and then Washington director of the ACLU for twelve years, Charles Morgan, Jr., wrote in his book, *One Man, One Voice:*

> As Thomas Jefferson knew, no rights can be secure for those whose work depends upon the whim of others. For years the ACLU had retreated from "forty-acres-and-a-mule" questions of economic rights. It still does not recognize the birthright of every person to food, shelter, clothing, health, and legal care—simply because they are born here; that employees have rights against the "private" corporate governments for which they work; that people should have freedom not to travel, the right not to be forced by economic necessity into a faraway city's suburbs or a big city's slum-ghettos; that it is people who have a right to the land, not ever-growing corporations; . . . that corporations ought not have the same rights as people; that multinationals must obey the people's laws.[33]

Glasser, as a long-time civil liberties activist, recognizes much of this. He wrote in 1978, "Most large employers, and certainly most large corporate employers, are nothing less than minigovernments. Many have more income, more expenses, produce more goods, control more land and assets, and have more people subject to their jurisdiction than all the thirteen colonies did 200 years ago. More than a few are larger, have bigger budgets, and control more land and people than some individual states today. Some multinational corporations exceed the budgets, gross national product, assets, and populations of entire countries.

"More people depend completely on their corporate employer today than many people did on government 200 years ago."

Yet the ACLU, which risks unpopularity and loss of financial support in its courageous battles against *government* actions, has never taken on these corporate minigovernments. The private companies have a more vital stranglehold on individual rights and individual lives than does government, but the ACLU has not plunged into the battle.

Glasser tells the story of a man who was fired by his company in the early 1970s because he was working actively for the impeachment of President Nixon. Yet the civil liberties union sent him away. "We couldn't help because the employer was private," wrote Glasser. "No law—not the Constitution, not any statute, not any regulation—limits the discretion of private employers to fire employees because of their politics."

The lack of a law supporting their position has not stopped ACLU lawyers in the past; they have attempted to "make new law" in the courts to uphold individual rights. But this effort has centered almost exclusively on abuses *by government*.

Where Is the Press?

Not only has the private sector escaped the scrutiny of aggressive civil liberties lawyers and organizations, it has largely escaped close scrutiny by the press.

In the 1970s we all learned of government intrusions upon constitutional rights, because of the concentrated efforts of news reporters. The Watergate disclosures led to the punishment of several persons responsible. And they led to reforms in the way government performs its functions and informs the public. We are less aware—if at all—of the same abuses in the private sector: wiretapping, dossier-collecting, unreasonable searches, "enemies lists," industrial spying, arbitrary use of power, bribery, intrusion upon the personal lives of individuals. All these continue in the private sector without regular press scrutiny.

The federal Freedom of Information Act and comparable legislation in the states provide some assurance that citizens and their representatives in the press will have access to documents and other materials used by government agencies in their policymaking. But except for certain required disclosures to the Securities and Exchange Commission, there are few comparable obligations imposed on businesses to disclose information to the public about their activities.

The Federal Advisory Committee Act and similar "sunshine legislation" in many states mandates that meetings of government agencies be open to the public. There is no similar requirement for private businesses. Publicly held corporations hold a single stockholders' meeting a year—usually in a remote location and always carefully controlled by the current management.

To be sure, laws passed in the 1960s and the 1970s have required corporations to submit to government agencies masses of data about their racial composition, lending policies, conflicts of interest, pension plans, real estate transactions, environmental hazards, and more. But the data is scattered and deceptive, and very few reporters are skillful enough—or so inclined—to use the data to gather substantive knowledge about corporate abuses, including what it's like to work for one of these companies. Even fewer reporters are able to present stories about private businesses in a way that will attract most readers' sustained interest. Consumers of news are lax here too. They will absorb everything they can about abuses in government— Watergate, Abscam, the Korean bribes, the sex and alcohol scandals in Washington—but will virtually ignore more shocking disclosures about private organizations.

Most daily newspapers do not have business reporting staffs. They rely on press releases and reporters who also cover other news. In 1980 fewer than a third of the newspapers in the U.S. had even one person assigned full-time to cover business news; only one out of ten newspapers had two or more full-timers assigned to covering business news. In 1976 the *Des Moines Register* beefed up its business news staff to six, only to have business executives in the community react with horror, claiming that the coverage was biased or inflammatory.

Most of the notable disclosures about corporate abuses in the past decade have come not from tough investigative journalism but from voluntary disclosures by a disgruntled member of the family—a "whistle-blower." And there are few laws to protect these whistle-blowers from getting fired for their disloyalty.

The relative lack of press scrutiny of large employers is particularly unfortunate in view of the fact that there are few factors more instrumental in reforming corporate practices than bad publicity. According to a recent study, nearly half of the public relations directors of large corporations feel that hostile press reports would evoke "extreme concern" by their corporate executives, almost as large a percentage as those feeling that an adverse decision by a government regulatory agency would bring the same reaction.

Today's Semi-Capitalism

Executives for large employers often say that press scrutiny and constitutional protections are not necessary in the private sector because businesses are regulated by the forces of the competitive marketplace. This is less and less true today.

Right now, it is government that feels the greater pressure to reduce expenditures, to be "cost-effective."

The average government executive, for example, is faced with a per diem reimbursement of only $50 (up to $75 in certain cities) when he or she travels on government business. If the government executive spends more than that on food, lodging, tips, and other expenses, it comes out of his or her pocket. By contrast, the executive in private industry simply charges his outrageous hotel, travel, and food bills to a company charge account. The traveling executive is not motivated to shop for the best rate. In fact, the reverse is true. The executive often opts for the more lavish accommodations to impress business acquaintances. The company personnel and accounting people pay only lip service to savings in this area. Expenses of this type are tax deductible by businesses and so there is no overwhelming motivation to save money here.

Also at a time when the government has shown a willingness to bail out failing companies with major loans or guarantees, there is a lessened motivation to be cost-effective or fiercely competitive. Since passage of a law in the summer of 1981, private businesses have been able to "sell" tax credits, which often result from mismanagement in the first place, to another company that needs them to offset taxable profits. Where is the motivation here to run a more efficient, more productive operation than the "competition"? In this new capitalism, where is the motivation to treat your employees with greater dignity than the "competition"?

Nor, as John Kenneth Galbraith and others have observed, do *profits* motivate the large majority of today's corporate decision makers. The entrepreneurs of small businesses are still motivated by the drive for increased personal earnings from a cost-effective, profitable operation, but executives for today's large corporations are not.

They are salaried; and even though their large salaries are perhaps keyed indirectly to the success of the company, their possibilities for personal advancement and increased earnings are enhanced not by efficient, productive operations, but by empire-building, expansion, and establishing new "profit centers" that generate income, not necessarily profits.

Andrew Hacker, author of a widely used textbook on free enterprise, has written:

> Ours has become a generation where status comes more from providing services than fervidly pursuing profits. . . . You find your peers in your fellow professionals; a nationwide guild devoted to truth, progress, quality. Your touchstone is service to society rather than profits or special interests. In a sense, professionalism serves as America's variant of socialism, but within a capitalist context. People want esteemed status, comfortable incomes, and what we generally think of as the good life. But they also wish to believe they are advancing justice, benefiting society, and remaining true to their conscience. But being a professional means you are less than completely loyal to the organization for which you work.[36]

In other words, the most important on-the-job fringe benefits that corporations provide today may be the permission and the funding for an employee to attend yearly conventions of a professional association. The trend Hacker identified may mean that American businesses are dominated by a cadre of professionals who are getting their job rewards from professional associations, not their employers. They have given up on reforming the hierarchy they are responsible for; in regaining dignity in the workplace, it is now every person for himself.

In this contemporary corporate environment, where

manipulating statistics and protecting one's own bureaucratic turf are more important than maximizing profits, the modern corporate executive has little motivation to attract the very best people to his organization, to fight for his subordinates' dignity and work conditions, to equate healthy employee morale with increased productivity. Furthermore, workers are hardly motivated to leave the company because they believe, probably rightly, that they will encounter the identical bureaucratic morass at the "competitor" across the street. It's important to remember that both Adam Smith and John Stuart Mill regarded *worker mobility* among different workplaces as an essential ingredient in the free marketplaces they envisioned.

Thus, corporate executives are as much victims in this system as are the people who work for them. Demoralized leaders make poor leaders, or no leaders at all. This is one reason that employees have gone outside the company—to courts and legislatures—for improvement in work conditions. They are not persuaded that true change is possible from within the organization.

The Effect of the Multinationals

Most of the large employers in the United States also do business in several foreign nations. More and more, these multinational corporations are showing disdain for the regulations of mere sovereign nations. The multinationals, after all, supercede national borders. They find national laws an inconvenience to their operations and often have the economic clout to alter them more to their liking. The large employer used to depend on the good will of the people in the community where it was located, and have an interest in developing skilled and inspired employees. Nowadays interstate companies can simply transfer employees like so many pieces of furniture, close down an entire operation and move it elsewhere, or bring to bear national pressure on an individual municipality or state. Multinational companies have even more leverage to alter the regulatory environment in which they conduct business—and in the process tyrannize the people who work for them.

The individual's position in this current age of bureaucracy, complex government regulation, limited constitutional protection, and almost nonexistent press coverage can be described in a word: vulnerable.

PART II
FOURTEEN FREEDOMS IN THE WORKPLACE

Employees are now seeking improvement in their work environments, as much or more than increased salaries. As employees see that inflation or taxes wipe out most of their pay increases and as holding on to a job takes on more importance than squeezing more money out of it, employees want to make sure that the place where they spend a significant amount of their waking hours is more tolerable. They are "drawing the line."

For most, paternalistic offerings from the boss will not do, for these can be withdrawn at will. They want to bargain as equals. They want rights. "Rights are what no one can take away from you," according to Ramsey Clark, a former attorney general. Employees have discovered that an offering from the company, like flexible work hours, can disappear just as quickly as it appears, but an established job right, like safety on the job or equal opportunity, is theirs as a matter of law.

The process of increased employment rights really began with passage of the Civil Rights Act of 1964, Title VII of which prohibits discrimination in employment based on race, color, sex, religion, or national origin. This marked the first recognition of substantive rights in the workplace whether or not the employees were organized in a bargaining unit. Previously, labor laws protected the interests of collective bargaining units (not individuals) or set basic rates of pay. Although blacks were the intended beneficiaries of the Civil Rights Act, they were not the only beneficiaries of the liberalization of the workplace that followed Title VII. Executive orders, regulations, new laws, and court decisions followed, establishing lots of do's and don't's for employers—protecting occupational health, prohibiting the uses of some surveillance devices, vesting certain fringe benefits, regulating pension plans. What private employees could not win through interpretations of the Constitution by the courts, they began winning through statutes passed by Congress and the states. And in other instances, they have begun to win recognition of additional rights through individual court decisions not based on constitutional grounds. The impact of these legal changes are only now becoming apparent to employees and employers.

Beyond these legal rights, discontented employees have won other changes in company policies simply because of their persistence and their numbers. In order to attract the kind of people they need, some employers have had to accommodate these new demands, even if they are not required by law. Company-sponsored day care is an example.

The status of the individual in the workplace in the 1980s, then, is shaped by a combination of new laws and court decisions, voluntary changes in company policies, and assertions by groups of employees that certain working conditions are simply their entitlement. But the work environment is also shaped by continued resistance to change by employers, especially those companies that have traditionally ignored social realities that affect their employees' morale and productivity.

Claims for the individual rights of employees can be grouped in a manifesto of Fourteen Freedoms in the workplace. They are:

Freedom to be hired fairly and openly
Freedom to be trusted
Freedom to speak freely
Freedom from intrusions into one's person and
    effects
Freedom of safety and health
Freedom from stress
Freedom in off-hours
Freedom from sexual harassment
Freedom of information about the company and
    about one's own records
Freedom from company propaganda
Freedom to participate in company decisions
Freedom in fringe benefits
Freedom of due process in adverse actions
Freedom from abusive firing

The sections that follow will look at each of these more closely: As rights we have, and rights we *thought* we had—and also as rights to fight for.

4

Freedom in the Hiring Process

The tyranny begins, of course, before the "servant" is on the payroll.

John R. Wareham, president of an executive search firm, "a headhunter," recommends that top business executives use intense psychological warfare in the first luncheon interview with a job applicant. "You will usually offer your guest a prelunch cocktail, which will normally be accepted," Wareham advised executives in an article in the *New York Times* in 1979. "A refusal will be of immediate interest.

"A candidate's refusal of alcohol may indicate deficiencies—possibly a certain lack of savoir faire, for example, or an inability to adapt and conform to the conventional practice of drinking in moderation on social occasions. The executive who accepts only fruit juice may be inclined to go his own way when it comes to making other decisions that will affect not only his own constitution, but the morale and well-being of the group he manages.

"Any discussion about the family leads naturally enough to where they live; find out how many rooms he's got, when he bought the house and how much he is paying for the mortgage—clues to his business acumen and his economic security.

"If you want to put a little pressure on the candidate, question him on some patently important point when he is distracted by the waiter, or by a mouthful of food. If you want to increase pressure a little further, you can then apologize for having 'caught him with his mouth full.' These ploys may seem both gratuitous and a little childish, but. . . ."

Imagine the dilemma of the applicant who now holds a job, or is hoping to get a job, at the New York City brokerage house of Johnson & Higgins, which in 1982 notified its employees to shun alcohol during the workday because "noontime drinking tarnishes your professional image" and "contributes directly to reduced productivity."

The tools of the tyrant with regard to rank-and-file employees are more blunt. They are called application forms. There seem to be no limits to the information demanded—spouse's name and occupation, number of children, source of funding for your education, credit references, household goods owned, make of automobile, long-range ambitions, marital status, date of marriage, date of birth. The medical questions can run to several pages. Many forms ask for information that is unnecessary until the individual is hired: Social Security number, persons to notify in an emergency, current insurance.

"We were getting a lot of data we really didn't need. It was cluttering up the files," admitted the chairman of the board of IBM, Frank T. Cary, in 1976. Thousands of companies were doing the same, but IBM Corp. was one of the few to do something about it. In the mid-1970s, it sharply pared down the size of its application forms—to name, address, previous employer, education, and a few other basic facts, including any criminal convictions (not arrests) in the prior five years. Many of IBM's personnel people were appalled; they felt naked without all that information on a job applicant. But they discovered along with the rest of the company that cutting down the amount of information demanded from applicants did not lower the caliber of their selections. They simply made a point of asking *the right questions*.

Some personnel people ask everything they possibly can; others are confused about recent nondiscrimination and privacy standards and they avoid asking for the information they need. "Everyone has the wrong impression about how many questions you can ask," says Susan B. Nycum, an attorney who advises companies how to prevent breaches of security in their computer operations. Her advice is sound. "Just don't go about it in an awful way. Avoid setting up what can be viewed as a pattern of discrimination. Ask questions closely related to the job the potential employee is applying for. Then get his or her signature okaying the fact that you can verify the applicant's claimed background. The problem now is that many employers went too far in the past and asked all kinds of personal questions not related to the job."[37]

There are two possible grounds on which an employer's preemployment inquiries would be ruled improper—as an invasion of privacy or as discriminatory on the basis of race, sex, national origin, or age. There have been challenges to inquiries on application forms as an invasion of privacy, but none of them successful. One court said that even probing into an applicant's psychological history may not be an invasion of privacy.[38]

The laws on nondiscrimination are more subtle than most people suppose. Some state laws prohibit certain preemployment inquiries, but more commonly state and federal laws prohibit use of the information for a discriminatory purpose once it is collected by the employer.

This means that in most places there are no hard and fast rules about what may and may not be asked. It is the use of the information and its relevance to the job that are important in assessing whether the inquiry violates nondiscrimination laws. There are countless inquiries by an employer that are legally asked and just as legally not responded to. An employer may ask for an applicant's race, sex, or national origin. (In fact, it may have to ask this information because of a federal requirement that it operate an affirmative action program to increase its hiring of minorities or women. It can neither do this well nor test the effectiveness of the program without cumulative statistics on numbers of persons applying and numbers hired.) By the same token, an applicant is not required to respond to such inquiries and would be the victim of discrimination if his or her refusal were the reason for not getting a job.

Asking on an application form whether a person is male or female and whether the applicant is known as Mr., Mrs., Ms., or some other designation is permitted under federal law if the inquiry is made in good faith for a nondiscriminatory purpose. An employer may ask for an applicant's age, but may not discriminate on that basis. The same is true of pregnancy. An employer is entitled to know whether there are physical limitations on the applicant's ability to do the job, but under the Pregnancy Discrimination Act of 1978, the employer may not deny employment or promotion on that basis. The same act prohibits discrimination based on childbirth or related conditions, and that includes abortions. An employer may ask about fluency in English, but only if that is related to the job in question.

Federal law prohibits employment discrimination based on religion. Since it is unlikely that a company would have an affirmative-action requirement with regard to hiring persons of a particular sect, an inquiry on religion is one that is most likely to be declared discriminatory and illegal. A question about sexual orientation on an application form or in a preemployment interview could hardly be justified as job related, but it is not regarded as discriminatory under the Civil Rights Act.

There is an important exception to the general rule that there are few legal restrictions on private employers asking for personal information upon application. That involves information about the applicant's criminal activity, most often his or her arrest record (as opposed to conviction record). California, for instance, flatly prohibits an employer from asking about arrests that did not result in convictions. Most inquiries about arrests are prohibited in the District of Columbia, Illinois, Maryland, Massachusetts, Michigan, New York, Pennsylvania, Utah, Virginia, Washington, and Wisconsin. Connecticut law limits who at the company may look at arrest information on an applicant, and New York has restrictions on asking for conviction information and for fingerprints. (One other restriction: Employers in Massachusetts and Maryland may not ask about mental health backgrounds.)

Many workers, especially those in the chemical fields, are alarmed that there are so few restrictions on preemployment inquiries because some major companies are now planning to put applicants through genetic screening. This would require applicants to be tested for their genetic makeup on the theory that the process will detect persons whose genes make them predisposed to serious illnesses caused by materials in the workplace. Many experts question the validity of the theory, and many labor representatives feel that the tests shift the responsibility for occupational illness away from the company, putting the blame on an individual employee's "faulty" genes. Representative Albert Gore, Jr., of Tennessee, who is investigating the trend, said genetic screening "has the potential to serve as a marvelous tool to protect the health of workers or a terrible vehicle for invidious discrimination." About sixty major corporations have told Gore that they will begin genetic testing in this decade.

In an earlier age, it was said that the boss could refuse to hire someone because he didn't like the way he parted his hair. In a future age, it may be said that the boss can refuse to hire someone because he doesn't like the arrangement of his genes.

The Decision to Hire

Beyond what may be requested of an applicant, however, there are of course definitive prohibitions with regard to the decision to hire or not. The traditional notion that an employer could hire whomever he wishes has pretty much been obliterated with the coming of collective bargaining and the equal employment opportunity laws. In the 1980s, the hiring decision is made in a complex environment of government regulations. Many employers have been obligated to develop affirmative action plans with regard to hiring more minorities and women. Some employers have turned this obligation into an opportunity to open up and systematize their hiring practices. In these cases jobs that were formerly filled by word of mouth are now publicly advertised. Positions that were ill defined and offered little chance of promotion now have clear definitions and are part of an advancement ladder within the company. Standards that once were taken for granted have been found to be discriminatory and have been abandoned.

On the other hand, as white-male-dominated institutions, many companies have made the affirmative-action obligation a mismanaged debacle that has turned blacks against whites and men against women. White males have been led to believe that they have missed out on jobs because of their color or race. Blacks or women have been led to believe that their hiring or promotions—or even consideration for work—have been the result of favoritism forced on the company by the government.

In the 1970s, employees and their representatives became aware of the subtleties of the laws and worked them to their advantage. Martin Luther King, Jr., once said that racial discrimination was a cancer on the body politic. If that is true, and most students of American history have to agree that it is, then the equal employment laws should be used as delicate surgical instruments to heal the situation, not as meat cleavers.

Clearly federal law prohibits a decision whether or not to hire to be based on race, color, national origin, religion, or sex.[39] Also pregnancy.[40] Also age, between the ages of 40 and 69.[41] This includes both obvious, overt forms of discrimination, as well as subtle or informal methods. The law prohibits any practice, even if it appears to be neutral, that has a discriminatory impact—usually against minorities or women. This would include policies against hiring married women, preferences for (or against) hiring relatives of present employees, hiring only those with high school diplomas or other kinds of certification, certain height and weight restrictions, policies against hiring applicants with children, and policies against hiring persons with arrest records. An employer possibly could continue using standards like these (even if it had a disparate statistical impact on minorities or women) if it could persuade the government that the standards were a business necessity. The employer would have to *validate* that its standards were directly correlated with performance on the job.

A very few number of jobs are appropriately filled by certain applicants because their race or sex is a *bona fide occupational qualification*. Actors and actresses are the best example.

If five women and a man apply for a job and the man gets the job, this in itself is not proof of discrimination. To show discrimination, a complainant would have to produce a statement uttered by the employer's representative that was discriminatory, or cite a practice, however subtle, that tended to favor men over women. It could be that the policy of having interviews itself has a disparate impact on women and doesn't have anything to do with future job performance.

It is not a valid defense to a charge of discriminatory hiring that a company's present employees or customers prefer whites, or men, or younger people, or any other category of individual. Nor may an employer refuse to hire a person because he or she has exerted rights under the law. Nor may an employer pretend to be color-blind and accept employees referred by a labor organization or employment agency that is discriminatory in *its* procedures.

Courts have held that the Civil Rights Act of 1964 does not prohibit employment discrimination against homosexuals, although someone someday may persuade a court that such discrimination has a disparate impact on men. A couple of dozen localities, like Tucson, Seattle, Detroit, Minneapolis, San Jose, San Francisco, Wichita, Miami, the District of Columbia, and the State of Wisconsin, prohibit discrimination against homosexuals in private employment. The California Supreme Court ruled in 1979 that the state constitution may provide a remedy for homosexuals at a "state-protected public utility" like the telephone company.[42]

An employer may not consider age as a factor in making employment decisions about applicants who are between the ages of 40 or 69, according to the Age Discrimination in Employment Act. This means that a company may not have a mandatory retirement age less than 70, nor a policy of not hiring employees over a certain age (between 40 and 69). An exception to the law permits companies to retire high-level executives after age 65 if they provide them healthy pensions. This law applies to companies with twenty or more employees, and the Civil Rights Act applies to companies with fifteen or more employees.

Companies with federal contracts incur additional obligations to go beyond nondiscrimination and implement an affirmative-action program. A court or government agency may also impose an affirmative-action plan on a company with or without government contracts, if it has been shown to have discriminated in the past.

An affirmative-action program, obviously, requires the employer to be conscious of race and sex in employment decisions and to overcome the effects of past discrimination, but a valid affirmative-action program does not involve hiring only minorities or women over other candidates. It does involve a comprehensive analysis by a company of its work force to determine which job categories have fewer minorities or women than one would expect based on the availability of qualified minorities or women in the relevant job market. The employer is then required to set short-range goals with specific time deadlines as part of a long-range plan to reach minority and female representation comparable to that in the market. Part of such a plan must be recruitment efforts to attract members of the group in question; a systematic effort to reorganize work and jobs to permit newcomers to enter and advance in particular job classifications; revamping selection methods that have not been shown to be relevant to job performance (in order to reduce the discriminatory effect these methods may have had); making special efforts for employees stuck in dead-end jobs; and setting up a system for monitoring progress of the program and for making necessary adjustments. If a company meets its goals within the time set, clearly its plan is working. If it fails to meet its goals, it must be able to show the government that its program is working well and that it has instituted all of the changes it promised. Women and minorities who meet the fair qualifications for various jobs are the obvious beneficiaries of an affirmative-action program. But all applicants and employees who have not been in the mainstream of a particular company's hiring are also beneficiaries. Whether men or women, minorities or not, they become aware of job openings (and the qualifications) that formerly were not publicly advertised, and they can take advantage of redesigned jobs and new "career ladders" that have been established.

Far from "favoring" minorities or women, properly designed affirmative-action programs open up the hiring process to all comers so that women, minorities, and anyone else who had formerly been excluded from the process have an equal chance to compete. Affirmative action has brought hiring out of the back rooms.

Employers with certain federal contracts have additional obligations with regard to hiring veterans. In addition, the U.S. Employment Service is required to refer veterans to employers on a priority basis. There are also tax credits for hiring Vietnam veterans, as well as certain economically disadvantaged persons.[43]

Employers with federal contracts must also take affirmative action to employ and advance qualified handicapped individuals.[44]

Finally, when a person has been hired or is under active consideration, it is not unusual for the person to be given a notice like the following:

> I hereby recognize that the company may conduct an investigative consumer credit report which may contain information pertaining to my character, general reputation, personal characteristics, modes of living, credit standing, and personal habits. I recognize that the investigation, if conducted, will be based on personal interviews with those who know me or know of me. I realize that I have the right to submit a request in writing to the company to know the nature and scope of the report that has been requested on me.

A notice like this is required by a federal law, the Fair Credit Reporting Act, whenever an employer procures an investigative report on an applicant from some outside firm.[45] No notice need be provided if the report is to be used for an opening for which the individual himself did not apply. Upon a written request from an applicant or employee, the investigating company must then disclose "the nature and substance" of the investigation requested by the employer. If an individual is turned down for employment because of an outside report, the employer must notify the person of this and supply the name and address of the firm that prepared the report. The person then has a right to call, write, or visit the firm and be told what information was in its report. (The law does not require that the individual be given a copy of the report, nor must an employer give the reasons for rejecting an applicant.)

Rates of Pay

The nondiscrimination laws protect an employee, of course, once he or she is hired, including the decision about rates of pay. Title VII of the Civil Rights Act of 1964 prohibits different rates of pay based on race, sex, or the other prohibited grounds. Further, the Fair Labor Standards Act requires certain minimum rates of pay in most jobs, in concert with state minimum wage laws, and it requires that workers be paid one and a half times the usual rate of pay for overtime hours beyond forty hours a week.[46]

The Equal Pay Act of 1963 prohibits the payment of lower wages on the basis of sex for equal work unless the pay rates are based on seniority, a merit system, per-unit production, or some other differential not based on sex.[47] The Equal Pay Act applies to employees covered by the Fair Labor Standards Act, and under both acts aggrieved employees may file lawsuits on their own behalf, without first complaining to the Department of Labor or the Equal Employment Opportunity Commission.

Advocates for women workers have argued that Title VII, because it was amended to incorporate the standards of the Equal Pay Act, requires not only equal pay for equal work, but also equal pay for "comparable worth," even though the tasks involved may not be identical. For instance, female matrons at a prison in Oregon argued that the act entitled them to wages equal to those of male guards. The women admitted they did not perform work equal to that of the males. The men supervised about ten times as many prisoners as the matrons did and the females did lots of less valuable clerical work. But the Tenth Circuit Court of Appeals said that the only reason for the different pay scales was the sex of the employees, and the U.S. Supreme Court agreed in 1981.[48]

The Supreme Court said it was not considering the "controversial" issue of comparable worth, but it did say that Title VII suits may be brought even if no member of the opposite sex holds an equal job with higher pay. The only reason the Court could find for the disparity in Oregon was sex, and this is discriminatory. Even so the "comparable worth" advocates took heart from the decision. They have argued in other court challenges that jobs requiring comparable but not identical skills and responsibilities should be paid equally. They say that predominantly female job classifications deserve pay equal to the wages of predominantly male job classifications if the requirements are comparable, even though the type of work might be entirely different. The U.S. Circuit Court of Appeals in the Third Circuit in 1980 accepted this reasoning in a lawsuit by the International Electrical, Radio, and Machine Workers against Westinghouse Electric Corp.[49] Minnesota has included the concept in its labor code.

But in Denver, city and county nurses said it was discriminatory to base their rate of pay on nurses' salaries at private hospitals. They wanted to be paid what the city and county paid other city workers who needed comparable qualifications and skills. (The city was paying male tree trimmers and male painters more than nurses.) The Tenth Circuit Court of Appeals rejected what it called the nurses' attempt to have the city "reassess the worth of services in each position in relation to all others, and to strike a new balance and relationship."[50] Employers apparently are able to consider market factors in setting rates of pay.

Labor and feminist groups are pushing the concept of equal pay for comparable worth, however. A municipal strike in San Jose in 1981 was the first over this issue. In the last year of the Carter administration, the Equal Employment Opportunity Commission held hearings on whether to revise its regulations on equal pay. Under the Reagan administration it has taken no action on this issue.

Once a person is hired, he or she is usually handed a company handbook that lists the marvelous benefits that the company provides. A professional employee at McGraw-Hill Co. in New York believed what he read. When he was dismissed from his job in 1977, he sued the company for breach of contract. The company handbook was not just a propaganda handout, the man argued, it was part of his work contract with McGraw-Hill. After all, when he joined the company he was asked to sign a statement saying that his employment was subject to the provisions in the handbook.

The handbook said that an employee would not be dismissed or transferred before his shortcomings were discussed with him. Also, it said that an employee fired for lack of qualifications is eligible for separation pay. The man claimed that he was not informed of his shortcomings, nor did he receive severance pay.

A majority of courts thus far have held that an employee handbook or a company manual is merely an expression of company policy that may be withdrawn or altered by the company at any time. There is a trend, however, for courts to recognize the commitments made in such company materials as part of an enforceable work contract that the employer must live up to. A New York State appeals court ruled in 1982, for instance, that McGraw-Hill was obligated to live up to what it had stated in its company handbook, just as if it were part of an enforceable employment contract with the man who was fired.[51]

5

Freedom of Trust

A few years ago, a man working at a manufacturing plant was recommended for promotion by his foreman, but the personnel department turned down the request without giving a reason. The man filed a grievance and the case was heard by an arbitrator. The head of personnel was asked at the hearing why he passed over the employee for promotion. His response was that he considered the man not to be a responsible person. Why? Because, explained the personnel chief, when he was touring the plant once with corporate VIPs he saw the man standing idle. "I looked up and saw him standing on a ladder with his arms folded when he should have been working."

Then the employee was given an opportunity to give his side of the story. He said that he was working on a high ladder moving heavy pipe across a narrow passageway. When the personnel director and the VIPs started to walk down the passageway toward the ladder the man wisely stopped handling the pipe so that there was no possibility that a piece might fall on the plant visitors. "And when I stand, I usually fold my arms," he told the arbitrator.

Because all of this was worked out in a relatively rational forum, the story had a happy ending. The employee was awarded his promotion, and the personnel officer realized the misunderstanding and was pleased to restore the morale of a productive employee who might otherwise have quit or become apathetic. Still, the question remains. Why did this matter have to go to arbitration?

The story is an example of the thousands of misunderstandings that occur in the workplace every day because of a lack of trust between supervisors and workers. Where there is a grievance procedure, these matters are sometimes ironed out in a rational way, even though there is inevitably a loss of work time and of good feeling on both sides. More commonly, companies let the misunderstandings fester. Or worse, they try to take a shortcut—by delegating to a machine the task of determining which employees can be trusted. Seeking to avoid direct human confrontation and the difficult fact-finding that may be necessary in these cases, corporations ask a polygraph machine to settle questions of trust. They might as well delegate this decision to the flip of a coin. Just about all respected studies of the "lie detector" device show that its accuracy rate is little more than mere chance.

Still, thousands of American companies, faced with increased losses from pilferage and from unreliable employees, have turned to the polygraph. This simply compounds the misunderstandings. The country is littered with innocent victims.

A young woman working for a California food store, for example, found herself accused of defrauding her employer. The store manager suggested that she submit to a polygraph examination. Reluctantly, she agreed. When asked by the examiner, "Did you check out items to your mother at a discount?" the woman answered no. The examiner analyzed her answer as a deception. She was fired. Her union conducted an investigation in preparation for a grievance proceeding. It discovered that the employee's mother had died several years earlier. The woman may have shown stress in her answer, but not deception.

A young clerk at a grocery store in Lima, Ohio, agreed to take a polygraph examination when $1,000 was reported missing from the store. He was asked whether he took the money. He answered no, but with hesitation (because in his subconscious he had a vague suspicion as to who had taken it). The polygraph recorded the hesitation. The man was suspended, and only a concerted effort by his union cleared up the misunderstanding and won his job back.

A bookkeeper at S.S. Kresge Co. in Detroit knew she was innocent of wrongdoing. In fact, she herself reported a $150 cash shortage. The company asked her to take a polygraph examination and she agreed (even though Michigan state law permits an employee to refuse, without consequences). She was taken to a motel in a scruffy part of town and plugged into the machine. She was shocked to be told she had "failed" the test. Five years later she collected $100,000 in damages from the company for the trauma inflicted upon her.

Combustion Engineering Co. in Stamford, Conn., was trying to track down which of its professional employees had leaked documents to the *Wall Street Journal*. A half-dozen employees were subjected to polygraph tests, which abruptly ended when the *Journal* ran a story about the testing. On the basis of the tests, company executives felt they had identified the culprit. The man singled out said later, "My associates, my peers, believed that I was the person. They would not confide in me any longer. I just felt I could not work in that type of environment." At that point began a steady decline in the man's mental health, family life, and professional employment. *Wall Street Journal* reporter Jonathan Kwitny and his *real* source at Combustion certified that the man forced to resign by the polygraph test was innocent of any contact with the press. By then it was too late.

Two laborers for a construction contractor were required to submit to polygraph examinations before they could work on a project at a nuclear power plant in Iowa. The two men answered all of the questions truthfully. And so they were cleared of any antinuclear attitudes—screening out such types was the purpose of the testing. But the two men lost their jobs anyway. In the course of their questioning, they were compelled to reveal prior felony convictions. Perhaps moved by testimony from representatives of the contractor that both men were good workers, an arbitrator ordered the men reinstated because they were not guilty of any misconduct on the job.

In spite of these and many more abuses documented in congressional testimony, periodicals, union records, litigation, and arbitration hearings, several hundred American businesses continue to rely on the polygraph to check on the trustworthiness of their employees and applicants. Trucking firms are big users; so are fast-food franchises, drug chains, retail stores, taxicab companies, security firms, car rental companies, airlines, taverns, and locally owned small businesses. Many of these companies ask job applicants to submit to a polygraph test. Some require employees once they are hired to submit to periodic testing, as a way of deterring pilferage on the job. Other companies call in the polygraph examiners only when there is a suspicion of wrongdoing and there is no clear suspect.

Those persons designated for the tests are usually sent to a private security agency that does the testing for the employer. The person to be interviewed is asked some preliminary questions, made to feel relaxed and simultaneously assured that the machine is infallible. (A person who thinks the machine cannot detect falsehoods will generally foul up the results.) The individual is then attached to the machine—a strap across the chest to measure breathing patterns, electrodes attached to the hands to measure increases in skin moisture, and a medical cuff around the upper arm to measure changes in blood pressure and pulse. These various indicators are marked on a graph by a moving stylus. As the examiner asks a series of questions, some of them innocent, others directly related to the individual's application form or to the crime under investigation, he notices the physiological changes as they are plotted on the graph. The examiner is interested in significant changes when the interviewee is answering pertinent questions. These are supposed to be indicators of stress—at least to the believers in this technique—and stress is supposed to indicate dishonesty.

Companies pay no more than $20 or so for a preemployment test, and so they get in return a once-over-lightly interview with a hasty conclusion by the examiner that the person is deceptive or not deceptive. The applicant is usually not informed of the results, merely told later that he or she will not be hired.

Experienced polygraphers say their questions on preemployment tests simply verify information on application forms, but most tests subject applicants to other embarrassing disclosures. At Adolph Coors Brewery, the questions have included:

Are you having sexual relations?
Have you had sex with more than one person?
    What kind of sex?
Are you a communist?
Have you ever committed an undetected crime?
How often do you change your underwear?
Have you ever done anything with your wife that
    could be considered immoral?
Have you ever been involved with homosexuals?
Is there anything that you know of for which you
    could be blackmailed?

An AFL-CIO spokesman in 1979 put it simply, "The cheap, quickie lie detector test achieves just what employers really desire: an intimidated, scared worker, rather than a certified, blemish-free background."

The results of lie detector tests are inadmissible in just about every court in the country, even when both sides agree to their use. Scientific testimony is admissible only when it has "gained general acceptance in the particular field in which it belongs." That is the standard set by a federal court in 1923 and accepted ever since by courts. The court in 1923 said flatly, "We think the systolic blood pressure deception test has not yet gained such standing and scientific recognition among physiological and psychological authorities as would justify courts in admitting expert testimony."[52]

When asked to admit polygraph testimony, courts have regularly stuck by this 1923 standard. Polygraphy has not advanced much since then and its "acceptance" among physiologists and psychologists is even less now than in the 1920s. In the 1970s, courts in Michigan, Maryland, California, and elsewhere reaffirmed the inadmissibility of polygraph evidence. Only in Wisconsin and New Mexico (when both sides agree) are polygraph results admissible. The constitutional rights to remain silent, to be free of unreasonable searches, to maintain one's beliefs free of government intrusion, and to confront one's accuser—all of these argue against admissibility, even if the tests were accurate. The Constitution, then, protects a criminal suspect from going to jail for "failing" a polygraph test or declining to take one, but what protects a person from losing gainful employment for the same reason?

In half of the fifty states there is no protection. The states of Alaska, California, Connecticut, Delaware, Hawaii, Idaho, Maine, Maryland, Massachusetts, Michigan, Minnesota, Montana, Nebraska, New Jersey, Oregon, Pennsylvania, Rhode Island, Washington, and Wisconsin, plus the District of Columbia, prohibit the use of polygraphs as a condition of employment. Arizona and Vermont require that the subject be told the test is voluntary. In Arizona, New Mexico, Virginia, and Vermont, certain questions are disallowed. In Utah a person can't be fired for refusing to take a test.

Even in these states employers get applicants and employees to "volunteer" for polygraph tests, as a way of circumventing the law. (And some interstate companies test employees in states without antipolygraph laws, then transfer them to sites within antipolygraph states.) In 1973, the New Jersey Supreme Court said unequivocally, after comparing the safeguards present when a criminal defendant takes a test:

> There is no judicial control when an employer subjects his employee to a lie detector test and there is no licensing or other objective method of assuring expertise and safeguard in the administration of the test and the interpretation of its results. Nor is there any assurance of true voluntariness, for the economic compulsions are generally such that the employee has no realistic choice.[53]

Most disputes in employment are settled not in court, however, but in arbitration hearings. Most collective-bargaining contracts include an agreement by both labor and management to submit disputes arising under the contract to an arbitrator, an independent referee selected by both sides. Arbitration is less formal than a court trial. The arbitrator has more latitude in accepting evidence than does a judge, and he or she does not have to be bound by the precedents set by previous arbitration decisions. Still, arbitrators do get together in an attempt to bring some uniformity to the process. The attitude of the typical arbitrator toward accepting evidence of polygraph tests is, "I'll consider it for what it's worth"—a clear indication that it isn't worth much.

"It is obvious that an 'overwhelming majority' do reject the polygraph as valid evidence," according to Edgar A. Jones, Jr., law professor at the University of California, Los Angeles, in a well-documented and searing indictment of polygraphs at the 1978 annual meeting of the National Academy of Arbitrators. He also quoted one of the "bibles" of the arbitration business, *How Arbitration Works* by Elkouri and Elkouri, saying that the "overwhelming weight of arbitral authority" bars penalizing employees for refusal to take a polygraph test and "where an employee does submit to lie detector testing, the test results should be given little or no weight in arbitration."[54]

Jones recognizes the dilemma of an arbitrator who is supposed to stick to the four corners of a labor agreement in making his rulings. The contract itself may even permit management and union representatives to agree to lie detector testing. But, Jones points out, the Supreme Court has ordered arbitrators to stick to the contract *unless it violates a clear underlying policy of federal law labor.* "Suppose," he asks, "a security-intensive employer were to obtain a contract provision that provided, 'The Director of Security of the Company may at any time and under any circumstances order any, some or all of its employees, regardless of sex or other characteristics, to undergo a stripped-down body search in the Company's maingate guardroom to be conducted by guards on duty under the supervision of the Supervisor of guards. The Chief Steward or his representative shall be present. A refusal to comply with such an order shall constitute just cause for immediate termination.'

"Could an employer reasonably be advised to expect an arbitrator to uphold the discharge of a female employee who had refused an order to comply with that provision?" Jones asks. Yet, that is what thousands of employees, whether oganized or not, are required to agree to as a condition of employment—to have their minds stripped naked before an untrained polygraph "examiner" to satisfy some employer's shortcut to the truth.

The machine has been discredited in just about all rational circles:

The U.S. House of Representatives' Committee on Government Operations in 1965 and in 1976: "There is no 'lie detector,' neither machine nor human. People have been deceived by a myth that a metal box in the hands of an investigator can detect truth or falsehood."[55]

The U.S. Department of Justice in 1974: "A useful adjunct . . . in certain limited circumstances in a very small percentage of matters. . . . We view the results of such examinations with caution and oppose their introduction into evidence."[56]

David T. Lykken, psychologist at the University of Minnesota and foremost student of polygraphing, in 1981: "A polygraph examiner who asserts that a respondent 'showed deception' or 'gave a deceptive response' on a particular question is making either a misstatement or a false statement."[57]

R. J. Weir, Jr., onetime president of the American Polygraph Association, in 1974: "I have even heard experienced examiners get mousetrapped into a discussion as to whether there is some mysterious difference between the reactions created by lies and those from strong emotions such as fear or anger. All I know is that I know of no way to make this distinction merely from the chart patterns."[58]

The U.S. Privacy Protection Study Commission in 1977: "Federal law [should] be enacted to forbid an employer from using the polygraph or other truth-verification equipment to gather information from an applicant or employee."[59]

Business Week in 1978: "One thing that many businessmen do not seem to have taken into account is that lie detectors are only as good as the people who conduct the tests, and the employers victimize themselves as well as workers when testing is slipshod."[60]

Seldom have such sophisticated people been hoodwinked by such mysticism as when personnel and security officers buy polygraph services. Some even believe in a "voice stress analyzer" that measures tremors in the voice as an indicator of stress. This device, of course, can be used without the knowledge of the subject, and some believers even try to use it on telephone calls or recorded voices. The states of New York and Wisconsin prohibit use of the device by employers, and another dozen states effectively prevent its use because of the wording of their polygraph licensing laws.

Pen-and-Pencil Truth Tests

Faced with legal, labor, and scientific obstacles to polygraph use, many employers turn to "pen-and-pencil" lie detector tests that are marketed by polygraph companies.

The first of these, the Reid Report of Chicago, advertises that "it is particularly helpful in states that prohibit polygraph or for companies with a large number of employees where the cost of administering polygraph would be too high."

The Reid people have their own notions about the "honest" and "dishonest" answers to the dozens of questions asked in the test booklets they sell to personnel departments. (The results are then "graded" in Chicago.) For example, one question on the test asks, "What percentage of people do you think steal from employers?" The Reid people say the honest answer is "from 1 to 5 percent." The dishonest person, they say, estimates that a large percentage of people steal. He thinks, "Everybody does it."

The Reid firm, owned and operated by polygraph examiners, has its own ideas about the proper answers to these questions as well:

"A judge in a recent case blamed the boss for paying low wages and freed the worker who took the money. Do you think the judge did right?"

"Did you ever think you had a good reason for cheating a company out of some merchandise?"

"If you found when you got home that a salesgirl failed to add a $1 item that you bought, would you return the next day and pay the $1 to the store?"

The Reid company says, "As compared with honest applicants, dishonest ones tended to rate their own honesty lower. Honest applicants believe that most of their fellow workers are honest; dishonest applicants think a large proportion of their fellow workers are dishonest." Those who "flunk" the test and are not hired are free to take a polygraph test to "prove their innocence," the company says.

Another company markets a test of 100 true-false questions designed to test "trustworthiness." These questions are even more subjective, related not to tendencies toward crime but to individual opinions that may validly differ among different persons. For example:

"Our society seems to be going downhill morally."

"Employee theft is chicken feed compared to income tax evasion by company executives."

Other tests pry into personal matters in an attempt to screen out unstable applicants.

"Were you a bed wetter between the ages of 8 to 14 years?"

"Do you frequently suffer from bowel problems?"

"Do you always sweat and get tied up in knots during examinations?"

It's hard to know the right answer to one of the questions asked in a Sears, Roebuck and Co.. preemployment test: "Are our modern industrial and scientific developments signs of a greater degree of civilization than those attained by any previous society—the Greeks, for example?" Sears psychologists say that there is no right or wrong answer with regard to getting hired, but that a "yes" answer on this question might make you a prime candidate for the hard commercial side of the operation and a "no" answer might channel you into the decorative or creative side.

What all this has to do with working in a warehouse or making hamburgers or programming computers is not at all clear. And so employment testing fell in great disrepute during the 1970s after a Supreme Court decision in 1971 said that the Civil Rights Act of 1964 requires "that any tests used must measure the person for the job and not the person in the abstract."[61] Where any job standard has a disparate impact on minorities and could not be shown to be significantly related to successful job performance, it was illegal. "Nothing in the Act precludes the use of testing or measuring devices; obviously they are useful," the Court said. "What Congress has forbidden is giving these devices and mechanisms controlling force unless they are demonstrably a reasonable measure of job performance."

By 1976, IBM Chairman Frank T. Cary could proudly report: "We have stopped excursions into applicants' emotional and private lives through the use of personality tests. We don't use polygraphs in hiring or at any other time—we never have. But we use aptitude tests and consider them useful. Some tests have credibility, for instance, in forecasting a person's aptitude for programming, or typing, or certain other types of occupation. Also, this sort of information isn't so personal or sensitive. It's more job-related than personality tests are. [General intelligence] tests don't help us much either. Many of the people we hire have college backgrounds, and their records in college seem to be as good an indicator as any IQ test. So here again, since there are other ways of making the evaluation we need—ways that can't be called intrusions—we use them instead."

As government pressure for equal employment opportunity seems to have lessened, testing in the job place has made a comeback in the 1980s. The trend is away from general IQ tests and personality exams and toward aptitude testing designed to predict performance in a particular job skill. Still, with so many companies taking shortcuts, testing in employment is subject to great abuses. Unfortunately, the experts and organizations that monitor developments in this field are currently focusing their attention on academic testing for higher education, not for employment.

An important consideration in employment testing is a Supreme Court decision in 1979 that an employee has a privacy interest in the results of psychological tests. In permitting Detroit Edison Co. to withhold test scores from a bargaining agent that requested them, the Court said:

> The sensitivity of any human being to disclosure of information that may be taken to bear on his or her basic competence is sufficiently well known to be an appropriate subject of judicial notice. . . . Accordingly we hold that the order requiring the Company unconditionally to disclose the employee scores to the Union was erroneous.[62]

But psychological testing remains in vogue in many places, as in Minnesota where the Vikings, the professional football team, requires personality and psychological tests of its players.

"This is ridiculous," said a pilot for Delta Air Lines after he was subjected to psychological testing. "What do these tests have to do with whether I'll make a good pilot? What the hell does it matter whether I like to sing in the shower?"

6

Freedom of Speech

Freedom of speech in the corporation—or lack of it—comes in two varieties. The first, speech involving work-related issues, has received increasing attention in the past ten years as a new generation of workers demonstrates a new level of concern about organizational behavior. These concerns have included environmental protection, the integrity of business dealings, equal opportunity, consumer protection, and the quality of goods and services. This free speech has found itself a name, "whistle-blowing."

Less is said, however, about an employee's freedom of speech in matters not directly related to work. There have been few court cases and few advocates protecting the right of persons to hold a job regardless of their expressed views on *or off* the job.

Of all the new rights asserted by employees, "whistle-blowing" has been the most difficult for management to accept. In World War II you didn't question the company commander; you were proud to be a member of the team. How can well-paid employees feel so ungrateful to the company as to express complaints openly within or especially outside of the company, top executives wonder. How can you run an effective organization if there's one loose cannon? James M. Roche, chairman of General Motors, seemed shocked in 1971 that Ralph Nader, the consumer advocate, would urge employees to speak out about abuses they saw. Roche responded:

Some of the enemies of business now encourage an employee to be disloyal to the enterprise. They want to create suspicion and disharmony, and pry into the proprietary interests of the business. However this is labeled—industrial espionage, whistle-blowing, or professional responsibility—it is another tactic for spreading disunity and creating conflict.[63]

There should be little wonder that a bitter worker at one of Roche's plants in Ohio was saying at about the same time, "Every time I passed through those plant gates to go to work, I left America, and my rights as a free man. I spent nine hours in there, in prison, and then came out into my country again."

Nor should there be much wonder that GM shortly afterward fired the head of a mechanical development department when he complained about deceptive practices inside the company, refused to join his colleagues in sending false information to the government, and tried to correct the misrepresentation made to the government by the company.[64]

The situation had not improved much in 1981 when the Reagan administration took over federal agencies in Washington. The president's appointee for secretary of housing and urban development faced some of the 14,300 employees he supervises in the department. Do you plan to protect whistle-blowers? he was asked. (Federal law requires this.)

The secretary, Samuel Pierce, thought for a moment, then said, "Do you mean squealers?"

This, from a man who had sat on the boards of General Electric Co., International Paper, Potomac Electric Power Co., Prudential Insurance Co., Public Service Electricity & Gas, and U.S. Industries.

Peter Drucker, the guru of American management, is

even harder on employees who expose wrongdoing. "Informers," he calls them. In 1981 he wrote:

> Whistle-blowing, after all, is simply another word for 'informing.' And perhaps it is not quite irrelevant that the only societies in Western history that encouraged informers were bloody and infamous tyrannies—Tiberius and Nero in Rome, the Inquisition in the Spain of Philip II, the French Terror, and Stalin. . . . For under 'whistle-blowing,' under the regime of the 'informer,' no mutual trust, no interdependencies, and no ethics exist.[65]

Drucker goes on to argue that in any relationship, like that of employer-employee, obligations must be mutual and balanced on both sides. His use of whistle-blowing as an example of this is curious. Employees rarely resort to the practice unless they perceive a breach of that mutuality on the part of their employers. In the minds of some management apologists, apparently, it is appropriate for company executives to "go public" about lack of productivity among workers, about the ill effects of government regulations, and the pressure of salary and wage demands, but it is inappropriate for rank-and-file employees to do the same with regard to issues that concern them. Would anyone seriously argue that a company president should be curtailed in publicly expressing chagrin about a practice within his industry? Yes, say some, if his "free speech" hurts the company. But, while we implicitly trust the company president to make the right judgment with regard to that, we do not generally trust an individual employee to do the same.

In fact, whistle-blowing is not at all akin to "informing." The informer usually acts out of selfish motives; he is often paid for his information. He is not asked to document his charges, yet is allowed to "finger" another individual for disloyalty. He can often act in secrecy, with immunity from repercussions. The informer's victim is usually an individual with no resources to fight back. Compare this to the corporation that is a "victim" of "whistle-blowing"—a corporation with monetary assets, a public relations and research staff, and legal expertise to tell its side of the story—or worse, to get revenge.

Far from being informers, whistle-blowers are like referees in a sports contest who "blow the whistle" when they spot an infraction of the rules. Many corporate executives may view it as strange that *a member of the team* may blow the whistle when he or she spots an infraction of the rules, but in corporate America this is both moral and necessary. More is at stake than a game between two teams, more is at stake even than fierce competition between two corporations. And besides, there is no system for having a "referee" monitor a company's activities to make sure it does not take unfair advantage of a competitor, or worse, the public. The "whistle-blower," by reporting perceived problems to higher-ups, to the press, or to the government, becomes the public's only way of becoming aware of corporate misdeeds that have an effect on us all. The public interest is involved, because a cost overrun, a bribe, waste, the manufacture of an unsafe product, employment discrimination, and other "internal" corporate infractions have an impact on society at large.

Employees who make cost-cutting suggestions are rewarded, but employees who focus attention on corporate problems that could turn into disasters later are generally vilified. And they soon become former employees.

Some examples:

A research manager in a large company spoke out in a management meeting and in social groups when he felt that his employer was making a weak effort to comply with antipollution laws. He was ostracized and eventually quit.

A bus driver complained to his superiors about unsafe conditions in the company's vehicles, then he went to a local television station. He was fired.

Another employee wrote a letter to the company president complaining about a lemon television set he had purchased himself from the company. He threatened to tell the Better Business Bureau. The man was fired.

A research doctor opposed her company's use of children in tests of a drug with a high saccharin content. She was demoted and soon saw that she had no alternative but to resign.

An Eastern Airlines pilot alerted the company to a defect in the jet the company was using. He got no response and complained to a federal agency. Eastern responded by demoting him, and later grounding him.

The principal design engineer at Ford Motor Co. in the early 1970s continually got a deaf ear inside the company as he dispatched memoranda about violations of federal law he detected in the company's testing of its Pinto automobile. "I was expected to be loyal to the company's policies and to ignore my own uneasiness about the safety of the cars we were approving," he said. His judgment was later vindicated, but his frustrations caused him to leave the company in 1978.

Whistle-blowing would seem to be extremely hazardous to your health in the workplace, but in fact more and more workers are boldly speaking up when they discover what to them appear to be unethical or unsafe or unbusinesslike practices. At the very least, they are forcing corporate management to take notice of the problem. If fired, they often manage to tie up the company in lengthy arbitration or litigation. And occasionally they are winning awards of back pay or damages.

When it occurs in public-sector jobs, the practice of whistle-blowing clearly is protected by the courts. This is true whether the complaints are made internally or outside the employee's government agency, and whether or not the employee "first went through channels." In 1968 the U.S. Supreme Court recognized legal protection for public employees who make complaints about their employers in public before going through internal grievance procedures.

The case involved a high school teacher in Illinois who wrote a letter to the editor of a newspaper criticizing the school board's funding preference for sports programs. The teacher was fired for disloyalty, but the Supreme Court ruled that speaking on issues of public importance cannot be the basis for dismissal from public employment.[66]

A psychiatric nurse in a Pennsylvania state mental hospital was fired after a news article quoted her as critical of the hospital. Because she worked for a public employer, which may not curtail a person's First Amendment right of free speech, the nurse won her lawsuit against the hospital.

When a policeman reported to superiors that colleagues were pocketing stolen property recovered on the job, he got no satisfaction and so he cried "cover-up" on a Chicago television program. He was fired for making "derogatory comments reflecting on the image or reputation of the Chicago Police Department." Because he was a public employee, a federal court ordered him reinstated.

An elementary school teacher with more than twenty-five years' experience went public with her concerns about an incinerator on the school playground. And she helped students compose a letter suggesting changes in the school lunch menu. For this, she was not rehired. Because she was a public employee, the court ruled in her favor, saying her superintendent "demanded blind obedience to any directive he gave."

A group of social workers in the Department of Welfare in New York City took a grievance to a federal agency and were suspended. The suspended employees were right; they did not have to go first through the department's complaint mechanism, according to a court in 1969. Because they were public employees, they were vindicated.

A fireman in Northbrook, Ill., accused the fire marshal of mismanagement and was fired. Because he was a public employee, the court sided with him.[67]

But what about employees for private organizations?

What are their rights when they speak their minds? Can employee newsletters have as much editorial freedom as junior high school newspapers? Can workers have unlimited access to work-site bulletin boards without interference?

Thomas I. Emerson, the retired Yale law professor who is a preeminent authority on constitutional law, wrote in 1970:

> A system of freedom of expression that allowed private bureaucracies to throttle all internal discussion of their affairs would be seriously deficient. There seems to be general agreement that at some points the government must step in. In any event the law is moving steadily in that direction.[68]

Indeed there is a trend in the courts to modify the traditional notion that a private employer may fire an employee "at will" without any valid cause. Nowadays, if the reason given by an employer for a discharge is that the employee was disloyal in his complaints, courts may well consider that arbitrary. There seem to be two bases on which a court will protect a private-sector employee from dismissals of this kind: if the dismissal violates sound public policy or if it is based on retaliation for a legitimate activity.

For instance, a court in West Virginia in 1978 recognized that a person has a right to sue for being wrongfully fired "where the employer's motivation for the discharge contravenes some substantial public policy principle. . . ."[69] The state and federal legislatures had clearly stated that sound public policy required certain conduct by banks, and in this case the dismissed employee had merely notified his superiors that the bank where he worked was violating consumer credit protection laws. In Pennsylvania, just four years earlier, a court had refused even to allow a lawsuit by a salesman who was terminated for complaining that his company's product had not been adequately tested and presented a serious danger. He was told to keep selling. The man took his complaint to a vice president, and the product was eventually withdrawn from the market. The salesman was fired anyway. The court said:

> The praiseworthiness of [the employee's] motives does not detract from the company's legitimate interest in preserving its normal operational procedures from disruption. In sum, while we agree that employees should be encouraged to express their educated views on the quality of their employer's products, we are not persuaded that creating a new non-statutory cause of action . . . is the best way to achieve this result. On balance, whatever public policy imperatives can be discerned here seem to militate against such a course.[70]

Perceptive lawyers recognized this language as an invitation to legislatures *to create* a right of action (a right to bring a lawsuit) when a discharge is based on an employee's speech or behavior that is in the public interest. And it is an invitation for courts in later years to declare a "public policy" against such firings if the facts in the particular case are especially compelling. In 1980, a court in Montana picked up the ball, even though it ruled against the dismissed employee in the case. It said, "In a proper case a cause for wrongful discharge could be made out by an employee."[71] The Montana court recognized that a "whistle-blowing" victim at least had a right to be heard in court, a right rejected in Pennsylvania in 1974.

Now, California (especially), Massachusetts, Michigan, New Jersey, New York, Oregon, Pennsylvania, and West Virginia (to a tentative extent) recognize by law an employee's right to sue when abusively discharged by a company in violation of a recognized public policy of the state. The doctrine is applied sparingly—and notably in cases involving an employee's doing what he was legally obligated to do (like obey the law and report wrongdoing to authorities) or what laws of the state give him a right to do (like file a claim for worker's compensation).

There is an additional theory to sustain a lawsuit in these cases. Some employees, notably in Massachusetts, have prevailed on the theory that firings of this sort violate an employment contract, which after all implies good faith and fair dealing by both sides.[72] If an employee takes this route, his or her damages are limited to lost wages under the contract. To date this theory has not been applied to firings involving free speech or "whistle-blowing," but it may provide fertile ground in the future.

Making Specific Complaints

In a sizable portion of the American work force, individual employees are protected when they complain within a company or outside a company *on specific work issues* like safety, equal opportunity, or collective bargaining: the National Labor Relations Act protects organized workers who speak out against work rules and other work conditions. Such speech is protected under the act to the extent that it does not disrupt work.[73] Still, it is important to remember that the act "protects protest only when it is related to wages, hours, and working conditions, and is the concerted action of more than one person. Hence, the single person seeking to prevent a company from marketing an unsafe product may get no help from the [National Labor Relations] Board."[74]

Title VII of the Civil Rights Act of 1964 bars an employer from discriminating against any person who "has opposed any practice" that is unlawful under the civil rights law or who "has made a charge, testified, assisted, or participated in any manner in any investigation, proceeding or hearing" to enforce nondiscrimination in employment.

The Equal Pay Act, the Fair Labor Standards Act

(minimum wage), and the Age Discrimination in Employment Act make it unlawful for a company to discharge or in any other manner discriminate against any employee who attempts to secure rights under these acts. The Coal Mine Safety Act prohibits discrimination, including discharges, against employees who report suspected violations of the act to the government, or who file suit or testify in court. The Occupational Safety and Health Act has a similar provision.[75]

What About Free Speech Off the Job?

While these laws protect the worker as a specific complainant, there is very little protection for the employee who chooses to be an individual on or off the job—by speaking out on an issue of concern.

For instance, a chemical engineer at DuPont Co. was fired for writing a fictional account of a chemical company's attitudes toward its professional employees.

Charles Morgan, Jr., was pushed to resignation as Washington director of the American Civil Liberties Union because of a quotation from him about the 1976 presidential campaign that appeared in the *New York Times*. Morgan had said that Northerners were biased against Jimmy Carter because he was a Southerner, and the ACLU management objected to Morgan that his views could be misinterpreted as those of the organization. And so he quit. The same ACLU, a few years earlier, had heard from a man in New York City who was fired from his job because he publicly advocated impeachment of President Nixon.

A California man with twenty years' service was suspended indefinitely from his job at a Libby fruit warehouse because he wanted to display in his office a poster with the incidental caption, "Viva la Revolucion."

The State Supreme Court in New York City in a 1978 case opened the possibility for an employee to have a remedy against an adverse action based on outside political activity. The man involved was fired by American Telephone & Telegraph Co. after he was arrested driving his van recklessly at a political rally. The court accepted the man's argument that discharges for outside political activity violate public policy. Ruling against the man "is not to say that such a public policy does not exist; it is merely to say that [the employee in this case] has not sustained his burden of persuasion."[76] The court ruled against the man because he had not persuaded the court that he was actually fired for political activity, but its language will be helpful to an employee with stronger proof.

A few states have found it necessary to enact legislation prohibiting an employer from interfering with employees who wish to engage in certain outside political activities. These include Arizona, California, Massachusetts, Minnesota, Missouri, and Wisconsin. California's law, on the books since 1915, says, "No employer shall make, adopt, or enforce any rule, regulation, or policy . . . forbidding or preventing employees from engaging or participating in politics or from becoming candidates . . ."[77]

In 1974, the Texas Department of Public Safety kept an eye on Robert Pomeroy, an outspoken opponent of nuclear power development and principal spokesperson for a citizens group opposed to the construction of a nuclear power plant near Dallas. It kept Pomeroy under surveillance and compiled a file on him. A DPS agent then went to Continental Airlines, where Pomeroy was employed as a pilot, and turned over to the company the DPS files on him. After it was caught, the Department of Public Safety apologized, saying it had no evidence that Pomeroy was engaged in illegal activity. It admitted that its agent had no business turning the information over to the man's employer. Also, an engineer working with Pomeroy's antinuclear group was told by his employer to quit his outside political work. The man said that a DPS record on him found its way to his company as well.

Luckily for Pomeroy, Continental Airlines did not demand that he choose between his job and the antinuclear campaign he believed in so much. "I've got a good job and I like what I'm doing," he said at the time. "If I thought I was going to lose it, I'd have to think awfully long and hard. Airline pilots are pretty useless when they leave the employment of one airline. You're done when you're fired from an airline."

Continental's decision to avoid a confrontation with its employee's off-hours freedom of speech is the kind of action that prevents lawsuits.

7

Freedom from Intrusions

From the moment your employees entered the front gate until they left for home, they've always been on their own. And no matter how dependable they were it's been almost impossible to hold them accountable for their actions and their whereabouts.

The Identification Network from Rusco Electronics gives you accountability for people and facilities that you never thought possible. It monitors and reports employee whereabouts and actions. And gives you an accurate, immediate record of who, what, where, and when.

Now basic data entry is available anywhere. For instance, you can control the locking and unlocking of doors on a pre-programmed time schedule.

Parking lot entrances and exits can be tied into the Identification Network. So you can always find out if an employee is on the premises.

You can account for the use of the copying machine and know how many copies each employee makes.

You can create an electronic time and attendance log of your employees' ins-and-outs for automatic payroll processing. You can even restrict after-hours elevator use. For certain key people and certain floors.

Those are just a few examples.

Each of your employees gets an Identification Network Entry Card with a personalized code. Each room or piece of equipment that requires accountability has a single, compact CARDENTRY reader. You simply tell the Identification Network which employees are allowed into each room and which employees are authorized to use each piece of equipment.

If someone attempts to enter a room or use a piece of equipment that's off limits to them, the door will not open or the machinery will not work.

And a central printer immediately tells your security people that an attempted unauthorized entry has occurred, where it occurred, and when.

It's that easy to account for (and control) unauthorized access and activities. And that easy to save money.

That warning is from the manufacturer of an electronic protection system for industries, in an advertisement appearing in *Datamation,* a trade magazine, in November 1979. Its tone sounds like an elementary school principal discussing his or her pupils. Most employees, at all levels, are treated like children or criminals, or both, says industrial psychologist David Sirota. And children must be watched. Employees, then, feel scrutinized, monitored, distrusted, and put upon from the moment they walk in the door in the morning until they leave at the end of the day. "The most severe labor conflicts are due not to financial issues but to disrespect," says Sirota.

The Company Cops

All of this watching requires sophisticated computer hardware and lots of sets of eyes. The number of persons employed in private security work exceeds 1.5 million, far in excess of the number employed as sworn police officers for municipalities and states. The smaller police force (the one supported by public tax money) is limited by a large body of constitutional law developed under the Fourth Amendment which prohibits unreasonable searches and seizures. The larger force is not even registered with the government, much less regulated in its work by state laws, court opinions, or constitutional principles.

Most of these private guards serve as "company cops" to keep employees in line. In fact, they possess no more authority to make arrests or use weapons than any other private citizen, but most employees do not realize that.

The manager of an agency that provides guards to industry was quoted as saying, "It's a real joke the way some agencies operate. . . . The majority of guards can't protect themselves, let alone the property. For the minimum wage, you can't expect a man to risk his life."

The *Richmond Times-Dispatch* said in 1976, "This industry is virtually unregulated and without industry-wide standards. Who is the young man who couldn't get a police job and now is guarding a department store, and how qualified is he to have a revolver strapped to his side? And who is the arthritic old man who has to supplement his pension with part-time security work, and how will he react to an emergency?" It quoted one young guard as saying, "I'll tell you, if I was hiring me, I'd be a little concerned. What am I qualified to do? They give me a gun, and the people who hire us expect us to be as qualified as the cops."

A commission sponsored by the U.S. Department of Justice in 1977 recommended that all states license companies selling security services and that all security personnel be registered by the state after satisfying certain qualifications with regard to age, physical fitness, intelligence, character, and training. Currently thirty-four states require licenses of private security *firms*, but there are virtually no requirements for an *individual* hired by these firms as a "rent-a-cop."

Limiting Personal Searches

More and more, employees are taking matters into their own hands, by challenging in court or in arbitration excessive physical intrusions in the workplace. In many instances they have been successful. A grocery store clerk recovered $25,700 in damages for false imprisonment after she was detained by security personnel at a Kroger Co. store in Texas. The woman was accused of stealing money from her cash register. She was interviewed at length by security men and asked to accompany them to her bank. Although the victim was never touched by her questioners and did not even ask to end the questioning, a jury found that she had been falsely imprisoned.[78]

At a K mart department store in Oregon a cashier was accused by a customer of taking four $5 bills from her. Even though the customer made no effort to see whether in fact she was missing the money, she made such a fuss that the store manager checked the cash register. As the complaining customer kept an icy glare on the proceedings, the manager found that the cash in the register balanced perfectly. But the manager ordered his employee to strip for a search in a back room. An assistant manager conducted a strip search in the presence of the unhappy customer. A state appellate court ruled in 1981 that "a jury could find that the K mart manager, a thirty-two-year-old male in charge of the entire store, after concluding that the plaintiff did not take [the customer's] money, put her through the degrading and humiliating experience of submitting to a strip search in order to satisfy the customer, who was not only acting unreasonably, but was creating a commotion in the store."[79]

In a similar suit, a General Motors employee won $25,000 for defamation, assault, and false imprisonment.[80] He said that security guards at a plant in Maryland detained him because they suspected him of carrying auto parts home. The detention may have been proper but the guards yelled at him and shoved him around. He was awarded damages.

Confronted with a memorandum saying that more than $40,000 worth of small tools had disappeared from CH Chemicals, Inc. in Bartow, Fla., that company's director of industrial relations posted himself at the front gate to watch the homebound employees. He noticed lots of workers carrying their personal plastic coolers through the gates. He figured the men would not stand for daily searches of each and every cooler and so he posted a notice saying, "No more coolers." The employees were outraged, because for years they had brought their lunches in large coolers. Banning the coolers was a basic change in working conditions, the employees argued in an arbitration hearing. But the arbitrator ruled otherwise, saying, "The management of the company has an obligation to discourage thefts of its own property, and therefore it is not unreasonable for the company to issue the rule it did."[81]

On the other hand, a woman in New York was able to collect unemployment compensation after being fired for objecting to a company search. After a year on the job as a sales clerk at a Casual Corner store in Rochester, the woman reported to work and was told the new company policy required her to open her purse for inspection. She said she would not cooperate and so she was fired. A New York Department of Labor referee ruled that the woman was entitled to collect unemployment benefits because "in view of the fundamental personal interest involved, I hold that claimant did not commit an act of misconduct sufficient to disqualify her. . . . Items of a personal nature are often contained in purses."[82]

A manicurist at a Lord & Taylor clothing store in

Washington, D.C., was stopped by a store plainclothes security guard after she stepped from a changing room. She had a blouse in her purse. The female guard said she had spied on the employee through one-way louvers in Lord & Taylor's dressing room, as was her custom. The guard accused the manicurist of shoplifting; the woman claimed that she had brought the blouse to the store to exchange. She was physically detained, formally charged with theft, and promptly fired. During her detention her purse and her wallet were searched and her cash was counted. She was forced to strip to her underclothes for a body search. A jury awarded her damages for the invasion of privacy.[83]

According to Washington attorney Robert R. Belair, "The outcome of recent lawsuits suggests that the courts are increasingly receptive to damage actions for detentions and other types of physical interference." He recommends that companies not permit their security personnel to use force or verbal intimidation in investigations of employees.

If similar searches were to arise at a police station, a public school, or a city hall, the victim of course could raise a constitutional issue, claiming that the search violated the Fourth Amendment prohibition against government-sanctioned unreasonable searches and seizures of "persons, houses, papers, and effects." The only remedy for a private employee is usually arbitration, in which the employee and the company have agreed in advance to abide by the decision of an independent referee who hears both sides, or a private lawsuit based on some wrong committed by a person or organization who owes some duty to the victim, in this case a duty of noninterference with one's freedom.

The general rule, according to the U.S. Supreme Court in a 1921 decision, is that a search by a private party does not fall under the Fourth Amendment protection *unless* there is government instigation or participation.[84] This means that whenever a company involves the municipal police or the Federal Bureau of Investigation in its investigation, even if only informing the police of its suspicions, the company had better make sure that any searches it conducts meet the strict requirements of the Fourth Amendment and the court decisions flowing from it. Otherwise, the evidence may well be excluded at a subsequent criminal trial.

Because the Constitution provides no protection against unreasonable searches by private employers, many Fourth Amendment scholars are now pushing for court decisions or legislation that would extend search-and-seizure protections to cover private security guards, who, after all, outnumber the tax-supported variety.

In a 1969 case in California involving a search conducted by a credit-card company investigator and police together, the judge added in a footnote (even though he found in this case there was clear government participation):

> We are not called upon to decide whether searches by private investigators and private police forces should be held subject per se to the commands of the Fourth Amendment on the ground that one of their basic purposes is the enforcement of the law. Searches by such well-financed and highly trained organizations involve a particularly serious threat to privacy.[85]

It is in footnotes like these, especially footnotes in California cases, that progressive attorneys take heart.

Golden Gate University law students, writing in California five years later, proposed this change to the California code:

> Private police shall have no authority to search any person unless such person be taken into custody pursuant to a lawful arrest. Search incident to such lawful arrest is limited to a search for "offen-

sive weapons" as prescribed by Section 846 of the Penal Code. In the event that said arrest and or search results in a criminal prosecution, the private policeman shall be deemed a "state agent" and his actions shall be limited by the prohibitions of the United States Constitution's Fourth Amendment.[86]

In a book generally advocating greater freedom for private citizens to make arrests, law professor M. Cherif Bassiouni discusses the court rule that evidence seized in an unconstitutional way must be excluded from a trial and concludes:

> In light of the magnitude of the private police force in the United States, the exclusionary rule should be made applicable to them in some form, to ensure the protection of the people's constitutional right to be free from unreasonable searches and seizures. Since the majority of states have enacted both citizen's arrest and shoplifting statutes, it would seem incumbent upon the state legislatures to enact legislation which would clarify the scope of search and seizure allowed by private persons.[87]

The line between the public police and private police is increasingly blurred in real life, as a significant number of government law enforcement personnel moonlight in private security jobs and as many more take private jobs just after retirement from public jobs. Employees at Armstrong Cork Co. in Lancaster, Pa., had to put up with regular searches of their lockers because the man who ordered the searches was the firm's security chief, a "private person," and thereby not limited by the Fourth Amendment. The man, in fact, was the former chief of police for the city of Lancaster. In that former capacity, he would have had to secure a warrant from a judge before conducting the locker searches.

The Supreme Court, as mentioned in Chapter 3, has applied the principles of *First Amendment* free speech to a privately owned "company town" because the owner opened the property for use by the public in general. Thus far, courts have not gone as far with regard to Fourth Amendment search-and-seizure protections at similar sites. For instance, in 1977, the Supreme Court let stand a decision by the Fifth Circuit Court of Appeals that security guards at Disney World in Orlando, Fla., were not limited by the Constitution in conducting a search of three visitors that resulted in a criminal trial for passing counterfeit bills. "If the owners of this amusement park impose in an illegal manner on their clientele, such an imposition . . . would subject the owners to a civil suit on behalf of the injured person. Such illegal conduct would not, however, give [the victim] the protection of the Fourth Amendment and the exclusionary rule which has developed from it."[88]

A civil suit, then, not a constitutional challenge, remains the remedy for an employee whose privacy is intruded upon by company personnel. This would be especially true if in their search company agents went beyond articles related to the company's business into the personal articles of the individual employee. This is true of lockers, desks, and private offices.

One further point remains to be made about searches in the workplace. A police search is reasonable under the Fourth Amendment if the custodian of the premises gives consent. Thus, company management can give valid consent for the police to search the work space of an employee. But there are limits. A court in the District of Columbia has said that a company official may give consent if access is related to the business of the company. The company may not give valid consent for police to search into an employee's purely personal belongings. For such a search, the police would generally need a court warrant.[89]

Wiretapping

The federal law against wiretapping unequivocally applies to private companies, but many continue to monitor their employees through electronic surveillance. The law permits electronic surveillance "where one of the parties to the communication has given prior consent," and this provision has often, although not always, been interpreted to permit a company to tap its own telephones without violating the law. The law also permits electronic eavesdropping by the "operator of a switchboard . . . for mechanical or service quality control checks."[90] That implies that the wiretapping must be for the purpose of *equipment* quality control, but a federal court in San Francisco once ruled that Macy's Department Store there did not violate the law when it tapped its own phones in order to catch employees who were pilfering merchandise. Preventing pilferage, the court decided, was "quality control." (However, some state wiretap laws are *more* stringent than federal law.)

Regardless of the rationale, many companies have been caught snooping with electronics. American Motors Corp. plant security admitted bugging meetings of the United Auto Workers in 1972.

Members of the textile workers union accused J. P. Stevens & Co. in South Carolina of doing the same thing.

The owner of a small factory in Cleveland installed microphones in the women's washrooms and thereafter became known around the plant as the "crapper-tapper."

A Baltimore firm went even further, installing a hidden camera pointed at the toilet in the women's rest room. This was to prevent thefts, the management said. A secretary in the firm quit when she discovered the video surveillance, and a state appeals board upheld her right to unemployment compensation, ruling that she had left her job for good cause.

A building management company in the suburbs of New York City admitted in 1979 to tapping its own phones to discover who was making unauthorized long-distance calls. (The taps revealed that the culprit was a man working in security.)

A woman in Philadelphia was ordered by her employer, an employment agency, to tape-record her telephone conversations with all callers. (She refused and won a lawsuit to recover unemployment compensation after she was fired.)

The owner of a small business in Memphis had a "consultant" install a microphone and tape recorder under the desk of an employee.

The branch manager of an air filter company in Atlanta was told by his receptionist that one of his employees had regular conversations with a friend who had left the company to work for a competitor. The receptionist said that at one time the two were discussing trade secrets. The branch manager overheard the next conversation on a extension telephone and recorded the conversation with a recording machine attached to the telephone. The branch manager confronted the employee with the incriminating tape recording and fired him. A federal court ruled that this did not violate the wiretap law because the eavesdropping was not part of a regular monitoring program and because the call involved business, not personal, matters. Similar cases have been decided the other way.

The wiretap law as it now stands covers only interception of *oral* or wire conversations. Videotaping of employees in the workplace is not governed by that law. Several employers are resorting to this kind of surveillance, to cut down on pilferage or to keep an eye on the productivity of employees. In a Syracuse plant, employees first spray-painted the lenses, then destroyed the cameras of the company surveillance system. "The mere fact that you scratched your behind was preserved on videotape," complained their union representative.

Courts thus far have upheld the right of employers to

use video surveillance, dismissing claims of invasion of privacy by employees. And labor arbitrators have been doing the same. For one thing, if a union contract reserves to management the right to measure work standards, the surveillance is often permitted; at other times arbitrators have ruled that the cameras may be used only for security, not for monitoring purposes.

There is a point at which courts will recognize such conduct by an employer as an invasion of privacy entitling the victims to sue. "In order to sustain a cause of action for invasion of privacy," said a New York court in articulating what remains the current standard, "the plaintiff must show that the [other person's] conduct was truly 'intrusive' and that it was designed to elicit information which would not be available through normal inquiry or observation." That court (in a case not involving employment) said that unauthorized wiretapping and eavesdropping clearly fall into the category of "intrusive."[91]

Surveillance in the workplace will remain a sore point between employees and employers. In a survey by Louis Harris & Associates in 1979, two-thirds of the *public* polled said the practice should not be used to monitor productivity. By contrast, slightly more than half of the persons *in managerial positions* thought it should be used. Nearly half the public thought that cameras ought not to be used in the workplace to prevent theft or vandalism. By contrast only a fifth of the managers thought so. But fully 83 percent of the public surveyed disapproved of monitoring conversations and even 70 percent of the managers disapproved.[92]

Employers' intrusions upon the dignity and autonomy of employees take other forms as well. Two matters that have caused tension at work are company standards for dress and hair length and company rules about an individual employee's work space.

Hair and Dress Codes

At the Continental Congress in 1789, one of the delegates was arguing against the need to spell out every single right that Americans would have under their Bill of Rights. His colleagues, he said, "might have declared that a man should have a right to wear his hat if he pleased . . . but, [I] would ask . . . whether . . . it necessary to enter these trifles in a declaration of rights, in a government where none of them were intended to be infringed."[93] And in a case upholding the right to travel in 1958, the Supreme Court said that right "may be as close to the heart of the individual as the choice of what he eats, or wears, or reads."[94]

However, the Supreme Court ruled in 1976 that a hair-length regulation by a public employer does not deprive a person of the liberty guaranteed under the Fourteenth Amendment. The case involved uniformed officers of a county police department.[95] Prior to that, several lower courts had ruled that grooming and hair codes were unconstitutional in public-sector jobs like teaching and administration, as distinguished from a uniformed police force, but there were just as many court opinions going the other way. It is likely, therefore, that reasonable—and even unreasonable—restrictions on facial hair and hair length and on certain clothing *by private employers* will be approved by the courts. An exception to this would be a hair or dress code that could be shown to be discriminatory on the basis of sex, race, or other prohibited grounds. Any rule, for instance, that had a disparate impact on blacks or on females could probably be successfully challenged in the courts.

A black man tried to do this in the early 1970s when Continental Illinois National Bank and Trust Co. of Chicago instituted a rule against facial hair. The man refused to trim his sideburns, saying that facial hair was a symbol of black American masculinity. He was fired because he had signed a statement upon employment promising to abide by any rules the bank may adopt. A federal district court rejected his claim that his firing violated the Civil Rights Act passed in 1866. "The dismissal from employment based on 'bias' as to the mode of dress and grooming is not a violation [by itself] of an individual's constitutional rights or the Civil Rights Acts." The court was simply not convinced that the "no-hair" rule had a discriminatory impact on blacks.[96]

In 1982 in Missouri a woman was unsuccessful in trying to convince a court that her company's rule that she had to wear slacks as a safety precaution in the plant compromised her religious beliefs and was in violation of religious nondiscrimination laws.

The nexus between an employer's grooming code and discrimination was apparently clearer in a 1981 case in which a federal district court in New York agreed with the Equal Employment Opportunity Commission that a real estate company's requirement that each attendant in an apartment building lobby wear a "revealing and sexually provocative" uniform violated Title VII of the Civil Rights Act of 1964. Each lobby attendant was required to wear a skimpy red, white, and blue Bicentennial poncho that revealed her midriff, buttocks, and upper arms as she walked. This prompted a series of lewd comments from passersby.

The prevailing view in the courts seems to be that when a grooming regulation tends to have a disparate impact on one group over another, the company must justify it as necessary to its business. Safety and cleanliness are often regarded as adequate justification, if supported by facts. This is one instance where negative customer reaction to an employee's appearance may be a factor in supporting an employer's hair or dress code. In other contexts, customer preference is not a legitimate defense for a discriminatory employment policy (as Pan American World Airways tried to argue in 1971, saying that its customers' preferences for women in airplane cabins justified its stewardess-only hiring policy).

In the 1970s when arbitrators as well as judges were

confronted with a barrage of cases involving hair, John H. McGuckin, Jr., an attorney in San Francisco, analyzed the arbitrators' rulings and concluded that most supported employers' demands for neatness and cleanliness. Many arbitrators recognize safety hazards as a reason for hair codes, but thought that employers could agree to reasonable alternatives, like wigs or hair nets. "Most arbitrators will not countenance a complete ban on beards," and mustaches are allowed except when "excessive," according to McGuckin.[97] "Many arbitrators are not moved by the plight of an employer who, seeking to make competitive inroads, decides to cut his employees' hair rather than prices."

The number of these cases has declined in the 1980s as employers reflect the more tolerant attitude toward different individual grooming tastes—and as long hair has become less popular.

The problem, however, has not entirely disappeared. In 1981, in a television interview, a janitor at Macy's in California said he was not allowed to wear sneakers. In the same year a four-year veteran of the District of Columbia Fire Department was suspended when he grew a beard. The department said that safety was not a factor, because firefighters are protected by face masks; the department simply wanted all of its men to look the same. In the summer of 1982, the Cincinnati Reds baseball team was still enforcing its longtime ban against mustaches and beards on its players.

At the new Honda plant in Smyrna, Tenn., workers on the line may not wear caps or badges identifying them as members of the United Auto Workers, in contravention of common labor practices in the United States.

Personalizing Office Space

Employees in the front office are demanding their prerogatives, too, and this usually means the right to decorate their own work space as they wish. A 1981 study for GF

Business Equipment asserted the importance of this to the individual worker. "Maintaining this control is vital to our mental health," the report said. "Personalizing space—stamping it with your identity—is one of the best means of protecting your privacy, particularly in places where you normally carry out tasks that require some concentration. It strengthens your position by helping you achieve two separate goals: psychological escape and personal recognition. The presence of personal memorabilia—pictures, postcards, trophies—provides a visual reminder of other areas of your life."

One of the specialists participating in the GF study, Frank Becker of Cornell University's Department of Design, commented, "People bring in all kinds of things that both tell them, 'This is where I work, this is where I live,' and tell others, 'This is what I'm like'—and in essence, help structure the nature of interactions with these other people by saying, 'This is the kind of person that I am.'"

The report strongly advised office workers to "stake a claim" in their surroundings by personalizing their work space and erecting barriers, even if intangible barriers, to reduce unwanted interruptions. Bare walls and empty desk tops can create significant morale problems in the office, according to Robert Sommers, another expert in the GF study. He thinks personalizing offices makes good business sense. Workers become more creative. They feel important. Their individuality is recognized. A person can be more productive in a tense environment if he has a sense of privacy. Also the employee has a sense of belonging permanently to the organization, according to Sommers.

Still, a large number of supervisors will not permit any of this. A cartoon in the *New Yorker* in the fall of 1982 showed what is a common attitude. "Each employee can have one plant or one poster," says one executive to another as they survey the communal office. "But they can't have both."

8

Freedom of Safety
and Health

A remarkable number of reforms in the workplace originated in the developed nations of Europe before they came to the United States. Most European nations, for instance, adopted state-supported pension systems long before Social Security legislation was passed in the United States in the 1930s. Paid vacations were required as a matter of law in Europe in the late nineteenth century before American businesses began to offer them as a fringe benefit in the early part of this century. The U.S. is the only industrialized country without legal protection against arbitrary firings by employers. In 1951 West Germany passed an Act to Provide Protection Against Unwarranted Dismissals, and England, France, and Sweden subsequently developed similar protections.

This trend has been true with regard to safety in the workplace, as well. In 1884 Germany passed a law to award compensation for lost work if the worker could show that he was injured on the job. Great Britain followed in 1887. After first legislating limited protections for injured railroad workers, the U.S. passed the Federal Employers' Liability Act in 1908. The Supreme Court of that era had declared an earlier version an unconstitutional infringement on the rights of company owners. Prior to that time, an employee who was injured on the job could sue at common law to recover damages. The worker would have to show negligence on the part of the company and show that he himself was unaware of the danger. He could not recover if his employer could show that the employee had contributed to the accident by his own negligence. This was a difficult standard of proof, but there was no real limit to the amount of damages a jury could award.

Under the current system set up by workers' compensation laws, the worker waives his right to sue in court, and the amount of his recovery is limited by law. He goes before a compensation tribunal, not a court, and must prove only that he works for the company in question and that the accident that injured him happened on the job.

At first, workers' compensation awards were made for "personal injury by accident," but gradually compensation boards and courts have dropped the "by accident" qualification. And occupational disease is now recognized as a basis for compensation, if the disease can be distinguished from what someone would run into outside of the workplace. One worker for a utility company was awarded compensation for illness caused by exposure to countless pigeon droppings, but a factory worker was denied an award for an allergic reaction to hand soap he used at work.

The workers' compensation system created lots of gory hearing transcripts and lots of employment for attorneys. It did not cure hazards on the job. Throughout the 1960s, the lack of industrial and office safety remained a major social problem in the U.S. Each year, accidents and job-related diseases resulted in lost wages of $1.5 billion and a drain on the gross national product of $8 billion. An estimated 14,000 workers were dying and 2.2 million were becoming disabled each year, according to Department of Labor statistics at the time. The department estimated that in 1967 65 percent of the workers in 1,700 plants were potentially exposed to hazardous conditions, and only a quarter of them had any protection. There was alarm about the effects in the workplace of lead and mercury poisoning, asbestos materials, cotton dust, pesticides, new toxic substances, as well as the atomic, laser, ultrasonic, and microwave technology then coming into use. Two-thirds of all collective bargaining agreements included clauses on health and safety, but labor representatives came to believe that workers were entitled to good health and safety without having to bargain away other benefits in negotiations.

In a truly bipartisan effort, Americans proceeded to do what is rare in this country; we passed legislation that is intended to be preventive. At the end of his term, President Lyndon Johnson proposed an occupational safety and health bill. At the beginning of his term, President Richard Nixon endorsed the idea. Upon signing the final act in 1970, he proclaimed, "This bill represents in its culmination the American system at its best." Republicans and Democrats worked for its passage and, in fact, the only arguments seemed to be which federal agencies would enforce the new standards for safe working conditions.

The Occupational Safety and Health Act of 1970 is a procedural law. It gives no private right of action to individuals, and it does not affect rights under state and federal workers' compensation systems.[98] About 90 percent of the work force is covered by workers' compensation plans, which still pay out about $18 billion a year in benefits.

The law states that all employers, regardless of size or type, "shall" provide a safe and healthful workplace. Employers *and* employees "shall" comply with safety and health standards issued by the federal government. A new agency, now in the Department of Health and Human Services, was established to conduct research in the workplace and to establish standards. It is called the National Institute of Occupational Safety and Health (NIOSH). A separate agency, the Occupational Safety and Health Administration (OSHA) in the Department of Labor, is responsible for inspecting workplaces and issuing citations for violations of the standards. OSHA's 1,200 inspectors are authorized to enter workplaces and to question employees. Upon demand of an employer, an inspector must have a search warrant but the warrant need not be based on the strict standard of a criminal investigation ("probable cause" that a crime has been committed). The agency proposes civil penalties for violations and, if the violation is "willful," criminal penalties. The Occupational Safety and Health Review Commission outside of the Department of Labor reviews about 5 percent of the penalties, and sometimes a court is asked to review the commission's determinations. In reviewing one such determination, a federal court ruled that there are no penalties for *employees* who violate the act, even though the law says that they, like the company itself, must comply with federal standards.[99]

OSHA also requires employers to keep records, and these can be voluminous, including a daily log of all injuries and illnesses. Employers in certain hazardous industries must keep work-related medical records on employees exposed to dangerous materials or environmental conditions and on the effects of such exposure. An OSHA regulation requires that this information be kept on each employee for thirty years, and that a record be made available (within fifteen days) to the employee or (with consent) his designated representative. And the information must be provided to OSHA or NIOSH upon request. Workers are permitted also to see company analyses of exposure or medical records.[100] Three times federal courts have ruled that the government's access to this information is legitimate, in turning down challenges by Westinghouse Electric Corp., General Motors Corp., and E.I. DuPont de Nemours Co.[101] In 1982 the Reagan administration moved to lessen these medical record keeping requirements.

In 1977, a dozen workers at an Occidental Chemical Co. plant in California happened to discover over their conversation at lunch break that they all suffered from sterility. This prompted an investigation by occupational health officials, who traced the problem to a pesticide. The affliction would not have become as widespread, they said, if the company had kept better records, and shared them with employees, unions, and government agencies. A representative of the Oil, Chemical and Atomic Workers Union says that companies keep sparse health records. A third of the places where his members work have no health professional to keep accurate records, even though union members work with countless sensitive substances.

The Safest Jobs

The chemical industry, for its part, claims to be one of the safest in the U.S. It points to a listing compiled by the National Safety Council each year.

The list shows that the chemical industry in 1981 reported 0.74 cases of occupational illness or injury per 100 full-time employees, far better than the average for all industries—2.21 per 100 full-time employees. The communication and aircraft industries had records just about as good. Here are the National Safety Council rankings for 1981, based on the fewest number of cases involving days away from work and deaths:

Chemical
Aircraft
Communication
Pipeline transportation
Textile
Electrical, electronics equipment
Agricultural chemicals
Oil and gas extraction
Petroleum and coal products
Primary nonferrous metals
Motor vehicles
Steel
Rubber and plastics

Cement
Electric service
Machinery, excluding electrical
Wholesale and retail trade
ALL INDUSTRIES (average)
Bituminous coal
Nonferrous rolling, drawing
Water transportation
Furniture and fixtures
Gas
Fabricated metal products
Printing and publishing
Paper
Leather
Services
Metal mining
Nonmetallic minerals
Construction
Stone, clay, and glass
Air transportation
Food
Iron and steel foundries
Railroad equipment
Railroad transportation
Lumber and wood products
Ship and boat building
General government
Meat products
Transit
Trucking

According to the council, trash collection is by far the most dangerous line of work, and handling textile fibers seems to be the safest. The figures show that office work is not significantly safer than other types of work.[102]

Each employee has a one-in-twelve chance of suffering

from job-related illness or injury, according to the Department of Labor's statistics for 1981. The department recorded 5.3 million work-related injuries in 1981, and 126,000 illnesses. The figures for the first two years of the decade represent a significant improvement in the nation's occupational safety and health record. (The department still feels that occupational *illnesses* are underreported because employers and physicians often are unable to recognize ailments as job-related. Skin diseases account for most of the total, because they are more readily observable than other illnesses.)[103]

At the time the Occupational Safety and Health Act was passed, there were an estimated 18 job-related deaths per 100,000 workers; ten years later the rate had been reduced to 13 per 100,000. And there is evidence that nonfatal job disabilities have decreased as well. The preventive legislation of 1970 may be working.

Still, the two federal agencies concerned with occupational health have replaced the civil rights agencies as the major *bêtes noires* for American industry. When the Reagan administration entered office, businessmen zeroed in on OSHA and NIOSH as primary targets. They challenged the safety standards through the courts and within the administration. They viewed the safety standards as trivial exercises in bureaucratic meddling. President Reagan's appointee to oversee government regulatory affairs, Christopher C. DeMuth, said, "Most people . . . would agree that government should not force citizens to spend enormous sums of money to make themselves enormously safer in the workplace than they are driving or walking to work." Easy to say for a man who works behind a desk.

Indeed, the extent of the two agencies' reach into the workplace is impressive. In the decade since the act was passed, the government has issued standards in the following areas, and far more:

Fire protection
Ship construction
Emergency escapes
Use of hand tools
Power presses
Sanitation
Physical hazards
Posting notices
Flammables and explosives
Noise abatement and hearing conservation
Compressed gas and air
Materials handling and storage
Cranes
Woodworking machines
Office equipment
Walking and working surfaces
Ladders
Air, ventilation
Radiation
Hazardous gases and chemicals
Personal protective equipment
Powered industrial trucks
Welding equipment
Electrical wiring

Concern about safety and health is not limited to industrial and agricultural sites. Labor unions representing office workers began in the early 1980s to press for OSHA inspections as well. Computer workers became aware of hazards in their work. According to Karen Nussbaum, president of Working Women:

> The health of office workers is threatened daily by the machines we use, the chemicals in common office products, by the design of our offices, and by the very structure of our work. A member of

Working Women in Pennsylvania had her lungs virtually destroyed by exposure to a copying machine. A switchboard operator in a Cleveland insurance company developed coronary heart disease at the age of twenty-seven after being forced to carry two work loads. An executive secretary suffered permanent hearing loss from exposure to noisy office machinery.[104]

In a book called *Office Hazards,* Joel Makower identified several health hazards in the office. Computer terminals with video displays, he said, may cause eyestrain, loss of visual acuity, changes in color perception, back and neck pains, stomachaches, and nausea. A combination of glass and steel design, modern air conditioning, synthetic products used in furniture and decorations, and miscellaneous pollutants have made the air inside office buildings dangerous to health. Contemporary design and new electronic equipment have produced barely tolerable noise levels in offices. Lighting in offices is designed for cost efficiency, not for good health. Modern office equipment may be emitting dangerous amounts of radiation.

The Occupational Safety and Health Act permits employees, whether they work in an office, in a factory, in a vehicle, or on a farm, to file complaints with local offices of OSHA alleging violations of standards or requesting an inspection. The complaint must be signed, but the identity of the complainant and others involved is supposed to be deleted by OSHA in reports it releases to the employer and others. Employees, on their own time, and their representatives may accompany federal officers on their inspection tours and may be represented in the officers' conferences with company management. The act provides safeguards for employees who feel they have been fired for having filed complaints.

In 1978, a paint company in Cleveland fired a worker after just ten days on the job when it received a report from

a consumer investigating company that the man was responsible for an OSHA inspection at his former place of
employment. The paint company and the consumer investigating company that supplied the information finally
agreed to comply with the government's demand that they
not continue to compile or use information about prior
OSHA complaints.

Smoking on the Job

Since the publication in 1972 of medical evidence that
cigarette smoke is harmful to the health of nearby
nonsmokers, there has been a move to eliminate smoking
in the workplace. Laws in Colorado, Minnesota, Montana,
Nebraska, and Utah specifically prohibit smoking in the
workplace (and Oregon prohibits it in state government
facilities). The "Clean Indoor Air" laws on the books in an
additional thirty states prohibit smoking in certain areas
that sometimes include work situations. These laws
usually exclude from their coverage smoking within the
confines of a private office.

Even before the Occupational Safety and Health Act,
courts recognized that all companies have a general duty
to provide a safe place to work. A court in Missouri in
1982 declared that Western Electric Co. had breached this
duty by not providing a smoke-free environment for an
office worker adversely affected by tobacco smoke. The
court ordered the company to provide such a workplace
for any non-smoker who requests it.[105]

Many employers, like Thomas Edison, have imposed
a no-smoking rule on workers. Some companies use a
carrot instead of a stick: they pay bonuses to employees
who quit smoking.

Increased consciousness of employee health and
safety has altered the way some courts have viewed
workers' compensation awards. It used to be that a
worker injured on the job received compensation based on

a schedule set by state law, and in exchange the company was then immune from a lawsuit by the employee. But in a 1982 case involving a chemical worker named Edward Blankenship, the Ohio Supreme Court ruled that victims could collect workers' compensation for illness or injury caused by company negligence *and* could sue on alternative grounds for *intentional* harm caused by the company. California courts permit this dual recovery also.

Despite attempts by the Reagan administration to cut back the powers of the Occupational Safety and Health Administration, the provisions of the 1970 law are here to stay. Allegiance to certain standards to protect the life and good health of the people who work there has become a fact of life in the American workplace.

9

Freedom from Stress

The warning from the 1972 government report *Work in America* said in fact that our work is killing us:

> Satisfaction with work appears to be the best predictor of longevity—better than known medical or genetic factors—and various aspects of work account for much, if not most, of the factors associated with heart disease. Dull and demeaning work, work over which the worker has little or no control, as well as other poor features of work also contribute to an assortment of mental health problems. But we find that work can be used to alleviate the problems it presently causes or correlates with highly. From the point of view of public policy, workers and society are bearing medical costs that have their genesis in the workplace, and which could be avoided through preventive measures.[106]

Subsequent medical and demographic research has further documented that lack of contentment in the workplace—whether the employee is actively conscious of it or not—can have serious and lasting effects upon the mental health and physical health of an individual.

The headlines of the 1980s told the story:

STRESS, HEALTH HAZARDS LINKED TO CRT USE
JOB BURNOUT: IT'S BECOMING AN EPIDEMIC
ONCE-UNFLAPPABLE AUTO EXECUTIVES SHOW
    STRESS SYMPTOMS
BLACKS FIND JOB-RELATED STRESS RISING
MIDDLE-CLASS MIDDLE-LIFE STRESSES & THE
    SUICIDE CONNECTION
WORK-RELATED HEALTH HAZARDS ARE MENTAL
    AND PHYSICAL

Whenever a problem reaches this level of recognition and when there is evidence that a specific organization, like an employer, is causing the problem, you can expect people to begin filing lawsuits. And that is what has happened in this area. Employees are filing, and winning, claims for workers' compensation based on stress in the workplace. They are also suing employers for intentional infliction of emotional distress.

Stress is defined by Webster's Dictionary as "a physical, chemical, or emotional factor that causes bodily or mental tension and may be a factor in disease causation." The condition was first identified by a Canadian doctor named Hans Selye in 1946. He defined stress as "the nonspecific response of the body to any demand made upon it." Stress, then, may not necessarily mean nervous tension or adverse reaction to difficulty or a stomach "tied in knots." It is simply the body's way of reacting to occurrences, whether good or bad, in order to keep the body functioning. Properly channeled, stress can be a positive force for many people at work. In fact, those who talk about stress the most—high-powered executives and professionals—may cope a lot better with it than rank-and-file workers who face relatively few vital decisions each day. Executives, just in identifying stress in their business lives, may go a long way toward channeling it properly. Many corporations provide fringe benefits, from transactional analysis and saunas to tropical retreats, for executives to deal with stress. Rank-and-file workers have no such opportunities, and so their stress comes home with them from the workplace.

The National Institute for Occupational Safety and Health undertook in 1977 to determine which occupations produced the most stress. The institute chose to measure stress by analyzing three categories of 22,000 records in Tennessee: death certificates, hospital admissions, and mental health center admissions. The institute was particularly interested in evidence of heart and artery disease, hypertension, ulcers, and nervous disorders.

By this measure, it determined that the following occupations showed the highest incidence of stress-related disease:

Laborers
Secretaries
Inspectors
Clinical laboratory technicians
Office managers
Foremen
Managers/Administrators
Waitresses/Waiters
Machine operators
Farm owners
Mine operatives
House painters

The incidence of stress among laborers was far more than twice than in the occupation that ranked second, secretaries.

Among the other occupations with high levels of stress, according to the NIOSH study, were health technology technicians, practical nurses, nurses' aides, musicians, dental assistants, teacher aides, computer programmers, bank tellers, health aides, social workers, telephone operators, hairdressers, warehousemen, sales managers.

clergy, sales representatives, police, railroad switchers, meat cutters, electricians, firemen, plumbers, structural metal craftsmen, guards and watchmen, machinists, mechanics, and public relations persons.

The researchers noted that several of the "stressful" occupations are in the field of health care, which requires "interaction on a continuous basis with persons who are ill, which can produce a feeling of being emotionally drained. . . . In addition they all have a great deal of responsibility for the welfare of their patients without the authority to have complete control over that welfare." The researchers also noted the presence on the list of blue-collar jobs that are normally regarded as skilled, well-paid, and satisfying. It cited an earlier study that showed that many of these workers are dissatisfied, bored, anxious, sleepy, and depressed on the job, and said the earlier results "indicate the fallacy of implying that a job should give satisfaction just because some skills are involved." In addition, the study listed a large number of public service occupations, which are vital to the community but low in public recognition or gratitude. Several jobs high on the list, like sales, involve constant pressure for production and success.

Even though the occupations that appeared on the list varied greatly, the NIOSH researchers generalized from their studies that there are a couple of common characteristics of stressful employment: a fast work pace with little chance of relief, and long working hours with repetitive and/or boring tasks that produce an overall feeling of tension and anxiety with little or no outlet for these feelings. "It is possible," said the researchers, "that an overall sense of distress . . . can be exacerbated by stressors specific to each occupation, thereby increasing the overall stress level to such a point that the outcome is a significant health strain."

The occupations found to produce low levels of stress-related diseases include stitchers, checkers and examiners, stock-handlers, freight handlers, craftsmen, maids, farm laborers, heavy equipment operators, child-care workers, package wrappers, professors, personnel and labor relations officers, and auctioneers.[107]

Thanks to portrayals on the screen by Charlie Chaplin, Lucille Ball, and others, we have all become familiar with the terror of working on a job where the machine sets the pace—and where a representative of management is always trying to speed up the pace. Experts seem to agree that these "machine-paced" jobs produce the most stress. Research for the government at the University of Michigan in 1975 found that supposed sources of stress like long hours, heavy work loads, pressing responsibilities, and bureaucratic tension actually produced less anxiety, depression, and physical disorder than did assembly-line work, where there were normal working hours and freedom from vital decision making. On the assembly line, there was also boredom and bondage to a machine.[108]

Collecting Compensation for Stress

In fact, it was a harried assembly-line worker who won a ruling from the Michigan Supreme Court in 1960 that set the precedent for workers' compensation recovery for mental or emotional disability on the job. Until that point, workers could mainly recover compensation for the loss of earning capacity caused by a *physical* injury or illness. The court opinion told the story:

> Plaintiff had worked as a machine operator for defendant, General Motors Corporation, with intermittent layoffs, since 1953. On October 8, 1956, he was recalled to work after a 5-month layoff and worked for 4 days on a "brace job" and then was transferred on October 12th to a "hub job." This operation required him to take a hub assembly (consisting of a case and cover) from a nearby fellow employee's table to his own workbench,

remove burrs with a file and grind out holes in the assembly with a drill, and place the assembly on a conveyor belt. Plaintiff was unable to keep up with the pace of the job unless he took 2 assemblies at a time to his workbench, and he feared another lay-off should he prove unable satisfactorily to do the work. He was instructed repeatedly by his fore-man not to take 2 assemblies at a time because the assembly parts became mixed up on the conveyor belt when he did so. However, plaintiff continued having trouble "getting on to the job" as it was supposed to be performed. Thus, when he took only 1 hub assembly at a time, he fell behind; when he fell behind, he took 2 assemblies; but, when he took 2 assemblies, he got the assemblies mixed up and was berated by the foreman. We are told that the dilemma in which plaintiff found him-self resulted on October 24, 1956, in an emotional collapse variously described as paranoid schizo-phrenia and schizophrenic reaction residual type. He was subsequently hospitalized for a period of 1 month, during which time he received shock therapy. In July of 1957 he filed an application for hearing and adjustment of claim for compensation under the workmen's compensation act. It should be noted that there is not involved in this case a psychosis resulting from a single fortuitous event nor is there involved a psychosis resulting from a direct physical blow to plaintiff's body. Instead, there is involved a psychosis claimed to be the result of emotional pressures encountered by plaintiff daily in the performance of his work.[109]

A referee awarded the man compensation; an appeals board and the Michigan Supreme Court upheld the award, in a case that was regarded as ahead of its time

Courts have generally been receptive to claims of "traumatic neurosis" caused by some abrupt work-connected physical event and to the opposite claims, in which a mental shock causes a disabling physical reaction. And they have even upheld awards when there is no physical injury, when the worker undergoes a mental shock or fright and develops a disabling nervous condition. An Illinois woman who witnessed a fellow worker lose a hand in a machine won an award after she suffered severe psychological reactions. Likewise a Maine hospital executive who attended sensitivity group training sponsored by his employer recovered damages for a schizophrenic illness requiring hospitalization because of the "emotionally tense atmosphere."

As more attention is focused on the problems of stress and "burnout," many judges are going back to their law books to find the Michigan precedent in 1960 and sustaining awards for emotional disorder caused by prolonged pressure at work, rather than a particular occurrence. This has been true in California, Hawaii, Illinois, Kentucky, Michigan, and New Jersey. Courts in a half-dozen other states will permit an award if the prolonged job stress is particularly unusual. Thus, in 1976, a Kentucky production worker was compensated for a "nervous breakdown" because his job required intense concentration. A woman working at Swiss Colony in Wisconsin was compensated in the same year for a schizophrenic reaction to her "nerve-racking" job, as well as the fact that her supervisor was harassing her and she had no vacations.

A foreman at a steel plant for twenty years was so frazzled by friction between the men he supervised and the bureaucrats who supervised him that he suffered a mental breakdown. The Supreme Judicial Court of Massachusetts ruled in 1979, "If an employee is incapacitated by a mental or emotional disorder causally related to a series of specific stressful work-related incidents, the employee is entitled to compensation."[110] The insurance company had argued that the man's breakdown was the result of gradual "wear and tear" on the job and thus was not compensable as a personal injury under workers' compensation law. The court disagreed, saying here was "a series of identifiable stressful work-related incidents occurring over a relatively brief period of time, compared with his twenty-year employment."

A court in Michigan extended this trend of the law even further when it said that nervous disorders are compensable not only if they are related to work by an objective standard but also if this is true *in the worker's perception.* "The potential of that approach is startling," said a treatise on this subject by Wex S. Malone, Marcus L. Plant, and Joseph W. Little.[111]

These principles have developed in cases in which an employee seeks compensation for a work-related "injury" under an insurance policy that state laws require the employer to maintain. There is another avenue available to victims of work-related stress, although it is a long shot. It involves suing for the tort of infliction of emotional distress. Lawsuits of this kind have arisen mainly after automobile accidents or harassment by debt collectors. In most jurisdictions, damages are awarded if physical injury accompanies the emotional distress. In some jurisdictions, recovery is possible without physical injury, if the victim can show that the infliction was intentional—or simply part of the intentional policy; that the employer's conduct was *outrageous in the extreme;* and that *severe* emotional distress resulted.

Stewardesses tried this tactic, when they complained to a court that Continental Airlines' sexually suggestive advertising campaign gave license to passengers and co-workers to make lewd comments to the women. A federal court in Illinois in 1979 rejected the claim because it did not find the ad campaign "extreme and outrageous."[112]

A Pennsylvania man made the same claim after his

company, he said, excluded him from important meetings, failed to tell him about his work performance, and hinted that the man's new assistant would be his replacement.[113] A federal district court rejected his lawsuit, but in the District of Columbia in 1981 a federal judge agreed to hear a claim for intentional infliction of emotional distress based on sexual harassment by a supervisor at work and over the telephone at home.[114]

The Effect of Computers

It it startling to note the number of women workers involved in these cases, and the number of female-dominated occupations on the "most-stressful" list. Women will probably continue to bear the brunt of work-related stress because they are present in large numbers in the machine-paced work of the 1980s—data processing and word processing. Perhaps one or two of every ten jobs now involves some use of computers or peripheral equipment. For many workers, the whole day is spent in front of a keyboard or display screen, whose pace is maddeningly technological, not human. On the assembly line, the problem seems to be that the machine pace of work is often too fast; in front of the computer, that may also be true. But more often than not, the machine has a delay of a split second that, over the course of a day or an hour, can be maddening: These "machine-paced" victims complain of eyestrain, backaches, neck pain, irritability, rashes, sleepiness, and anxiety. "It is almost impossible for a key-puncher, a copy typist, a data-control clerk to explain what she does all day or even organize it into a coherent reality in her own head," wrote Barbara Garson in *All the Livelong Day*.

Tarald Kvalseth, a professor of mechanical engineering at the University of Minnesota, concluded that workers seated in front of computer-oriented equipment often have to move their heads up and down continually by more than 30 degrees. There should be little wonder that operators of visual display terminals voiced more complaints about stress than any other occupational group studied by the National Institute for Occupational Safety and Health, according to Michael Smith of the institute's motivation and stress research project in Cincinnati. He says, "These jobs are repetitious and every little keystroke that an individual makes is recorded by the computer and a supervisor has only to look into a video tube to be able to key in on particular individuals and their performance. Partly as a result of this, VDT [visual display terminal] operators have the highest stress jobs that we've ever seen—and we've been in the stress business for ten years."

In addition to the difficulty of the work, industrial psychologists have discovered a significant fear of computers, and this is seriously affecting employee morale. Many companies have employed specialists to adjust their workers to new computer applications. If this isn't done, there's ample evidence to show that workers may sabotage systems, feed phony information, or make naive mistakes out of fear. Blue-collar workers, clerical workers, and professionals are all showing signs of computerphobia. Thomas B. Sheridan of Massachusetts Institute of Technology thinks many of us are alienated from computers because they tend to remove us from the ultimate task we are paid to do. Many midmanagement employees who used to be professionals have become assembly-line foremen supervising a staff of machines not persons. Ultimately just pushing the right buttons can make our jobs less rewarding than writing memos, attending meetings, and figuring out solutions. In 1982 virtually every trade publication in the computer field published prominent articles on stress, burnout, "professional suicide," and a series of other emotional ills in the workplace.

Stress Among Women and Blacks

Studies show that stress is particularly severe among women and minority-group members. Many women and blacks do find themselves in job categories where the stress level seems to be highest, including data processing and word processing, but beyond that, many women feel that their skills are underutilized and inadequately recognized in a male-dominated environment. Although they have worked their way into attractive jobs, women have not yet worked themselves out of the larger share of child-rearing responsibilities. If the babysitter does not show up or a child gets sick at school, this will probably cause anxiety at work more for the female worker than the male. Top management tolerates a failure rate among male employees but regards female failures as a reason to cut back on promoting women through the ranks, according to a study reported in *National Business Woman* in 1982. "This pressure to excel has increased stress for many working women," said the magazine.

Like women, black executives are relatively new to the middle and upper levels of the corporation and they feel that one slip is all it will take to tumble down. They don't feel entirely welcome in the top echelons. "Black professional organizations have booked me solid to speak on stress reduction; it's the problem of the eighties," said Frederick Phillips, a psychologist in Washington, D.C., who sees many black patients. "In order to keep their jobs and gain promotions, they've been forced to take on Caucasian characteristics in speech, life-style, and dress, losing their black identity in the process. Now, they literally don't know who they are." Referring to a study of black graduates of the Harvard Business School, a psychiatrist who sees many black professionals concludes, "Being black and holding a management position in a white corporation can be emotionally difficult." Black professionals get flack from white and black subordinates alike, perhaps for different reasons, and they feel under special scrutiny by higher-ups in the company.

All of this stress takes its toll in the company—in absenteeism, bureaucratic friction, pilferage, padded expense accounts, costly mistakes, hostilities, slowdown in productivity, and wasting of energy. It seems to infect workers at all levels of the organization. It affects the hours off the job, just as stress off the job affects performance on the job.

But of all the stresses in the workplace, none exceeds the stress of being without a job, at least for most people. A psychiatrist in the high-income Detroit suburb of Bloomfield Hills said during the depression in the auto industry in 1982 that many laid-off executives were in a state of despair. "Once their job is gone, they have no identity. Ego is attached to achievement, and achievement is directly related to what we call happiness. And when you cannot achieve, you cannot be happy." Her clients "are people who, up until now, have always felt in control of things. Suddenly the corporation is no longer perceived as a family that is going to protect them."

The wife of an unemployed forest worker in Oregon, who could not afford a psychiatrist to tell it to, said simply, "It's just depressing as hell." An unemployed coal miner said, "I go to sleep worried and I wake up worried." There's only one thing worse than the stress of holding down an unpleasant job. And that's the stress of holding down no job.

10

Freedom in Off-Hours

At the Bumble Bee seafood plant in Oregon, a woman explained the effect of her job on her home life. Her job was to pull the veins of dark meat to be used for cat food from the white meat used for human consumption.

"The loins come past me on a moving belt," she told Barbara Garson, author of *All the Livelong Day*. "I put the clean loins on the second belt and the cat food on the third belt and I save my bones." A supervisor comes by later to count the bones and thereby check on the woman's productivity.

"Do you talk a lot to the other women?" asked Garson.

"Not really."

"What do you do all day?"

"I daydream."

"What do you daydream about."

"About sex."

At this point her boyfriend interrupted the interview and said with a proud grin, "I guess that's my fault."

"No, it's not you," said the woman who worked the line. "It's the tuna fish."

Separating one's work from one's home life, even one's life in bed, has always been a problem for many people. For many workers, work itself is invigorating and exciting—even sexy. But more often, the tensions and the undone tasks at work intrude into the home, often making one less responsive as a lover. The hectic pace of modern industrial and bureaucratic employment has only made life more difficult for these people, with its insatiable demands for time and attention, its "crises" after work hours, its petty nitpicking, its tedium, or its complexity.

"Constant ego gratification for my husband by those surrounding him at work leaves sex unimportant and last," complained the wife of the chief executive of a Fortune 500 company to the *Wall Street Journal* in 1981. Another executive's wife told the *Journal* that the demands of her husband's career forced her to learn to be alone a lot and "accept not having a good sexual relationship." A third wife said that she constantly has to let her high-powered husband "unwind" at home. She was expected to understand his problems at work but he did not regard what was on her mind as problems at all. Such an imbalance does not make for a lasting and affectionate relationship.

A lot of wives of middle-management employees complain that their husbands get first-class pampering from secretaries and subordinates, airline stewardesses and waitresses. They stay in nice hotels, eat filet mignon when they wish, and generally enjoy civilized business meetings with their peers. Meanwhile, back at home the wife is eating hamburgers and coping with the kids and the supermarket. Husbands start to think they are pretty swell, simply because they are treated so well on business travel. They pay lip service to the virtues of staying home, of course, but often can't wait to hit the road again, where they will live the good life. If the husband has any guilt, he can come to believe that "my job makes me do this."

"If our welfare system places a monetary advantage on fathers' abandoning their wives and children, the expense account, with the Internal Revenue Service regulations on it, is making its contribution," according to Robert Seidenberg, a specialist on the problem of corporate wives. (He calls the wives "corporate casualties.")

The spouse who is employed outside the home sees the situation differently of course. To him, work is a constant assault on his self-esteem and sanity, making him barely able to think straight when he gets home, much less act like a responsible parent and loving mate. He sees a constant tug between the boss and the wife.

"If I didn't work so hard, I wouldn't have gotten as far as I did and I wouldn't have been able to support my family," says the data processing manager for a large manufacturer in the South. "My only regret is that, in the process, I think I've burnt myself out a little bit. I don't have the drive I used to. There's no doubt about it. The demands of the job did take their toll. Because of all the time I spent at work, we had little in common to talk about when I did come home. I feel I did do right by my family, but maybe I could have gotten by with a little less money and preserved the family life." The man is now divorced, and no longer can do much about preserving the family life.

A 47-year-old Californian, also in data processing, echoes the same concerns. His job has always come first because "that's what puts bread on the table." When the computer is "down" and he gets a phone call after work hours, he won't let it wait until tomorrow. The women in his life just didn't understand. He's been divorced three times now and says if he remarries a fourth time he'll find someone who also works with computers.

The tug-of-war between computer jobs and home has become so acute that one of the trade magazines, *Computer Decisions*, devoted a cover article to the problem in January 1982. The cover illustration showed a three-piece-suited young man being pulled on one side by his boss and on the other side by the wife and kids.

The magazine described one man who worked fourteen hours a day, usually seven days a week, for a three-month period, until his wife locked him out of the house. When that happened, the man called his boss and resigned. The boss' reaction the next day was, "How can you let your wife push you around like that?"

Professionals in the field say that data processing work presents special conflicts with home life. Fernando Bartolome, a professor of organizational behavior at the European Institute of Business Administration, who has conducted extensive studies of the career-family conflict, was quoted by *Computer Decisions* as saying, "Computers are not emotional. They're logical. There are rules to follow and controls that can be relied on.

"Not so in the home. There you're dealing with impulsive children and less than rational spouses. The culture shock can be quite severe. And, as a reaction to that shock, it's only natural that people start to spend longer hours in their offices and get more addicted to their computers." Also, computer management can mean crises at any hour of the day, and this puts a strain on relationships as well.

Mid-Level Managers

There are comparable conflicts in other lines of work, of course, regardless of the level. However, this problem of family sacrifice seems to afflict the middle levels of employment more than the highest or the lowest. A survey conducted by the *Wall Street Journal* and the Gallup Organization of 476 wives of top corporate executives showed that the women generally reported that the advantages outweighed the disadvantages. The survey, published in 1981, reported that the following advantages ranked high among the wives: financial security and material rewards, 64 percent; exposure to important people and events, 45 percent; opportunity to travel, 43 percent; pride in husband's accomplishments, 39 percent; status, recognition, and power, 33 percent; and opportunity to help their children, 16 percent. They ranked the disadvantages as follows: lack of time with husband, 40 percent; business dominating husband's life, 36 percent; confining nature of the wife's role, 22 percent; worry about the toll his career is taking on husband, 19 percent; and loneliness and isolation, 15 percent.

While most of the women questioned had favorable views toward their husbands and found them admirable models for their children, fewer than four out of ten wives considered their husbands to be romantic.[115]

One of the greatest problems seems to be the inability of busy executives to "leave their work at the office." After all, they are being paid to handle heavy responsibilities, and not just from 9 to 5. Being able to do a job and forget about it after leaving work seems to be one advantage cited by workers in the lower ranks of employment. "When I leave, my work is turned off," said a woman who makes table tennis bats at a plant in New England. "I don't see no bats in my dreams like some people. I have a house in the country. Takes me three-quarters of an hour, then I'm home. So it's not really not such a bad job." She is paid extra, like most hourly workers, when she must work overtime.

People in the middle levels seem to have the worst of both worlds. Their jobs won't permit them to block out their work-related concerns when they leave to go home; yet they are not compensated for extra work.

Jet airplane travel has only exacerbated the problem. One survey in 1982 found that managers use 14 percent of their work time in travel, more than any other exercise except talking on the telephone. Many executives spend from 20 to 30 percent of their workweek on the road. "The corporate husband who is home all the time is either a nonentity or in semiretirement," says Robert Seidenberg. "Many [executives] in fact have become elite hoboes." There is very little place in corporate life for the conscientious professional who dislikes air travel; very little choice for the man or woman who wants to spend 100 percent of his nonwork hours at home.

Like the hoboes who rode the rails in earlier years, these modern corporate hoboes have created their own community across the breadth of America. Their homes are called Ramada, Sheraton, Hilton, and Holiday Inn. They get their news not from the suburban daily where the family resides, but from *their* community newspapers— the *New York Times,* the *Wall Street Journal,* and sometimes the *Los Angeles Times, Chicago Tribune,* and the *Washington Post.* In 1982 a newspaper named *USA Today* was created to serve this community. They care not so much about the weather back home as about the weather in the city toward which they are headed. They watch the network morning news/talk shows for that. The weather between where they are and where they are going is irrelevant because the sun always shines above the clouds. Their meals are thawed steak and roast beef, and the pseudo-Continental fare of the hotels. The people with whom they spend the most time are fellow professionals around the country who frequent the same meetings, rather than the persons who live down the street or who work down the hall. The "family car" comes from Hertz, Avis, or National. The bus schedule for this community is the *Official Airline Guide.*

They spend most of their time not in a den at home but in conference rooms at company headquarters and in partitioned hotel "ballrooms" with straight-back chairs and crystal chandeliers.

Their concerns about the airlines, not surprisingly, are the schedules, the quality of food, the amount of legroom, and the friendliness of the cabin attendants. Price is not their concern (in fact, deregulation of airline fares meant to them only more crowded airplanes).

Their corporate community spreads across America but it touches only parts of it. It touches the urban freeways and the rental car parking lots and the front offices of America. It does not touch the parks and downtown theaters and the small-town inns of America.

From this world between Monday and Friday—and often Saturday and Sunday as well—the corporate hobo is expected to return home with his work behind him and his enthusiasm for family adventures at a peak. Instead, his soul, if not his body, is often back in St. Louis, where somebody brought him his food, made his bed, and washed his automobile. At its convention in 1982 one trade association included a session entitled, "As an Executive—Where Is My Office?"

Add to this frustration the frequency of transfers in the corporate world. The wife and kids are asked to join the hobo and uproot themselves to move to some other suburban community near another company facility and another airport. The 1980 Census statistics show that 64 percent of us no longer live in the state where we were born. An estimated 50 million people move each year, and much of this is caused by company transfers.

"For those who move a great deal, so that they never have the time or the energy to take root or make friends, the corporation for good or bad becomes the main interest," says Seidenberg, echoing what William H. Whyte, Jr., wrote in 1956 in *The Organization Man*. Like military families, the families of corporate America make new friends in new places but the relationships can never be too close, for somebody will be moving to another city before long.

One woman wrote to Seidenberg about her experiences:

> I wonder if it is the loss of *status* which makes it so difficult for some of us. In my own case it is more the loss of *dear* friends, the kind that take years to make and that are not easily replaced. Bonding is a process which is somewhat limited, I should think. In my new location, I have been able to make many new friends, but the relationships are still somewhat superficial and constrained by the fact

that most are wives of coworkers of my husband, which certainly makes confidences limited. This kind of superficial friendship does serve to pass the time pleasantly, but in time of crisis, is terribly inadequate.

Another difficulty is that in moving, the *only* seasoned relationships you take with you are [those] of the nuclear family. Perhaps most central is that of your husband, the reason you moved in the first place—to cleave unto him. If after this move, in which you have stripped yourself of the other old and true relationships, trouble arises with your husband, you are as alone as alone can be. In my case, my husband got involved with someone at the office. It's a recipe for collapse—in a marital crisis with no deep friends. The move makes you almost pathologically dependent on a single person; and inconstancy on the part of that person is devastating. In the old location, one is somewhat diversified in terms of relationships. Moving gives one person a monopoly; and that monopoly is dangerous.

I don't know what the solution is. Perhaps on our next move—this September—I'll try to move directly into a job, which will at least keep me from being so dependent upon my husband and preoccupied with him in a daily sense. But he will still be, because of the dynamics of moving, the emotional core, all others having been left behind once again. Certainly I never thought at age 34 to end up in a psychologist's office. But the *combination* of infidelity on the part of my husband with the loss of other relationships because of a move was devastating. The move seemed harmless as long as the marriage was not threatened. But threaten the marriage and the loss caused by moving becomes apparent.[116]

Another woman wrote to Seidenberg, "I refused to move. I am no 'shrinking violet'. . . . I love my home and my life. I don't care if my husband never goes any higher. He is a plant engineer of a large company, so he does better than I expected after living on a nurse's salary for years. I know that I would not get involved in Red Cross, church, PTA, and all those other organizations if I moved." And so she didn't move.

Perhaps this woman represented the transition period between the loyal wife who goes anywhere and the woman who has developed strong interests—and perhaps a career of her own—where she is. And she refuses to move. More and more, spouses are asking to stay put, and this is increasing the pressures between home and office.

In writing to Seidenberg, a male executive himself was sympathetic. "I believe that our large corporations would do well to apply the moral of this story to their own provincial practices of hopping managers and their families around the country (world) without regard to the traumatic effects on wives and children. Instability of family life, which includes the home location, certainly has its effects on the ability to perform. I've seen too many alcoholic wives, delinquent children, and misplaced souls in my life among the corporate movers. Perhaps some day our large corporations will consider the families of their employees. . . ."

Traditionally employees have not been in a position to resist company demands that they be transferred. If they object to moving, they may forego a promotion or a better opportunity. Employees have not yet gone to court to establish a "right not to travel." One executive did go to court to claim that his company had an obligation to transfer him out of an undesirable location. He was the victim of a kidnapping in Colombia, South America, and tried, after the fact, to pin the responsibility on his company because it did not respond to his requests for a transfer. The court said the company had no such obligation.

Keeping Personal Time Personal

While employees may not have gone to court to prevent the family disruption caused by transfers, they have gone to court to keep their companies out of what the employees consider their personal, off-the-job lives. A marketing manager with the Office Products Division of IBM was transferred from her job in 1979 because of the man she was dating. A twelve-year veteran with IBM in San Francisco whose loyalty and sales earning were not denied by IBM, the woman first became involved with the man when he too worked in the Office Products Division. He left for Philadelphia to join Exxon Corporation's company that makes and sells QYX typewriters in direct competition with IBM. Upon his return to San Francisco, the QYX man and the IBM woman resumed dating. As QYX district manager, the man began hiring away some of his former IBM colleagues. That was when IBM superiors raised objections to the woman's relationship with the man.

When IBM switched her out of the Office Products Division, she felt she was being put out to pasture. She then quit. Even though she loved the company for what it had done earlier for her career, the woman sued.

A jury in 1981 awarded her compensatory and punitive damages, in deciding that IBM had in essence terminated the woman without good cause and had invaded her privacy.[117]

That same year, a Tennessee woman was awarded damages after convincing a jury that her employer had meddled in her troublesome marital breakup. Both she and her husband worked at the same manufacturing plant in Knoxville. In the first half of 1980 the two were living under the same roof but had filed papers for a divorce. The woman began seeing a lot of an engineer at the same company. In September, her new companion told her that he had been fired, after supervisors at the company apparently heard a tape recording of a conversation over her home telephone between the woman and the engineer. Two days later, the woman lost her job. She alleged later that a fore-man at the plant had been following her around.

The New Hampshire Supreme Court in 1974 upheld a jury verdict for a woman who claimed that she was fired mainly because she refused to accept an invitation to go out with her foreman. She had good reasons to decline. She was married, with three children. She was attending col-lege. And she was working the night shift.[118] After this came several court rulings upholding the rights of a female to resist "sexual harassment" by fellow employees, even when it occurs after work hours.

The Merit Systems Protection Board, which decides cases involving federal employees' grievances, has said in its rulings that a federal agency, to justify discipline or dis-charge for off-duty activities, must show that the agency's action will promote the efficiency of the federal service. The burden of proof is on the agency to show a connection between the off-duty misconduct of an employee and the harm to the efficiency of the government agency. However, the board has said, some off-duty conduct is so abhorrent to society that it can be presumed to be detrimental to the agency's mission without further proof. Still, in these cases (which often involve violent crimes) an employee could present proof to overcome this presumption. Fraud and incest off the job have been found to be misconduct serious enough to impair federal service, but a conviction for pos-session of a small amount of marijuana has been found to be insufficient to do so.

Labor arbitrators in the private sector have generally made the same rulings in cases involving employees dis-charged for criminal convictions for possession of mari-juana off the job. While they have upheld company rules calling for automatic discharge for possession of illegal drugs, arbitrators often make exceptions for particular employees on a first offense or a minor offense. By contrast, arbitrators generally uphold the firing of employees caught *selling* drugs or regularly using drugs other than marijuana, even if off the job.

The standard that private arbitrators try to follow in these cases of off-duty activities was articulated in 1944 by arbitrator Harry Shulman in a case involving Ford Motor Co. and the United Auto Workers:

> The jurisdictional line which limits the company's power of discipline is a functional, not a physical line. It has power to discipline for misconduct directly related to the employment. It has no power to discipline for misconduct not related to the employment.

Thus, arbitrators have refused to permit the dismissal of two employees caught fighting, when the fight occurred outside the plant gates. "The proper and only authority over the personal lives of employees, once they leave their place of employment, is the civil authority," said one arbitrator in the auto industry in 1946. Arbitrators have similarly been tolerant of employees who moonlight at other jobs, even if a company has a rule against it, unless the extra job seriously affects performance on the principal job.

Also in the automobile industry, an arbitrator ruled that employees don't have to like the products they make. A Ford employee had been fired for buying a Rambler, but he was ordered reinstated by the arbitrator. A handful of states have laws prohibiting a company from directing its employees to buy, or not to buy, products from certain companies. (The chief executive officer of a major oil company once said that he did not want to see any employee of his company buying gasoline at a competitor's gasoline station.)

There are a few other laws on the books that prevent employers from making further intrusions into the off-the-job lives of employees. For instance, the Consumer Credit Protection Act prohibits the firing of an employee solely because his or her earnings have been subjected to garnishment for any one indebtedness.[119] A company must reasonably accommodate the religious practices of an employee unless to do so would result in undue hardship on the conduct of its business, according to the Equal Employment Opportunity Commission guidelines.[120] This includes observance of a sabbath or a religious holiday, needs for prayer breaks, special diets, or mourning for a deceased relative, and religious prohibitions against physical exams and union membership.

Even off-the-job obligations of citizenship like voting and jury duty are not always respected by companies. A woman in Oregon lost her job in 1973 because she served on a jury as required by law. The Supreme Court of Oregon upheld an award of damages to the woman for wrongful discharge. But an Alabama court in 1980 upheld the dismissal of a woman who missed work for jury duty.

The following states require companies to provide time off for employees to serve on juries (and many of the states say the same about military duty): Alaska, Arizona, California, Colorado, Connecticut, Florida, Hawaii, Idaho, Illinois, Indiana, Kentucky, Massachusetts, Minnesota, Nebraska, New Mexico, New York, North Dakota, Oregon, Pennsylvania, Puerto Rico, Rhode Island, South Dakota, Tennessee, Vermont, West Virginia, and Wisconsin.

The following twenty-nine states require that companies give time off to vote, in most cases with pay: Alaska, Arizona, Arkansas, California, Colorado, Georgia, Hawaii, Illinois, Indiana, Iowa, Kansas, Kentucky, Maryland, Massachusetts, Minnesota, Missouri, Nebraska, Nevada, New Mexico, New York, Ohio, Oklahoma, South Dakota, Tennessee, Texas, Utah, West Virginia, Wisconsin, and Wyoming.

Aside from these specific limitations, there are very few legal principles covering an employer's adverse actions for an employee's off-the-job activities. Only in government employment (17 percent of the work force) and in jobs where collective bargaining provides for arbitration (22 percent) is there much recourse for an employee. In the remaining work force, the individual employee can be controlled by his employer at home, as well as on the job. For these persons, the situation has changed only in degree since the boardinghouses of the Lowell textile mills in the 1830s.

11

Freedom from Sexual Harassment

Back in 1974, after four years of working her way up through the clerical ranks in the Department of Corrections in a major eastern city, Sandra Bundy was approached by her supervisor, who was interested in sexual relations. The supervisor, Arthur Burton, would call the woman into his office and ask her to spend the afternoon with him in his apartment. He began to question her about her sexual likes and dislikes. Then Bundy was approached by another supervisor, James Gainey, this one wanting to take her to a motel and then on a trip to the Bahamas. Bundy complained to Burton's and Gainey's supervisor but received no satisfaction. In fact, that supervisor *himself* asked her to have sex with him in *his* apartment. "Any man in his right mind would want to rape you," he told her.

Bundy didn't know where to turn, because she recalled that in 1972 another man who worked there sought sexual favors from her. He was now the director of the department. On April 11, 1975, Bundy met with the director anyway and presented him with a summary of her complaint. She alleged that she had been turned down for promotion because of her refusal to accept the sexual advances of supervisors.

Just a month earlier a federal district court in Arizona was telling a woman complainant, "There is nothing in

[Title VII of the Civil Rights Act of 1972] which could reasonably be construed to have it apply to 'verbal and physical sexual advances' by another employee, even though he be in a supervisory capacity, where such complained-of acts had no relationship to the nature of the employment." The same court said, "It would be ludicrous to hold that the sort of activity involved here was contemplated by the Act because [this would bring] a potential federal lawsuit every time any employee made amorous or sexually oriented advances toward another. The only sure way an employer could avoid such charges would be to have employees who were asexual."[121]

Prospects for Bundy were not very bright. Twice she saw female colleagues promoted to higher government-service levels to which she thought she was entitled. The men in her office were of no help in her attempts to work in an environment free of sexual pressure. The courts at that time only rarely recognized such complaints by women as a violation of law. Judges considered the complaints as frivolous, vague, or simply inevitable in any environment where there are both men and women.

But the situation changed sharply in 1977. On July 28 the decision in Arizona was reversed by the influential U.S. Court of Appeals for the Ninth Circuit, which sets legal policy for California and eight other Western states. The equally influential Court of Appeals in the District of Columbia issued a similar ruling the same month. Then in November came the Third Circuit in the Midwest. The Fourth Circuit, covering the Border states, had begun the trend in February.

And on August 3, 1977, Sandra Bundy filed a lawsuit against her employer. The district court that heard her case declared that sexual intimidation was a "normal condition of employment," but by January 1981 the U.S. Circuit Court of Appeals had reversed that decision.[122] Bundy's case has helped to propel the fastest growing legal movement in employee rights—sexual harassment.

"Sexual harassment in employment is rapidly emerging as one of the most significant and controversial labor relations issues of the 1980s and potential sexual harassment suits are becoming a substantial problem for employers. The development of this problem has occurred quite recently, virtually over the last two years," said Washington attorney Gerald S. Hartman at a 1981 meeting of lawyers to discuss employee lawsuits.

"The problem" Hartman was referring to presumably means lawsuits based on sexual harassment. "The problem" of sexual harassment itself has been with us for years. It is remarkable to see the parallel between the environment of the Lowell textile mills of the 1830s, described in Chapter 2, and the environment of today. In the 1830s, when a few women called for a strike at the textile mills, a supervisor called them "Amazons." In 1976, when a stewardess rebuffed the sexual advances of the captain of her crew, he retaliated by spreading the word (falsely) that she was a lesbian.[123]

It is not new that males seek to take sexual advantage of females nor is it new that females are subjected to teasing, joking, and suggestive remarks. What is new is that the law now recognizes the right of a woman to a remedy when this harassment affects her employment.

The fact that male-female interplay with sexual overtones—ranging from the casual to the cruel—has long existed in our society has led many employers to conclude either that sexual harassment in the workplace is harmless or that preventing it is impossible. In the early years of this litigation, judges reflected that attitude. "The attraction of males to females and females to males is a natural sex phenomenon," wrote a federal judge in California in 1976, "and it is probable that this attraction plays at least a subtle part in most personnel decisions. Such being the case, it would seem wise for the courts to refrain from delving into these matters."

That ruling was reversed in 1979 by the Ninth Circuit

Court of Appeals. By now all of the circuits in the United States recognize sexual harassment in the workplace as a violation of Title VII of the Civil Rights Act of 1964, which makes it unlawful for an employer "to discriminate against any individual with respect to his employment, because of such individual's . . . sex."

More is at stake here for both sexes than "the attraction of males to females and females to males." That attraction in society at large is a fact of life that each individual learns to live with, either enjoying it, avoiding it, or coping with it. But a woman has a right to expect that it will not adversely affect her livelihood. (According to one study, more than half the victims of sexual harassment are the sole supporters of their families or themselves.) All employees have a right to expect that they will be evaluated and promoted fairly and that sexual attractions between supervisor and employee, or lack of them, will not be factors. All employees are entitled to an environment that is conducive to productivity, not play.

And that is the law. Because claims of sexual harassment in the workplace arise under Title VII of the Civil Rights Act, which covers private and public employers equally, this is one area of employment rights where the law for employees in the private sector is just about identical to what has developed in the public sector. Although Sandra Bundy works for a public agency, the principles she eventually established apply equally to women working for private companies.

In November 1980, the Equal Employment Opportunity Commission, which enforces Title VII, issued regulations that prohibit sexual harassment, saying:

> Harassment on the basis of sex is a violation of Sec. 703 of Title VII. Unwelcome sexual advances, requests for sexual favors, and other verbal or physical conduct of a sexual nature consti-

tute sexual harassment when (1) submission to such conduct is made either explicitly or implicitly a term or condition of an individual's employment, (2) submission to or rejection of such conduct by an individual is used as the basis for employment decisions affecting such individual, or (3) such conduct has the purpose or effect of unreasonably interfering with an individual's work performance or creating an intimidating, hostile, or offensive working environment.

In determining whether alleged conduct constitutes sexual harassment, the Commission will look at the record as a whole and at the totality of the circumstances, such as the nature of the sexual advances and the context in which they occurred. The determination of the legality of a particular action will be made from the facts, on a case by case basis.[124]

The concern with this issue expressed by the Equal Employment Opportunity Commission and the federal courts reflected the increased sophistication of women's organizations who developed a legal strategy to move the law in this direction. It also reflected increased recognition of the debilitating effects in the workplace of sexual pressures and unwelcome sexual fun-and-games.

In testimony before a House subcommittee hearing on workplace problems in 1980, the Merit Systems Protection Board of the federal government reported that 42 percent of the women it surveyed reported harassment incidents, most of them severe. And 15 percent of the men said they had been victims. In a survey sponsored in 1981 by *Harvard Business Review* and *Redbook* magazine, 90 percent of 9,000 women claimed they had experienced sexual harassment. Seventy percent of the respondents in a study of New

York public-service employees said the same. "If, in fact, these women actually are experiencing sexual harassment, the pervasiveness of the problem may be attributable to the rapidly increasing number of women in the work force and the fact that only about 5 percent of all female workers hold managerial or administrative positions and thus women still tend to be in low-paying positions where they remain dependent upon the approval and goodwill of their male supervisors," says Gerald S. Hartman, who represents management in equal employment opportunity cases.

Whether or not the claims can be verified, it cannot be denied that there is a pervasive *perception* that the workplace is a place where women must submit to or resist sexual pressures, or must encounter lewd jokes or suggestions.

Most of the victims are unmarried or separated, and most of them are clerical workers not earning top dollars, according to Working Women's Institute in New Jersey. The director of the institute, Joan Vermuelen, says:

> As an assertion of power, sexual harassment serves to reinforce the notion that if a woman values her psychological and physical integrity, she must function within certain limits, both in terms of work choices and personal behavior.

> When a man sexually harasses a woman, he is saying that a woman's legitimate function is that of a sexual object, thus denying her role as a contributing member of the work force. This is dysfunctional for women workers in several respects. First, sexual harassment challenges a woman's right to function as a worker by underscoring the socially imposed incongruity between the roles of woman and worker and causes her to experience conflict, tension, and stress which may well interfere with her work performance. To the extent

that a woman internalizes this role conflict, it will affect her motivation and her belief that she can advance up the career ladder, thus preventing her from applying for promotions or openings that are perceived to be men's jobs. Further, reinforcing the primacy of a woman's sexual identity to her male colleagues will make it less likely that she will be viewed as capable of undertaking demanding work and, consequently, will make it less likely that she will be given demanding projects. Finally, to the extent that a woman is able to continue to function and, indeed, to succeed in such an atmosphere, her male colleagues are likely to attribute such success to sexual manipulation and to avoid acknowledging her ability as a worker.[125]

Ann F. Hoffman, attorney for the Communications Workers of America, is quick to point out, "Nobody is trying to prevent or punish the 'natural sex phenomena.'. . . If a man and a woman—or two men or two women—choose to enter into a serious or joking sexual relationship *voluntarily*, the courts and EEOC as well as employers, unions, and civil rights organizations will not and should not interfere—even if she is the supervisor and he is the employee. That's not sexual harassment."

"Such behaviors and relationships may reflect poor judgment, but they are not appropriately defined as harassment," says the Federation of Organizations for Professional Women.

What is sexual harassment in the workplace? Here are some examples that courts have been asked to consider in recent years:

A stenographer at a utility company in New Jersey was told by her supervisor that he wanted to discuss her promotion, over lunch, only to have the man say at the restaurant that he wanted to "lay" her and that he "couldn't walk around the office with a hard-on all the time." Having sex was "the only way we could have a working relationship," the supervisor said. "When I tried to leave the restaurant," recalled the woman, "he restrained me physically, and angrily declared I wasn't going anywhere except with him to the executive suite on the thirteenth floor of the hotel. When I protested again, he advised me not to seek help, that since he had 'something' on everyone in the company, including top management, no one would venture forth to help me."

The airline pilot mentioned earlier who resorted to rumors about lesbianism originally insisted that the stewardess join him for dinner. On the limousine trip to a hotel after their flight, he said that in the past it was easier to "get some ass." The woman continued to resist, but the man broke through her hotel room door and even tried to carry her downstairs to the hotel bar. Rejected, he falsely told colleagues that he had caught the stewardess in lesbian sexual acts.

One of only two females employed at a Continental Can plant in Minnesota was the target of sexually derogatory remarks and verbal sexual advances from male coworkers for three straight months. One of the men regularly patted her on the rear end. The woman complained once to a supervisor, without using names. When nothing changed, she felt she simply had to endure the indignities. She did so for another six months until one of her harassers grabbed her between the legs when she bent over machinery. Again the woman complained to management. After the woman's husband complained to the culprit, the couple found their automobile damaged in the company parking lot. The confrontations escalated until the woman filed a complaint with the state Department of Human Rights. One supervisor told her that a woman "had to expect that kind of behavior when working with men."

A Washington, D.C., woman was told flatly to agree to her male supervisor's demands as the price for holding her job. All executives "have affairs with their personnel," she was told.

An industrial engineer at Western Electric Co. in New Jersey was taunted by three men who placed bets on her virginity. One of them drew an obscene cartoon and placed it on her desk. She was told she should expect such jokes in "a working man's world." When she complained, *she* was moved to another office and then told to see the company doctor for psychiatric help.

Another Washington, D.C., woman employed as assistant manager at a hotel restaurant had to put up with the advances of the manager after she had been on the job only a few weeks. The manager would write her little notes about his interest in her, leaving them inside menus and slipping them inside the woman's purse without her knowledge. Then the manager began to telephone the woman at home, making leering remarks about her sexual life. When the manager's wife discovered one of these little love notes, *she* telephoned the woman and began threatening *her*. The man's harassment stopped for a time, but before long he was stroking her hair at work, touching her, and asking her to spend a night or take a trip with him, according to a lawsuit filed by the woman. After two months of this, the manager started excluding the woman from staff meetings, telling coworkers that the woman would soon be leaving, and "generally made it difficult for her to perform her job."

A third Washington woman was greeted in her first week on the job by the off-color remarks of the company president, and later by his sexual advances.[126]

The harassment ranges from the bothersome to the dangerous, and when it affects employment, courts will listen. Gerald Hartman summarizes the cases as follows: If submission to sexual conduct is implicitly or explicitly made a term or condition of the individual's hiring or continued employment, then it is illegal. If submission to or rejection of sexual conduct by an individual employee is used as a basis for employment decisions affecting that individual, then it is illegal. If the sexually harassing conduct has the purpose or effect of unreasonably interfering with an individual employee's work performance or of creating an intimidating, hostile, or offensive environment at work, then it is illegal. (In these cases, the harassment may be obvious, but the effect may not be.) It was in establishing this last principle of law that Sandra Bundy's case was significant. In January 1981, in Bundy's appeal, a federal court stated for the first time that a woman can sue her employer to stop sexual harassment without having to prove she resisted the harassment and that, in effect, sexual harassment in and of itself violates the law. Further evidence that the employee was penalized or lost specific job benefits is not necessary. Title VII is violated, said the appeals court, "where an employer created or condoned a substantially discriminatory work *environment*, regardless of whether the complaining employees lost any tangible job benefits as a result." This means that an employer can be held responsible for continued harassment by customers and other nonemployees.

The court asked, "How then can sexual harassment, which injects the most demeaning sexual stereotypes into the general work environment and which always represents an intentional assault on an individual's innermost privacy, not be illegal?"

The best defense for an employer, since the Bundy decision, is to establish a clearly understood policy against sexual harassment and seriously to resolve complaints that arise. Courts do not hold employers accountable for an isolated incident, and some do not hold them accountable if higher management was not made aware of the problem. Other courts rationalize occasional incidents that do not involve the supervisor-subordinate relationship. Courts are particularly intolerant of company management that heard about an incident of sexual harassment and did nothing to resolve it, or punished the complainant, not the perpetrator. "Prevention is the best tool," say the EEOC guidelines.

A federal court in Illinois in 1981 said clearly that a homosexual advance by a male supervisor to a male employee would also be encompassed in the prohibitions of Title VII. How about a male claiming heterosexual harassment at work? A jury in Wisconsin in 1982 awarded damages to a state employee who claimed that he was demoted by his female supervisor after he refused to continue a love affair with her that began one night in a motel room.[127]

The Equal Employment Opportunity Commission guidelines published in November 1980 generally coincide with the latest rulings of the federal courts, with one exception. The guidelines conclude by saying:

> Where employment opportunities or benefits are granted because of an individual's submission to the employer's sexual advances or requests for sexual favors, the employer may be held liable for unlawful sex discrimination against *other persons* who were qualified for but denied that opportunity or benefit.

This means that the commission will be receptive to a complaint from employees (presumably male or female) who felt they were qualified for a promotion or other job benefit that was given instead to a person who had responded affirmatively to the supervisor's sexual requests. The courts have not yet gone this far.

At least ten states, including California, Colorado, Illinois, Kentucky, Maryland, Michigan, Pennsylvania, Rhode Island, Washington, and Wisconsin, plus the District of Columbia have adopted laws or regulations prohibiting sexual harassment in the workplace. Other states are moving in that direction. Some of these state standards are stiffer on the employer than the Equal Employment Opportunity Commission's. Victims of sexual harassment may also be able to file a lawsuit based on the torts of assault, battery, abusive discharge, or intentional infliction of emotional distress. Or the victim may claim a breach of an employment contract. Libel and slander have been involved in other cases (and the victim runs the risk of a libel or slander suit against herself if she is not truthful in her allegation).

Male supervisors—and perhaps many females—remain skeptical about the claim of sexual harassment. For them it is either too difficult to prove, too tangentially related to work, or too subtle to prevent. They may think that a woman invites such behavior—simply by looking her best at work or by being polite to fellow employees and customers who happen to be males. But Ann Hoffman points out that a woman who pursues a sexual harassment complaint is destined for a difficult ordeal indeed. As we have seen, many complainants are told that sexual harassment is part of the job. Or the complaint is ignored or ridiculed. Or the higher authority in the organization joins in the inappropriate behavior. Judges are not always sympathetic; many pioneers in this legal area have lost at the trial-court level. Finally, even when a woman eventually prevails in court, it is not uncommon for a judge to refuse to order the woman reinstated, because of the hostility that has developed. A woman's reward may be that she has won her back pay, that she has tied up her company in lengthy litigation, and that she has strengthened the principles in this relatively uncharted area of the law.

"What this unsympathetic background means," says Hoffman, "is that any complainant who bothers to pursue allegations of sexual harassment in court will be determined to see the case through and, assuming good representation, armed for a tough fight."

And she adds, "The fight is on. Employers and unions resist at their peril. We would all be far better advised to be on the right side of this issue."

12

Freedom of Information

Many American employees know the workplace as, in Karl Marx's phrase, "a hidden abode of production." Information does not flow freely in American corporations, either outward to the public nor internally among employees. Consequently, very little is known about the true working conditions of many Americans.

This mania for secrecy is one of the legacies from the influx of military-minded veterans into American companies after World War II. Russell B. Stevenson, a Washington law professor, points out in his book *Corporations and Information,* "Many of the government bureaucrats who apply 'Classified' stamps to purchase orders for paint or toilet paper in the Pentagon eventually go on to jobs in industry where the habits of secrecy acquired in the government continue to influence their attitudes toward the use and misuse of information.

"Whether secrecy is prompted by the desire to conceal information from competitors, shareholders, consumers, the general public, or the government, or whether it grows out of the desire of individuals to advance their own interests within the bureaucracy," writes Stevenson, "the result is always a restriction in the amount of information that reaches decision makers to whom the information is essential."[128]

This self-imposed limitation on disclosure affects employees in at least three ways. They are denied information about the organization they work for and thus are less able to participate in guiding its destiny, or even in working effectively for its success. They are denied crucial information about their specific jobs within the organization, including information necessary to protect their own safety, health, and rights as citizens. Lastly, employees are left in the dark about information that is kept on them as individuals, in the personnel files of the front office, as well as about how that information is collected, maintained, and disclosed to others.

Employees are campaigning, then, for full disclosure of corporate information—with regard to information about the organization—and they are campaigning for fair information practices—with regard to the personal information that the company as employer keeps on file. As a citizen, the employee enjoys both of these informational rights with regard to his government. As an employee in the private sector, he enjoys neither (with a few exceptions).

The United States has always recognized the principle of free disclosure by government. ("A popular government without popular information or the means of acquiring it is but a prologue to a farce or a tragedy or perhaps both," said James Madison.) The Freedom of Information Act of 1966 provides citizens the right to have copies of documents that federal agencies use in their decision making. The Government in the Sunshine Act and the Federal Advisory Committee Act open up to the public many meetings held by federal agencies. There are comparable state statutes affecting state governments.

At the same time, the United States has always recognized the interests of private corporations to conduct their business in secret. The Constitution itself recognized the need for a system of patent registration to protect innovation on the part of inventors and businesses. Near the end of the last century, American courts recognized the interest of a corporation to protect its "trade secrets." To this day, protection of trade secrets provides one of the exceptions to the government's Freedom-of-Information policy: the law permits the government not to disclose information if it would compromise the trade secrets of the business that originally provided the information to the government.

Journalists, government inspectors, union organizers, and researchers—all have reported extreme difficulties in penetrating the boundaries of most workplaces. Access to an enemy prisoner-of-war camp is often easier. In her autobiography, the first director of the Woman's Bureau in the Department of Labor wrote of the period after World War I:

> I remember going to Bridgeport with a group of several men and one other woman to inspect some factories and see that production was facilitated by proper working conditions. The group never got into a factory. We waited for the head of our expedition to tell us when we could go into a factory to see what the conditions were. Day after day he put us off saying the management was "about" ready to let us in. After nearly a week of waiting we left in disgust.
>
> Another time, Mary van Kleeck and I stopped in Pittsburgh for one day to see conditions in some of the many ordnance plants there. We were met by an officer from the Ordnance Department the minute we got to the hotel, were taken to the office, taken to lunch, taken through one plant in the afternoon, taken to dinner that night. We were so closely chaperoned that until we took the train that night we could not so much as say "hello" to one another. Naturally, we did not find out much about the conditions of women's employment.[129]

Beginning with the securities and exchange legislation of the New Deal period, companies have had to disclose certain information concerning their structure and ownership. In the mid-1970s came additional requirements for disclosure, about interest rates, land sales, warranties, and similar business matters. Only one of these laws, the Employee Retirement Income Security Act, required disclosure directly relevant to the employer-employee relationship, although some employee representatives were able to use information disclosed under these other statutes to piece together a partial portrait of the company and its management.

Increased concern in the late 1970s about employee safety brought new pressure on companies to disclose relevant information to employees, especially about the substances they must handle every workday. The House Committee on Government Operations reported, "The problem of worker and employer ignorance of hazardous substances used in industry is far greater than previously supposed. The chief cause is the practice of identifying chemical compounds by trade names without the disclosure of ingredients, which thwarts even the most conscientious attempt to alert workers to exposures beyond specified limits."

And so, in its last week in office, the Carter administration proposed a tough regulation that would have required, among other things, the detailed labeling of hazardous chemicals in the workplace. Within four weeks, the Reagan administration had withdrawn the proposal. In March 1982, the administration offered an alternative Occupational Safety and Health regulation that deemphasized compulsory labeling and emphasized posting bulletins to advise workers of toxic risks and training workers to handle the toxic materials.

This right to know about hazardous substances that employees must handle is a part of state law in California, Connecticut, Maine, Massachusetts, Michigan, New York, Oregon, Washington, and West Virginia. All but Massachusetts, Oregon, and Washington include a requirement that employees have access to relevant company information. The city of Philadelphia has also passed right-to-know legislation, and a half-dozen other jurisdictions had it under active consideration in 1982.

Voluntary Disclosure

A corporate executive who was responsive to demands for more disclosure was A. W. Clausen, chairman of Bank-America Corp. He led the way in 1976 with a speech in San Francisco entitled, "Someone Has to Jump into the Icy Water First." And that is what he did that year with publication of the company's Voluntary Disclosure Code. It recognized that a variety of groups, including employees, are entitled to certain information to evaluate the company's operations, "to judge the value of BankAmerica's contributions to economic and social well-being and its adherence to legal and ethical standards." The code listed five objectives:

1) To provide the men and women who manage BankAmerica with a continuing guide that keeps effective disclosure a principal objective of corporate policy.
2) To facilitate disclosure of information that has been determined—not by the corporation but by its constituencies—to be useful and relevant in understanding and evaluating Bank-America's activities.
3) To encourage disclosure of information in ways which can be easily understood by all concerned.
4) To give the public ready access, to the extent permitted by law, to information the corporation currently provides in its routine reporting to regulatory agencies.

5) To define the limits of voluntary disclosure—
that is, to respond to the public's question,
"Why not?"

Few, if any, businesses have followed Clausen's lead,
and employees continue to be denied basic information
they need to protect themselves and their rights within the
workplace. In fact, some employees or their representatives file lawsuits not with the hope of prevailing but with
the intent of "discovering" corporate information they
need.

Few corporate executives realize that secrecy tends to
diminish the number of persons making informed decisions
to a very few. Secrecy excludes from the process other
personnel who could contribute significantly. Employees
denied information, and thereby denied an opportunity to
contribute the fruits of their own experience, become
isolated from, and hostile to, the decisions that are made.
Secrecy then becomes a two-way street. Rank-and-file employees deny to their superiors the information the superiors need for intelligent business decisions. The subordinates tell the higher-ups what they think the latter want to
hear. Information is covered up, like a smoldering fire that
will erupt when people least expect it.

"Businesses get into the habit of keeping documents
secret. That's understandable on the part of the business,
but it is questionable in light of the social issues," says
Russell Stevenson. As recently as 1971 a mechanical engineer for a lumber company in Oregon was fired for exercising his rights as a stockholder to inspect corporate books
and records.[130]

Opening Up Personnel Records

Employees seeking access to personal information
about themselves have had more success, thanks to increased concern in society at large about the effects of

large-scale information gathering on personal privacy. Here too the contrast with the rights of public-sector employees is striking. Every single employee of the federal government and those who work for state agencies in sixteen states have a right to inspect, and sometimes to correct, their own personnel files.

But a Virginia man had to go to court to compel his private employer to provide him with copies of his personnel files, including evaluations of job performance. The man had just completed six weeks of special schooling at the company when he was fired in 1977. He suspected that the reason for the firing was his complaint about unsafe office conditions during renovations. To prove his point, he needed access to his performance records, which he believed would show him to be a good employee.

A Chicago woman complained, "I asked personnel for the reason I was turned down for a promotion, in order that I might correct my deficiencies and move elsewhere. I was told that this was a just request. But I have heard no more."

A New York City man asked, "If I was the victim of chicanery during a promotion decision, how would I go about finding out the information, which is not likely to be given up easily by an employer? I do not like the idea of derogatory information sitting in my file that could be used against me."

An employee at IBM had to go all the way to the office of the board chairman, Thomas Watson, Jr., on his simple request to see his own personnel file. That was in the 1960s. Watson apparently could find no good reason to deny the man's request and so he let him look at the file. He also wrote to all IBM managers, saying that from now on employees are entitled to see their own files.

These examples show, and a 1976 study by a New York City management firm confirmed, that access to personnel files is an issue that concerns primarily professionals and managers at the higher levels of the organization. The management firm found that 90 percent of the factual information on file about an employee had been gathered at the hiring stage, and just about all of that had been gathered from the application form itself. "Thereafter, the most significant factual information accumulated about employees is their payroll, tax and benefits accounting, and their work and salary history within the company. The remainder is either evaluative or predictive," said the firm of McCaffery, Seligman, and von Simson. It found very little evaluative material on hourly employees and those represented in collective bargaining. There was a moderate amount of evaluative material on clerical workers, but most of the crucial evaluative material was on the 5 percent of the employees at the very top of the organization. This is the information that many top-level employees are eager to see, to check its accuracy or at least to know of its existence.

Health-Insurance Information

There was another trend in personnel record keeping in the 1970s that brought an additional rationale for employees to have access to their own records. Increasingly, health care and insurance benefits came to be administered through the workplace. The vice president of a small New York company points out, "We've had a lot of employee concern here about invasion of privacy in . . . company-run insurance programs that require the employee to submit claim forms with diagnosis to the company. Some who should be making claims are not submitting them."

It is not the medical insurance companies that insist on sending this medical information to personnel offices. It seems to be the employers themselves, who want to monitor insurance claims to make sure that the companies are getting the group coverage they are paying for. Companies doing this have discovered an incidental savings: employees concerned about disclosure of sensitive medical information to the personnel office are foregoing insurance claims to which they are entitled. They are paying for certain treatments, notably mental health care, out of their own pockets rather than filing claims for insurance reimbursement that may bring their conditions to the attention of the people at work.

Because of this practice, employers may be losing out on valuable additions to their staffs. A woman in Detroit said after interviewing for a job there, "I remember cringing when I realized that if I took the job I sought, I would have to turn in my medical bills to the personnel manager, to be forwarded to the insurance company. Instead, I took another job without this requirement."

Employees have been shocked to discover that information about their treatment for alcoholism, depression, minor cancers, or heart ailments has found its way to supervisors and personnel officers. A representative of the National Institute of Mental Health guessed in 1980 that 15 percent of adults covered by health insurance are depriving themselves of insurance reimbursement for therapy because of concern about disclosure to their employers (although accurate figures are obviously difficult to come by).

This is a concern that affects employees at all levels (for information about their dependents' treatments are recorded as well). A couple of medical organizations have experimented with numerical codes between doctor and insurance company to disguise the nature of the treatment. Some companies have agreed to a spot check of claims rather than collecting 100 percent of the claims filed by their employees.

The use and abuse of employee records was a primary concern of a privacy commission established by Congress in 1974. In its final report in 1977, the Privacy Protection Study Commission said, "There is no general framework in the private sector which could accommodate disputes about recorded information. . . . Most employers have not undertaken any sort of systemic review of their employment record-keeping policies and practices with privacy protection in mind."[131] The commission recommended that each employer articulate a policy of fair information practices, which should include limiting the collection of information to what is relevant for specific decisions, informing employees of the uses to be made of such information, adopting procedures for assuring accuracy and confidentiality, and permitting individual employees, former employees, and applicants to see, copy, correct, or amend the records maintained about them. The commission said that its open-access recommendation should apply to *all* information about an employee, including letters of reference and investigative materials. In fact, it said the position of many employers that certain records ought not to be disclosed to the individual was "difficult to defend."

In contrast to its recommendations in other areas, the privacy commission stopped short of recommending federal legislation to require that these policies be adopted in the workplace. Since the commission's report, legislation incorporating these recommendations has been introduced in Congress, and six states have enacted laws requiring that employees be entitled to inspect their own records— California, Connecticut, Michigan, Oregon, Pennsylvania, and Wisconsin. Ohio requires that an employee be able to copy any *medical* information in his or her personnel files.

An eighth state, Maine, passed its law in 1975, before the commission issued its report. Maine's law, the first in the nation on this subject, is an admirable precedent for federal legislation, because of its simplicity and clarity. It states:

> The employer shall, upon written request from an employee or former employee, provide the employee, former employee or his duly authorized representative with an opportunity to review his personnel file if the employer has a personnel file for that employee. Such reviews shall take place at the location where the personnel files are main-

tained and during normal office hours. The employer may at his discretion allow the review to take place at such other location and time as would be more convenient for the employee. For the purpose of this section, a personnel file shall include, but not be limited to, all formal or informal employee evaluations and reports relating to the employee's character, credit, work habits, compensation and benefits which the employer has in his possession.[132]

Maine's law is unique in that it is the only one of the eight to agree with the federal privacy commission's recommendation and not exclude letters of reference and investigative materials from what an employee may see about himself or herself.

Since the commission's strong recommendations, many large companies have adopted them voluntarily, at the behest of trade associations like the Business Roundtable. This has not been highly publicized, and many employees are unaware that their companies have publicly adopted policies permitting employees access to their own personnel files. Among the first companies to do this were: Aetna Life Insurance Co., Cummins Engine Co., Equitable Life Assurance Society of the U.S., Ford Motor Co., General Electric Co., IBM Corp., Manufacturers Hanover Corp., and Prudential Insurance Co. These open-access policies have exceptions to them, but in many instances the beneficiaries include customers, applicants, stockholders, and others in addition to employees.

Further, the Department of Commerce has urged large American companies to abide by the privacy guidelines drafted by the Organization of Economic Cooperation and Development (OECD), to which the governments of the U.S., Canada, Japan, Australia, New Zealand, and the European nations belong. The guidelines say, among other things, that individuals should be allowed to see data maintained on them and to challenge, correct, amend, or erase data. This includes employees, customers, and others whose names might be on file in a company. Personal data must be protected by reasonable security safeguards and should not be disclosed, except for the purposes originally specified for the information, without consent of the individual or by authority of law. Data about individuals must be kept relevant, accurate, complete, and up-to-date. The rules for handling personal data must be openly announced by the company. Here are some of the large companies that have notified the U.S. Department of Commerce that they intend to abide by the OECD guidelines:

Aetna Life Insurance Co.
Allstate Insurance Co.
Aluminum Co. of America
American Cyanamid Co.
American Express Co.
American Hospital Supply
American Telephone &
 Telegraph Co.
Armstrong World
 Industries, Inc.
Atlantic Richfield Co.
Avon Products, Inc.
BankAmerica Corp.
Bankers Life Co.
The Boeing Co.
Bristol-Myers Co.
Burroughs Corp.
Caterpillar Tractor Co.
Chase Manhattan Bank,
 N.A.
Chemical New York Corp.
Chrysler Corp.
Citibank

Commonwealth Life
 Insurance Co.
Conoco, Inc.
Control Data Corp.
Crocker National Bank
Cummins Engine Co., Inc.
Deere & Co.
Dow Chemical Co.
Eastman Kodak Co.
Equitable of Iowa
Exxon Corp.
Federated Insurance
Firestone Tire & Rubber
 Co.
Ford Motor Co.
General Dynamics Corp.
General Electric Co.
General Mills, Inc.
General Telephone &
 Electronics Corp.
General Tire & Rubber Co.
Hewlett-Packard Co.
Honeywell, Inc.

International Telephone &
 Telegraph Corp.
John Hancock Mutual Life
 Insurance Co.
Johnson & Johnson
Life Insurance Co. of
 Georgia
Marine Midland Bank
Massachusetts Mutual
 Life Insurance Co.
Merck & Co., Inc.
Metropolitan Life
 Insurance Co.
Miles Laboratories, Inc.
Mobil Corp.
Motorola, Inc.
Mutual Benefit Life
Mutual of Omaha
National Bank of Detroit
National Life of Vermont
NCR Corp.
New York Life Insurance
 Co.
Northrop Corp.
Norwich-Eaton
 Pharmaceuticals
Ohio State Life
Olin Corp.
Pacific Mutual Life
 Insurance Co.
The Paul Revere Life
 Insurance Co.

Perkin-Elmer Corp.
Philip Morris Inc.
PPG Industries, Inc.
Proctor & Gamble Co.
Prudential Insurance Co.
 of America
RCA
Reader's Digest
 Association, Inc.
Sentry Life Insurance Co.
Smith Kline Corp.
Sperry Corp.
Standard Oil Corp. of
 California
Sterling Drug, Inc.
Sunbeam Management
 Services LTD.
Texaco, Inc.
Texas Instruments, Inc.
Textron, Inc.
3M Co.
Travelers Insurance Co.
Travenol Laboratories,
 Inc.
TRW, Inc.
Union Carbide Corp.
United Technologies
 Corp.
The Upjohn Co.
Xerox Corp.

Employee Clearinghouses

In addition to information gathered and stored by the
employer itself, employees have been increasingly troubled

by information gathered by various clearinghouses that share the information with employers. A good example involves a young Maryland man, a Vietnam veteran, who applied in 1980 for a position as a bank manager in Annapolis. The bank notified him, as it is required to do, that it would ask for a third-party investigation to verify information on his application and to inquire into his character, general reputation, personal characteristics, and mode of living. The man signed a form authorizing the investigation, and the bank ordered an investigative report from a credit reporting company in Baltimore.

The man figured he had little to hide. He had received a general discharge under honorable conditions because of unsuitability for military service due to a passive-aggressive personality disorder. The discharge was honorable, even though he had faced a court-martial on minor offenses, and it had occurred in 1970. Since then, the man had completed college and had been gainfully employed.

In response to the reporting company's request for the dates of the man's military service, however, a low-ranking clerk at the National Personnel Records Center in St. Louis felt compelled to release two army psychiatric reports that discussed the personality disorder back in 1970 and a record of the man's summary court-martial. The clerk told the reporting company how it could get more information from the Veterans Administration in Baltimore. The reporting company had requested neither psychiatric nor disciplinary records.

The reporting company, naturally, notified the bank of the information it had gathered. Within a few days, less than two months after he had been hired by the bank, the veteran was fired. The bank told him that the investigative report showed he had a *dishonorable* discharge. It accused the man of lying on his application form.[133]

A woman in Wayland, Massachusetts, was similarly victimized in 1974 when she took a Christmas job selling cosmetics at a Boston department store. Then she was offered a permanent position. Within a month, a personnel officer told the woman that she was being discharged. He mentioned vaguely something about a shoplifting charge. In fact, the department store had checked with a clearinghouse that keeps track of shoplifting accusations in the Boston area. The woman's name appeared in the service's files, because of an incident five years earlier. The woman had been accused of taking clothing from a store, but she paid for the goods and was told the matter would be forgotten. Instead it was reported to the clearinghouse, even though the case was dropped without any adjudication of the charge.

Similar "blacklisting" services operate in most major cities. Elsewhere, firms keep track of workers' compensation claims filed by employees. For a fee, these firms will inform a company that a particular job applicant has filed a compensation claim in the past.

A 32-year-old offshore oil field worker in Louisiana found in 1974 that he was unable to find work in the South because he had collected damages on two previous work-related injuries. If he applied for work using his correct Social Security number, a clearinghouse named Industrial Foundation of the South, which files names and Social Security numbers of 20,000 workers in the region who have filed workers' compensation claims, would report to the employer that the man was in its "blacklist." The man was virtually "blackballed" in his industry. When he used a different Social Security number on a job application, he could often find work.

The Fair Credit Reporting Act is of only limited help to individuals haunted by clearinghouses that provide information to employers. It requires that the applicant or employee be told that the employer will check with the clearinghouse, that the person will be given an opportunity to know the nature and scope of the information provided, and that he or she will be able to amend the information if necessary. But the law applies only to organizations that *regularly* assemble or evaluate consumer information for purposes of furnishing reports *to third parties*. On this basis many private investigators and some clearinghouses escape the coverage of the law.

"Headhunters"

For the reason just discussed, and because the notice provision of the Fair Credit Reporting Act does not cover employment for which the individual did not specifically apply, the law does not generally reach executive "headhunters." These executive recruiting firms collect thousands of resumes—most of them submitted by the individuals themselves—of executives who may be prospects for high-level jobs in business. They also compile vast files of press clippings, proxy reports, annual reports, and trade publications. Some of them keep computerized data on half a million names or more. The persons who are named in the files or who come to the attention of the executive recruiters are checked out informally—usually without the knowledge of the individual. The person himself or herself usually does not even know he or she is under consideration by another corporation. There is a lot of word of mouth in this business, a lot of reliance on tips and hearsay from other executives. Whether the subjective information stored by these firms—and in the heads of their recruiters—is accurate or fair to the individuals involved is unknown, because there are virtually no safeguards on the activities of the headhunters, who earn thousands of dollars by landing the right person for the right job. In many large urbanized states the headhunters have managed to get themselves exempted from the laws requiring employment agencies to be licensed and regulated. The headhunters regard themselves as consultants to business, not as employment agencies. This means that they generally avoid the equal employment opportunity laws as well. The headhunter's stock-in-trade is secrecy, so that a client's competitors—or the executive to be replaced—do not discover just what kind of person a company is looking for. This means that the rising executive who wants to know whether the executive recruiters have an accurate profile of him or her is out of luck.

Connecticut has a law unique in the nation that prohibits a company from "blacklisting" an employee so that he or she may not get another job, but the employer is able to give "a truthful statement" about a present or former employee. "Truthful" is the key word here.

An employee, whether executive or not, has recourse in a lawsuit when derogatory information is circulated about him or her by an employer. The first recourse is an action for defamation (libel for written communications and slander for spoken communications). In order to prevail, an employee would have to show that the information circulated was untrue and that it tended to damage his or her reputation. Most courts have recognized that disclosures of this kind among organizations exchanging information for legitimate business purposes are *privileged*—that is, immune from lawsuits. This is a difficult, but not impossible, rule of law for the aggrieved employee to overcome.

One employee for Westinghouse Corp. did overcome this privilege even though the company representative did not disclose derogatory information *outside* of the organization. A Florida State Court of Appeals in 1976 ruled that a discharged employee could sue for slander when a company representative told an in-house meeting that the employee was let go for stealing company property.[134]

In 1980 a California court awarded $36,000 in a slander action against the airline pilot mentioned in Chapter 11 who bruited among his colleagues that a certain stewardess was a lesbian.[135]

A second recourse for employees when companies disclose information about them, even if it is true, is a lawsuit for invasion of privacy, but this is rarely successful. (Surprisingly, a court has ruled that company doctors owe no duty of confidentiality to employees.)[136] A privacy action may generally be maintained if embarrassing private facts are publicly disclosed or if information is portrayed in a way that casts the individual in a false light. A company's defense to a privacy action would be, first, that the disclosure was privileged as an exchange of business information or, second, that the employee consented. Thus, a company can protect itself from liability when it discloses information about employees, first, by being sure that it can prove the truth of the statement, and second, by securing the consent of the employee to make the disclosure.

Just as a company can be liable (although in very limited circumstances) for the information it discloses about an individual, an employee can be held liable for information he or she discloses about a company. This is mainly true of business information that is highly useful to competitors— trade secrets. In 1972, a federal court in Oregon held a regional sales manager for an insurance company liable for taking the names of customers and sales leads to a competitor when he switched companies. (The man also took with him fifteen of the first company's best agents and that displeased the court.) On appeal, the Ninth Circuit Court of Appeals said that "there is no proprietary right to customers or proposed customers" but courts will protect a company from competition by a former employee using written customer lists that he had no role in preparing.[137]

The "bottom line," as they say in business, is that there are virtually no limits on a company's demands for personal information about an employee and very few limits on what it may disclose about an employee. Only in gaining access to information in his or her personnel record is the employee of the 1980s making much progress to assure fair information practices.

13

Freedom from Propaganda

At a small textile plant in North Carolina, as at just about every other work site in the nation, employees are pressured each year to contribute to local United Way campaigns through payroll deductions. "Give your fair share" and "100 percent participation" are the rallying cries.

"One year, the boss man was going to get a TV set if we gave the most," recalls one employee of the textile plant. "He told us that if he won we could come up to the house and watch it!"

The boss man's method was only one way in which employers try to inspire employees to do what is expected. Pressure to give to the annual charity campaign is only the most intense, and to some workers the most irritating, of the propagandizing that comes from the front office. We usually think of propaganda ("the spreading of ideas, information, or rumor for the purpose of helping or injuring an institution, a cause, or a person") as the product of an overseas tyrannical government. We think of an endless drone of exhortations, trite inspirations, and deceptive "misinformation."

We have no government Ministry of Information in this country (although each government agency devotes considerable resources to public relations), and the American people have always had a healthy skepticism about what their government officials say. The dominant propaganda in

American society comes not from government but from the private sector, in the form of advertising aimed at consumers and management messages aimed at employees.

Employees at one telephone company in the Midwest had to sit through a carefully produced simulated television news broadcast showing the economic collapse of their company. "Golly," they said as they emerged from the film, "we didn't know it was that bad. What can we do to prevent that?"

"And that's exactly what we wanted them to say," said the man from personnel.

The history of the American workplace, in one sense, is the history of partial applications of new theories intended to motivate workers to new heights of productivity and company loyalty. Taylorism at the turn of the century was not the first such attempt but it was one of the most prominent. Few if any companies applied the theory of Frederick Winslow Taylor, also known as scientific management, in its pure form. Taylor's idea was that human beings could be organized and managed much like a well-oiled machine. Workers were subjected to partial applications of the theory, which was usually patched over the underlying flaws in the work environment. When these mutations of Taylorism did not work, it was discredited and managers looked for another panacea. There followed "welfare work," and when that seemed not to inspire workers to new heights it too was abandoned. The idea behind welfare work was that a package of paternalistic fringe benefits would motivate workers to greater productivity.

In the late 1960s and early 1970s American workers were subjected to a series of company-sponsored efforts to improve the workplace. After this blitz of propaganda, the employees began to greet each new workplace "innovation" with skepticism. The good intentions were then probably doomed from the start. Managers later discovered "humanizing work," then "work simplification," then "job enrichment." The latter was thought to be a cure-all for worker alienation in the sixties, but second-guessers now know that it was based on a faulty assumption: that "blue-collar" workers aspire to "white-collar" work. A large percentage of rank-and-file workers didn't want to take on new responsibilities on the job, especially if it meant no obvious rewards. "I don't want to be a foreman," "I don't want to think," "I don't want to take my job problems home with me," they said, according to industrial psychologist David Sirota of New York City. Still (often on their own time) they were subjected to program after program designed to convince them otherwise.

Then managers discovered sensitivity training, behavior modification, "quality of work life," "rap sessions," and transactional analysis. They figured the benefits of these techniques could be applied en masse in the workplace. At about the same time came the invasion of the industrial consultants, who told top management that they could make sure that employees stayed happy. Too often that simply meant keeping them away from union organizers. Employees, then, could not distinguish between sinister manipulations to bust unions and well-intentioned efforts to increase productivity and morale.

Like Frederick Taylor in an earlier era, an industrial psychologist named Charles Hughes became the guru of the new managerial movement to make workers happy. After ten years of "preventive" labor relations at Texas Instruments, Inc., Hughes produced a book called *Making Unions Unnecessary*. Through a system of positive and negative reinforcements, managers could persuade workers that they were better off with the company's benevolence than with collective bargaining. As with earlier theories, there were partial applications of Hughes's theories in many companies.

One West Coast labor relations consultant, paying lip service to Hughes, says, "If management is clever about the thing, it can also make the employees feel they are involved in some of the decisions made affecting them, even though the company had planned to do it all along." So much for Hughes's advice that companies succeed by "dealing with people as effectively as possible so that the dichotomy between management and labor does not arise."

The same labor relations consultant on the West Coast issues a manual telling its clients the importance of "indoctrinating" new employees. It is important to "shape their attitudes in healthy and productive ways during the first several months of employment and quickly discharge those who don't come around." This may explain why many of the victims of intimidation, forced resignations, discrimination, sexual harassment, and other ills in the workplace are new employees.

If union activity appears imminent, the influence of these consultants rises markedly. They send their people to the company, to schedule regular meetings with groups of employees (taking them away from their work incidentally) to persuade them that unions are not in their best interest.

In the 1970s a personnel director at McDonald's Corp., following the well-intentioned industrial psychologists' advice, instituted regular meetings similar to "employee committees" advocated by Hughes. The idea, of course, was to address common problems of employees and to resolve grievances before they became unmanageable. However, the personnel director admits to interjecting into the employee meetings a bit of the transactional analysis he had picked up. He would manipulate the attendees with flattery and "stroking"—and deliberately create competition among the attendees. Either as a direct or indirect result, McDonald's employees end up competing with each other in such events as the "National Hamburger Olympics" and are diverted from any collective action for their collective welfare, according to an AFL-CIO critic of such propagandizing.

Another device employed, according to this same critic, is the upgrading of individuals' titles, with no change in pay, status, or working conditions. Laborers become "staff technicians" and secretaries become "confidential assistants," but the work remains the same. This is one of Hughes's contributions to "making unions unnecessary."

Is there any wonder that these "innovations" in the 1970s were greeted with skepticism by representatives of organized labor? Said Daniel Zwerdling, author of the 1980 book *Workplace Democracy,* "The strategy is to give the employees the illusion of power by yielding control over usually menial decisions—'Should I bag dogfood today or hoist the bags on pallets'—without giving them power over the key decisions that shape their lives—how much they are paid and what benefits they get, who can work and who shall be laid off, what they produce and how fast they must produce it, and what to do with the profits of their work."

The Japanese Fad

In the 1980s, once again American workers are being asked to embrace a panacea for the workplace, this one from Japan. In the early 1980s, it seemed that American managers could not get enough of Japanese management techniques. "No doubt you've heard Japan is tops in productivity, balance of trade margins, new technology development and worker satisfaction," wrote *Data Management* in October 1981. At bookstores patronized by corporate managers, you could find titles like *The Art of Japanese Management, The Japanese Company, Japan as Number One, Type Z: An Alternative Management Style, Success with People, The Theory Approach,* and *The Japanese Are Coming.*

Employees girded themselves for the latest fad that was going to make them productive, loyal, diligent, and *happy.* Japanese workers, it was said, produce high-quality goods, work harder, and show extraordinary loyalty to the company. They also have lifetime assurances of employment, it was said. Equipment is the best, it was said. Government, management, and labor work hand-in-hand, it was said. Executives fraternize with assembly workers, it was said. And everybody sits around discussing new ideas for the workplace, it was said.

As American business executives discovered more about Japanese management, they discovered that many of the first reports were myths and that many of the techniques used in Japan work because of the cultural characteristics of that island nation. They discovered that one of the perceived quick fixes from Japan was actually born in America. The technique is called quality circles. The Japanese applied it to industrial management in the 1960s after American academicians introduced the theory to them.

Quality circles are regular small gatherings of workers and supervisors to develop serious suggestions for improving the quality of what is produced and, sometimes, to improve the immediate work environment. The idea is that "the superior doesn't have any monopoly on brains," according to an executive at Honeywell, Inc., the American company that uses quality circles perhaps the most. An estimated 500 American companies have instituted the meetings, a variation on earlier plant "brainstorming" sessions. Teams of ten to fifteen persons meet every week or two and discuss suggestions on improving specific work tasks from the persons who actually perform them. Some subjects are usually forbidden: management's performance, salaries, personalities, and gossip.

It is remarkable that such an idea took so long to arrive in the American workplace—especially in view of the fact that American theoreticians originated it—and that such a simple idea could be credited with such success in Japan. (Actually the experts say that quality circles are only a small part of Japan's current superiority in productivity.)

After three years of sponsoring quality circles at its Nuclear Division in Oak Ridge, Tenn., Union Carbide

Corp. reported only a handful of changes in the way work was done there. The main results from the quality circle discussions were, first, to clean up a storeroom, and second, to move a lamp so that a machine operator could turn it off without getting hurt.

Workers must wonder why we had to have the Japanese teach us that.

Union representatives are understandably cautious, because they have seen workplace fads before. "I'm all for unions getting involved with quality circles if they're going to improve the work environment," said a Communications Workers local president in San Diego. "But quality circles, or whatever new management techniques are adopted, may be just window dressing. If these things work, then I guess the companies won't ever have a union. But that's not human nature. Management usually ends up abusing worker rights."

The coordinator of quality circles at Hewlett-Packard, a company frequently credited with a good work environment, says the circles have made a big difference. "People need to be recognized as team players and as individuals. And they need to feel good about what they accomplish."

American workers may be even more skeptical as other Japanese customs are imported into the American workplace. Some Japanese companies like to call in the employee's whole family for an orientation on the need for total dedication to the company, whether at work or home. At the San Diego plant of Kyocera International Inc., a Japanese-owned and operated company, supervisory and line employees file out onto the parking lot at 7:00 A.M. for exercise. This is preceded by homilies over the public address system from a coworker who speaks on appropriate values for employees. Many employees like to begin their days this way, but whether it will work elsewhere in the U.S. is unknown.

Propaganda for Charities

As employees become more sophisticated about past efforts to propagandize the workplace, they are making efforts to resist. They feel manipulated, or deceived, or patronized. Nowhere is this more apparent than in employees' objections to their companies' enforced enthusiasm for the local charity drive. The situation at the textile plant in North Carolina mentioned earlier is pretty typical.

"The vast majority of American employees and executives involved in deciding to give to charity at their workplace are participating in the equivalent of a Russian election; they can give to the only candidate [the United Way] or none at all," according to David Horton Smith, a Boston College sociologist, in a study for the Commission on Private Philanthropy and Public Needs, a private group that issued a report in 1977. Also in 1977, the United Way secured commitments from 106 of the Fortune 500 largest corporations, which employ more than three million persons, allowing United Way to be the only charitable solicitation in the companies. Nearly nine out of ten of the local United Ways—there are 2,300 nationwide—have no competition at any of the companies that permit them to solicit employees for donations, according to Timothy Saasta of the National Committee for Responsive Philanthropy in Washington.

The stakes are high for United Way—formerly Community Chest or United Fund—which raises 61 percent of its approximately $1 billion yearly from employees, most of them signing pledges permitting the money to be deducted from their paychecks.

In a workplace with larger numbers of minorities, women, and young people who have their own ideas about philanthropy, this monopoly situation was destined not to last forever without controversy. The pressure to diversify at-work solicitations came from within the workplace, from employees tired of being coerced into giving, and from out-side the workplace, from minority-oriented charities that wanted an opportunity for those coveted payroll-deduction contributions.

International Business Machines Corp., for instance, now lets workers select the Black United Fund in New York *or* the United Way. In Philadelphia, many companies responded to United Way's refusal to finance feminist-oriented groups by permitting employees in 1981 to give through payroll deduction to groups not participating in the United Way campaign. This trend began in the federal government, where employees have had the right to designate non-United Way charities for years.

In many companies, contributions from employees to United Way increase, not decrease, when they are given a choice. In a 1976 study for Wells Fargo Bank, nearly half of the employees said they would give to charity, or give more, if given a choice other than United Way. A survey for the American Cancer Society in California the same year showed that 67 percent of employees preferred a choice.

The secret of United Way's great success, of course, has been its almost exclusive solicitation in the workplace. "Pressure is the name of the game," says Robert Bothwell, director of the National Committee for Responsive Philanthropy, which is trying to direct some charitable dollars to worthy groups traditionally left out of organized campaigns. "Companies can apply more pressure than anyone, since they have power over your job and future."

Unlike just about any other charity, United Way can use the same device that has worked so well for creditors and labor unions—payroll deductions. United Way's board of directors, made up of the business leaders in the community who are exhorting their employees to give, then decides which causes get to share the pot, and year after year the same causes get a share.

In the workplace, United Way can reach far more prospects at one time than elsewhere. This reduces the cost of solicitations—the United appeal spends only a fraction of what other charities spend to get their money—and it provides a captive audience, with peer pressure to produce 100 percent participation.

Employees are often marched into meetings for a sales pitch from a supervisor (and told that the president of the company sits on the board of the local United Way). Sophisticated computer printouts reveal last year's giving and this year's expected "fair share," based on 1 percent of income. Supervisors thus become aware of how much each employee has given. If a contribution is not high enough, or if an employee neglects to make a contribution, the supervisor pressures the individual to make amends.

Ohio Bell Telephone Co. once suspected some employees of making inflated pledges to keep supervisors and fellow workers off their backs and then submitting reduced or canceled pledges. The company circulated a computer printout of these pledge changes to supervisors and union leaders for "review." When a Cleveland news reporter asked the business executive who headed that city's United Way to reveal *his* personal gift, he refused, saying it was a "private matter."

In 1981 the president of First Federal Savings and Loan Association in Cumberland, Md., fired a newly hired teller who declined to make a United Way contribution. The president was outraged, because, "I've had 100 percent participation from my employees for years, and I'll be damned if one person is going to come along and change that.

"We never had a problem before. Everybody gave their 50 cents a month and that was it," he said.

But the intimidated employee had her own reasons for declining to make a "voluntary" payroll deduction. She suspected that United Way money was used to pay for abortions and to fund gay rights programs. Not even a meeting with the local director of the fund, who assured her that her fears were unfounded, could change her mind. And so she lost her job.

The bank president later agreed to have her back. The woman said that the coercion at work violated her right against discrimination based on religious beliefs, as prohibited by federal law.

The woman's resistance led in 1982 to the introduction in the Maryland state legislature of a bill to protect the rights of employees like her. The bill, which did not pass, would simply prohibit "coercion" of private or public employees to give to charity. Its sponsor was a state legislator who felt "coerced" by his employer, a large steel company.

Abuses like this plus the social concerns of new workers in federal agencies led to a liberalization of rules governing the Combined Federal Campaign, the United Way equivalent for federal employees. The rules change was also prompted by a lawsuit filed by sixty-five chagrined members of the U.S. Army Band at Fort Myer, Va. They objected when the army posted their names on a bulletin board as nongivers and when their supervisors pressured them to make pledges.

The band member who initiated the suit said that the Combined Federal Campaign violates his religious beliefs. "It mocks the very spirit of charity by publicly establishing the amount which one is expected to give and then designating the amount as an individual's 'fair share,'" he said. He and the others settled their suit in 1979 when the army agreed to stop posting lists of nongivers or givers, to stop the pressure for 100 percent participation, and to stop using supervisors to conduct the solicitation. The agreement allowed anonymous contributions for the first time.

The court-sanctioned settlement then led the federal government to alter its rules for all federal agencies. More and more unorthodox charities were able to participate in the campaign. The government was originally influenced by two significant court rulings on challenges from competing charities. In July 1982, the National Black United Fund successfully won an equal opportunity to the government-run charity drive. At the time, the Combined Federal Campaign had required participating charities to have affiliates throughout the nation and to have administrative costs below a certain percentage. The government did not appeal the case and allowed the National Black United Fund on its list of sharing charities. United Way, however, took up an appeal against the NBUF. Likewise, another federal district court in the District of Columbia ruled that the NAACP Legal Defense and Educational Fund and the Puerto Rican Legal Defense and Educational Fund could not be excluded from the Combined Federal Campaign.

In 1982, the Reagan administration repealed the liberalization in charity participation. Its new rules turned over most of the management of the Combined Federal Campaign to the United Way. This included the power to select which charities would share the annual booty.

There have been court challenges to United Way's monopoly participation in state employee fund drives in New • York and Illinois, and it may not be long before employees in the private sector begin their challenges.

Employees want the right to give to charities of *their* choice, not the company's choice. They want the right to contribute *privately* only what they can afford, just as executives at the company do. And they want a work environment where their views are welcomed and where there is freedom from propaganda and management fads.

14

Freedom to Participate

The 1960s and 1970s were decades of intense pressure on American businesses to change their ways—with regard to hiring policies, investment decisions, overseas operations, manufacture of unsafe, harmful, or martial products; and responsiveness to local community needs. The pressure came from the outside, from young people trained in the civil rights movement and the antiwar movement. Some employees of these companies may have given silent support or provided inside intelligence about their companies as best they could. But, for the most part, they did not participate directly in these reform movements.

Now the youthful agitators—products of the baby boom after World War II—are on the inside. They are the employees. And they are doing what they were raised to do—insisting on changing institutions to accommodate their perceptions of individual dignity and social justice.

In his book on the baby-boom phenomenon, *Great Expectations,* Landon Jones points out that the masses of young people in the baby-boom generation transform each institution through which they pass. In the 1980s, this generation has left the colleges and entered the workplace.

Arthur White, of the Yankelovich, Skelly, and White firm that has measured discontent in the workplace for many years, said in a 1982 speech that Americans have become more passive, less activist, in the 1980s. But, he adds quickly, they are preserving their insistence on equal opportunity and fairness. "Consumerism will continue to be with us through the 1980s and beyond because the American people are still concerned about getting true value, full value," he said. "They are going to resort to lawsuits."

"Business," White said, "has had one of the lowest ratings in the opinion of the American people for the last decade and now we're in the eighties and some things are changing, but that hostility and suspicion and concern is not fading away."

After the activist decades, American employees began to seek meaningful *participation* in company decision making.

In the 1970s, participation in company decision making may have meant preventing the manufacture of napalm, halting investments in South Africa, ceasing construction of a nuclear power plant, diverting resources to the poor, getting women and minorities on the board of directors. In the 1980s participation in company decisions means holding on to your job.

The employees' response at Continental Airlines in 1981 may have set the tone for this new participation. Texas International Airlines had to reckon with the concerted effort of angry Continental employees when it sought to take over Continental Airlines. Also, the closing of four major steel plants in Youngstown, Ohio, from 1977 through 1980 left 13,000 men and women out of work and sent shock waves through the ranks of employee groups and local governments throughout the country. Unions and residents of local communities dependent on a single large employer in town knew then that to avoid abrupt economic catastrophe in the community they had to have a role in major decisions to close work sites or transfer them. This led to the introduction of legislation in Congress. The first proposal, in 1979, would have provided that employees, labor unions, and local governments receive advance warning when a business plans to relocate. A similar proposal was made in the 98th Congress by Representative Robert A. Roe of New Jersey. His bill is a complex proposal that involves advance planning on the part of large employers and an intricate procedure to soften the blow when a plant closes down. Its preamble says, "Irresponsible and unnecessary changes of operation at establishments of business concerns disrupt commerce and cause unemployment to increase drastically in local areas. . . . It is the purpose of this Act to prevent or minimize the harmful economic and social effects of unemployment on employees and on local governments caused when business concerns undertake changes of operations."

The closing of a work site was until very recently considered the absolute prerogative of the private entrepreneur. Public services run by government might have to take into account the community's needs, but the privately owned company could simply close down if it chose to. The union might tell the company whom it could hire and at what rates of pay, and the socially minded groups could exert political and consumer pressure on the manufacture of certain products, but *nobody* could tell the businessman he had to stay open for business.

In a move that would have been unheard of earlier, perhaps even at the beginning of the decade, employees took legal action through their union when Pabst Brewing Co. notified them that it was closing down its facility in Peoria Heights, Ill., on the last day of 1981. Within four months, the Brewery Workers Union had a decision from a labor arbitrator saying that the company could not close the plant unless it paid $25 million in wages and benefits under its labor contract extending to July 1983. The arbitrator pointed to a clause in the company-union contract stating that the company "shall not reassign any work presently being performed by employees covered by this agreement, to other personnel to do such work who are not in the bargaining unit at this plant or other facility." The company argued that it was eliminating work in Peoria Heights, not reassigning it. The arbitrator said that the Peoria Heights facility was a "viable and profitable operation." And so Pabst employees, who had less than a month's notice that the brewery for which they were working would disappear, salvaged some compensation, if not their jobs.

Employees are demanding participation in major corporate decisions so that they can verify the profit-and-loss claims of management, explore alternatives to drastic reductions in force, and have adequate warnings of cataclysmic corporate decisions.

They also want to be convinced that the decisions made by management are valid business decisions. Six months before the Pabst closing, a meat-packing company in Denver dismissed 200 unionized employees and sold its plant. The new owners discarded the existing union contract, calling for wages in the neighborhood of $10 an hour, and hired recent Asian immigrants at $5.25 an hour. "The former employees were offered the same opportunity to be rehired as everyone else," said the new owner. The trouble is, the United Food and Commercial Workers Union suspected the entire sale of the company to be a sham. The union claimed that the plant is still owned by the same company, which merely changed its name.

In fact, in early 1981, Cudahy Foods Co., a subsidiary of General Host Corp., had announced it would close its Denver plant. Then in August, Cudahy sold the plant to a company named Bar S. However, as the union pointed out, Bar S is no more than a brand name of Cudahy, and trucks parked outside the meat-packing plant still show both names. The National Labor Relations Board rejected the union's claim that this was an unfair labor practice, but attorneys for the union say this technique is becoming common among meat-packing operations around the country and must be stopped.

Worker Involvement in Management

In spite of alleged abuses like this, American labor leaders traditionally have been reluctant to have employee representatives involved in company management. "Industrial democracy" caught on long ago in Europe, but not in the U.S. In Germany, the Netherlands, Denmark, and elsewhere, employees have the right by law to participate in work councils that make significant decisions regarding mergers, plant relocations, and shutdowns.

Most organized labor is leery of management involvement, and want to go slowly. In 1978, an assistant to AFL-CIO President George Meany was quoted as saying, "We do not seek to be a partner in management—to be, likely, the junior partner in success and the senior partner in failure. . . . [This] offers little to American unions in the performance of their job unionism role . . . and it could only hurt U.S. unions as they pursue their social unionism function. . . . We don't want to blur in any way the distinction between the respective roles of management and labor in the plant."

After all, under the leadership of Meany and others, American labor unions have always exerted more influence at the political nominating conventions and in the White House than in corporate boardrooms. Union representatives already sit down at the bargaining table with management representatives and have access to limited amounts of corporate information. Efforts by individual employees to participate in corporate decision making can only weaken this union-sanctioned participation.

The participation of United Auto Workers President Douglas A. Fraser on the board of directors of Chrysler Corp. is one of the few concessions by organized labor leadership in the U.S. to this worker-participation trend in the industrialized nations of the world. Even Fraser had to step down from the board when contract negotiations got intense in 1982.

"I don't want to sit on the board and be responsible for managing the business," says Glenn F. Watts, president of the Communications Workers. "I want to be free as a unionist to criticize management."

For an employee representative to serve on a corporate board clearly presents a conflict of interest between his obligation to the company and to the employees and it may require him to segregate in his own mind information received in each of his two roles. But some kind of participation in corporate decisions could clearly head off abrupt decisions that alienate employees or do not take advantage of their special knowledge of company operations. Labor unions seem to go to arbitrators or courts *after* the damage is done, instead of insisting on participation before unfortunate decisions are made, as their European counterparts often do.

One of the first observations of a visiting Japanese trade representative once was that American employees are reluctant to make suggestions to improve company operations. "In the United States," he said, "no proposals come from the bottom."

According to the *Harvard Business Review,* half of the companies in the United States would consider employees' advice on the proposed relocation of a facility, and a quarter would agree to consultation prior to accepting a controversial defense contract. An analysis by the *Review* in 1978 showed that joint committees of employees and management had met with some success. By consulting a small group of employees, for example, a manufacturer in upstate New York was able to add a new product to its line.

Organized and nonorganized employees have successfully provided advice on designing new or remodeled work facilities to avoid the nonsensical design mistakes that employees usually get to complain about years after the fact.

At a Midwest newspaper, reporters and editors have met regularly to nominate persons to be their own supervisors. The United Automobile Workers and General

Motors have ongoing labor-management committees to improve working conditions. Those with experience in these tentative labor-management projects warn that they work only when the participants are willing to abandon, or at least modify, their previously held fears and suspicions. And, these participants point out, these projects, even where they work successfully, generally involve a miniscule percentage of the total work force at a facility.

It should be emphasized that these plans can be terminated by management at will; they do not constitute true employee participation as a permanent part of the corporate structure.

As American courts and legislatures realize the damage done by business decisions without consultation with employees directly affected and as they seek to compensate for the damages, there will be a change in attitudes about employees participating in decisions that were once thought to be the exclusive prerogative of top corporate executives.

In assessing the situation in 1974, Phillip I. Blumberg of the University of Connecticut School of Law wrote:

> Except to the extent provided through the collective bargaining process, employee participation in corporate decision making in the United States is not a reality, and there is little indication that it will become a serious possibility in the immediate future. Until participative management and employee representation on the board are adopted as major objectives and vigorously pursued by American unions, they will remain theoretical suggestions. Nevertheless, there are powerful factors at work which in time could make these matters— entirely visionary at the present time—a more realistic possibility. Changing social values and employee attitudes, concern over the nature of the role of the major American corporations in American life, which is reflected in sharply increased

public expectations with respect to so-called corporate social responsibility, and the increasing momentum of the movement for employee participation in Western Europe constitute deep-seated underlying forces that could conceivably create a social and political climate in which employee participation could emerge as a matter of realistic concern in the future.[138]

Those factors identified by Blumberg loom larger in the early 1980s than they did in the early 1970s. It is ironic that employees in the United States have enforced their rights to dignity and security in the workplace through litigation, legislation, and collectively bargained contracts and not through direct participation in decisions that directly affect their dignity and security at work. As employees discover that their rights have been recognized by law and as corporate decision makers discover the high costs of resolving disputes *after* the damage is done, the 1980s may prove to be the decade when both sides recognize that joint participation in directing company affairs is in their mutual interest.

15

Freedom in Fringe Benefits

Morton Savodnik worked thirteen and a half long years for Korvettes, Inc., in New York. He received frequent promotions and salary increases; the company agreed that he was a model employee. Then at the age of 53 in 1977, Morton Savodnik was abruptly fired, along with other faithful employees. He suspected there was an ulterior motive; he suspected that Korvettes fired him to prevent having him work long enough at the company to earn credit toward its retirement plan. A federal district court in 1980 agreed with Savodnik's assessment, saying that Korvettes "does not deny this scenario—indeed, they seem to agree they discharged Mr. Savodnik for this very purpose, and urge that however contemptible such behavior may be, it is simply not illegal." The judge said that it was "unconscionable" that the company did not live up to its commitment to employees expecting pensions. He ruled that Savodnik had a right to sue his employer for "abusive discharge."[139]

A federal law passed in 1974, the Employee Retirement Income Security Act (ERISA), makes it illegal to fire an employee to deprive him or her of a pension.[140] The law also provides several procedural guarantees with regard to pensions, but it does not guarantee to every employee, regardless of how loyal and how senior in service, any pension at all. In fact, it's not uncommon, before ERISA or after, for an individual to work long and hard from age 21 to age 65 and not have any pension at all, even though each of the companies for which he worked in his lifetime has an attractive pension package.

Sixty million active workers are covered by a valid pension plan in the private sector. Only 9.1 million retirees are currently collecting any benefits from a private retirement plan. That's merely a third of the 25.5 million persons aged 65 or more in the U.S.

Getting fired at the "eleventh hour," just before any pension rights are realized, is just one of the pitfalls that the employee has to worry about with regard to retirement benefits. And retirement benefits are just one of many fringe benefits in the workplace that employees must stay on top of in order to secure their rights. Pensions are merely the most perplexing—and the least immediate—of all the fringe benefits.

"Pensions do not make fascinating conversation," says U.S. Representative Patricia Schroeder of Colorado. "Who wants to worry about retiring when the whole world is waiting to be explored?"

But it's a subject that many employees are forcing themselves to talk about. Because a lot can go wrong.

The employer could have no pension plan. The law doesn't require that an employer have a pension plan, only that whatever plan it has meet certain standards. One out of ten large corporations does not provide pensions, and thousands of small employers don't.

The employer could go out of business. In fact, the closing of Studebaker automobile manufacturing company in 1964, leaving 2,000 workers stripped overnight of their pensions, created the political pressure for a federal pension reform law ten years later. Studebaker had been paying pensions out of its operating funds, not out of a segregated pension trust fund. When the company ceased, there was no quasi-independent pension fund to carry on.

It is ironic that many of the pensionless workers who testified in behalf of reform received no benefit from the

1974 law. These so-called "pension-losers" have united in an attempt to persuade the government to provide them with pensions. The movement's leader is Ed Johnston, who was 62 years of age when the machine company he worked for in Springfield, Mass., went out of business in 1971. Like 250 fellow employees, Johnston lost not only his job but also his pension. He had to take on a job as a janitor. The Employment Retirement Income Security Act addresses this problem by requiring that employer contributions to a pension fund become the property of the fund itself, not the employer. The general rule of ERISA is that benefits earned by each employee up to the time the company goes out of business (or the fund is terminated) will be protected, but there are exceptions. A business about to go under may be given permission to cease contributions to its pension fund so that it can recover.

Financially troubled A & P Company attempted to do precisely this in 1981, by terminating its current pension fund (maintaining monthly payments to current retirees), using the surplus in the fund to finance corporate expansion, and then reestablish a new pension fund with different standards. An unhappy retiree has sued the company, claiming that beneficiaries should have gotten the fund's surplus.

Second, the 1974 law established a Pension Benefit Guaranty Corporation in Washington, to which administrators of pension funds must make contributions. If a plan is terminated, the corporation oversees the distributions of retirement benefits, including dipping into 30 percent of a company's total assets. As "insurer of last resort," the corporation then makes up the rest from its fund established through the years by employer contributions.

Still, there is nothing in the law that prohibits a company from terminating its pension fund. In fact, an estimated 34,000 companies did just that in the first two years after the law became effective.

An employee may be barred from participating.

ERISA permits a company to exclude employees under age 25 or with less than a year's service.

An employee may switch jobs regularly and be entitled to nothing when he retires. ERISA permits companies to adopt one of three schemes for determining when employees have put in enough years to receive a pension at retirement; most companies require ten years. The typical worker in 1963 kept a job for 4.6 years; in the 1980s, the average is 3.6 years. Thus, millions of workers—especially females—leave their places of employment before meeting the minimum-service requirements.

Frank Palmer, an electronics engineer, is a case in point. Since 1951, when he joined the Dictaphone Co. in Connecticut, Palmer has changed companies nine times, each time getting improved salary and positions. But he never stayed in one place more than seven and a half years. By 1978, at age 53, Palmer had settled in Cocoa Beach, Florida, with RCA International Service Corp., looking forward to a career first: in 1986 he would complete RCA's eight-year minimum service requirement and vest in a pension.

Job hopping for personal advancement is not unusual in high-technology fields like Palmer's, nor is it unusual for scientists, middle managers, journalists, many women employees, and teachers. The Institute of Electrical and Electronics Engineers says that engineers average just seven years with each employer, and four out of ten of its members are not vested in pensions.

Once an employee has put in the requisite number of years to qualify for a pension, a company may have complex rules for calculating *the amount of a pension,* based on years of service. A plan may require a full calendar year to count toward pension benefits, or it may not count service if it is less than full-time. Thus, an employee who has put in more than the minimum ten years to participate in a pension plan may still end up with no pension at all, or a tiny one, because years credited toward benefits are inadequate.

An expert who administers pension plans, Michael J. Casey, has stated the unhappy truth:

> It is totally possible for an individual to be constantly employed from the age of 20 to 65, to be constantly participating in a retirement plan during that entire period, to have his employers constantly contribute to various retirement plans on his behalf for the entire period, and yet for the individual never to qualify for a single dollar of retirement benefit.[141]

A truck driver named John Daniel put in twenty-two years on the road and when he was forced to retire in 1973 because of eye cataracts, he expected a monthly pension of $400 from the Teamsters pension fund (many pensions are administered by unions or professional associations). Instead, he got nothing.

Why? The pension fund administrators told him that according to its rules, a 100-day involuntary layoff during his career created a "break-in-service." Daniel complained all the way to the U.S. Supreme Court, but without success. ERISA now requires employers to have uniform "break-in-service" requirements, more often permitting a participant in a pension program to pick up where he left off when he returns to the same employer or union.

This does not help the employee who finds a better job elsewhere. Many employees are agitating for the right to take their "pension credits" with them when they change companies; "portability" it's called. Truckers, retail employees, and construction workers enjoy portability through multiemployer pension plans arranged by their unions. The employee accrues pension rights so long as he works for any company participating in the multiemployer plan. But if an employee goes to work for a company not participating in the plan, he or she is out of luck. Many company representatives see portability as an administrative nightmare. Besides, they point out, the idea of a pension is to keep employees with the company and to reward employees with the most longevity. People who switch companies don't deserve the same pension rights as long-timers, they say.

Teachers and professors have one of the most successful multiemployer pension plans in the country. A teacher who goes from a state university in the West to an Ivy League college, then to a church school in the South, will continue to accumulate years toward an ultimate pension, through the professors' Teachers Insurance and Annuity Association–College Retirement Equities Fund, TIAA–CREF, which involves 3,400 educational institutions. A college professor with the same career patterns as electronics engineer Frank Palmer would have accumulated more than $200,000 in potential retirement benefits at the same age (although perhaps not earned the same salaries as Palmer).

Once the employee retires, the actual monthly retirement payment may be meager indeed. This is especially true if the retirement plan is one that is *integrated* with Social Security benefits. Integrated plans deduct a portion of the individual's expected monthly Social Security payment from the anticipated company payment. Most plans deduct half the Social Security payment. This could well leave the retiree with no company payment, or very little. A woman in Minnesota received this letter from her employer in 1978:

> Your term of service with [the company] has been sufficient for you to qualify for a vested pension. In determining the amount of benefit, the one-half of Social Security paid for by the company [in payroll withholding] is deducted from the gross pension benefit because our plan is integrated with the federal retirement plan. In your particular

computation the amount of pension benefits based on the formula is $72.72. The one-half of Social Security paid for by the Company is $99.45. Therefore, no benefit is payable to you from the company pension plan. If you have any questions, please let me know.

Thousands of Americans receive letters like this as sixty-fifth birthday presents. In pension plans in which benefits are based on earnings at the company, this Social Security offset hurts lower-paid workers the most. Higher-paid workers are left with a healthy monthly benefit check even after one-half of their Social Security benefits are deducted.

Social Security was never intended to provide a livable pension by itself, but for low to middle-level employees, the monthly Social Security check is 100 percent of their pension benefits even though they worked long years for a company with a valid retirement plan. (Designers of retirement plans generally take care of themselves and their managerial peers.)

"An integrated plan can obtain a tax-preferred status," said W. Michael Blumenthal, when Secretary of the Treasury in 1978, "even though most or even all of the plan benefits go to persons earning more than the 'wage base' on which Social Security taxes are paid [$35,700 in 1983]. Consequently, a company's middle- and lower-income employees might get nothing from a pension plan while the tax dollars of those employees subsidize the pension benefits of the same employer's highly paid employees."

A poll by Louis Harris in 1979 showed that more than half of pension beneficiaries think integration with Social Security is unfair; three-fourths of all top executives liked the idea.

The employer's regular contributions to its employees' pension fund may be unwisely invested, leaving each re-

tiree with a reduced share. Most pension funds pay monthly benefits that are affected by the appreciation, or depreciation, of the pension fund over the years. The Employment Retirement Income Security Act requires that the administrator of a fund exercise "prudence" in making investments. The Department of Labor has an office to check on pension-fund investments. One unsuccessful investment may trigger the interest of the office, but generally it says it will look to the *reasonableness* of the total portfolio. The administrator of the office in 1979 set this standard: "The real test will be whether you applied and used reasonably prudent procedures and thought processes and checks and balances as opposed to the underlying gain or loss on a particular investment."

After the new law was enacted, the Department of Labor went after a money management firm that invested $4 million of the pension fund of a Teamsters union local in New Jersey—about 8 percent of the fund's assets—in loans to two businesses whose principal was behind bars for misuse of funds. About $20 million from pension funds of another Teamsters local, this one in New York, were to be loaned to build a casino in Las Vegas until the department stepped in. Most of the abuses in investments, says the Department of Labor, are found in small employer plans.

Beyond avoiding imprudent risks, fund administrators can't use pension funds for loans to friends, relatives, and business acquaintances, even if the outcome of the investment is comparable to what it would have been with a stranger. The theory is that a plan administrator might be less hard-nosed on interest rates and collection procedures with a friend than with a stranger. Companies and unions have pointed out that this often prohibits a fund from making loans to deserving employees, or to a supplier or subcontractor of the company. The law has an "escape clause" permitting the Department of Labor to make exceptions, but businesses are crusading to loosen this standard. A utility in Florida was accused of making eight loans. totaling almost $500,000, to executives of the firm who are also fiduciaries (trustees) of the pension plan. The Department of Labor made the executives pay back the loans, on the theory that it is unfair to employees and potential pension beneficiaries to have their funds used to make loans to company executives or their friends.

Secretary of Labor Raymond J. Donovan told a Senate subcommittee in 1982, "We intend to enforce vigorously the mandate of the law that the fiduciaries of funds act solely in the interests of the participants and beneficiaries."

The amount of money at stake here is far in excess of $200 billion. Investments by employee trust funds in the stock market exceed the combined total of investments by individual investors. The overwhelming majority of these vast assets are managed by the trust departments of twenty large banks—half of them in New York City.[142]

Until ERISA was passed in 1974, employees were totally in the dark about their pension plans—not only how the funds were invested but also how the legal language vitally affected the amount of their retirement benefits. ERISA's strongest provision, and its most influential, is the one requiring full disclosure about pension plans to participants. The law has not made pension plans any easier to figure out, but it has made information available to employees interested enough to try to understand.

Each employee is entitled to a brochure summarizing the plan, as well as a summarized financial report. Upon request, the participant may receive detailed information, including copies of all plan documents and a statement of his or her individual status with the plan. On file with government agencies are all of the financial records, all transactions, and the names of individuals responsible for managing the pension plan and its assets.

Naturally, this creates a lot of paperwork for companies and creates lots of questions among the plan participants, and so many firms have strongly objected to the disclosure provisions of ERISA. Legislation introduced in the Senate in 1983 would cut down on many of the reporting requirements (and also permit additional types of investments).

The rule of pensions remains what Professor Merton C. Bernstein, a consultant to the National Commission on Social Security, has articulated:

> The losses of many provide the funds with which the payoff is made to the lucky few—just as in any honest race track.[143]

On the other hand, the wonderland of retirement benefits has improved for the worker considerably since 1912 when American Telephone and Telegraph Co. introduced a pension plan that gave employees no rights until management decided they were qualified.

And it has improved considerably since 1959, when the Eighth Circuit Court of Appeals ruled that an employee discharged after forty-five years of satisfactory service and one year from retirement was out of luck.

Knowing About Benefits

Significantly, the provision of ERISA regarding *disclosure* to employees, claims and rights of appeal, and "prudent" investing apply not just to retirement plans but to all sorts of employee benefit plans. This can include health and hospital insurance, medical and dental plans, life insurance, vacation and severance pay, legal services, child care, scholarships, and other kinds of benefits. (Most provisions in the law, however, do not involve these fringe benefits, but are restricted to pensions.)

Employees who remain ignorant of these "fringes" (once thought of as employer "extras") do so at their peril. In the employer-employee relationship of the 1980s, they are as crucial a part of compensation as salary or wages. In fact, for major companies in the U.S., benefits equal an average of 37 percent of payroll, according to 1981 figures from the Chamber of Commerce of the United States.[144] Of 994 companies reporting figures to the chamber, the lowest benefits plan constituted 18 percent of salary or wages, and some companies reported up to $11,000 worth of benefits or 65 percent of salary. The average fringe-benefit package represented $6,627 per employee. The predominant benefits, as percentage of payroll, were:

Contribution to Social Security taxes (legally required)

Life insurance, death benefits, and health insurance premiums

Payments to pension plans

Paid vacations

Paid rest time, lunch periods, travel, or wash-up time

Paid holidays

Sick leave

Unemployment compensation taxes and contribution to workers' compensation (legally required)

Profit-sharing payments

Short-term disability payments

Dental insurance premiums

Bonuses and awards

Payments for National Guard duty, jury service, voting, or personal time off

Long-term disability payments

Payments for employees' education

Miscellaneous payments, including moving expenses and severance pay

Meals furnished by the company

Employee discounts on goods purchased from the company

Many of these benefits began because companies discovered that they were essential to attract and keep productive workers. As discussed earlier, the move for paid vacations began in Europe and caught on in the United States only later, before World War I. Pension plans began after the war, but the Depression wiped out many of them and also eliminated paid vacations. Vacations, like other "fringe" benefits, began not as gratuities from generous employers, but as the result of "bottom-line" business decisions that the interest of the company demanded them. They were hardly mentioned in labor negotiations.

After World War II, labor organizations claimed fringe benefits as their rightful entitlements. A labor arbitrator spoke for his colleagues in the field when he wrote in a 1948 case:

> In present day labor relations the granting of a vacation period to workers is so widely accepted that no industry or Company can claim to be exempt from the propriety of this practice. . . . The Company claims that it is not financially able to grant vacations with pay. Today, however, common practice decrees, in general, that those who employ workers assume the general obligation of giving them vacations.[145]

The same attitude applies to other fringe benefits. A few years ago, the National Labor Relations Board was ruling that a company could not begin withholding Christmas bonuses if it had paid bonuses so regularly in the past that employees began to expect them every year. By 1962, a speaker at the American Federation of Labor–Congress of Industrial Organizations (AFL–CIO) was proclaiming that *benefits* for a worker and his dependents, to cover illnesses and to provide security in old age, were just as real to him as dollars in his pay envelope. Employee benefits were no longer a fringe, but an entitlement.

By the 1970s, in the era of expansive civil rights law, courts regarded fringes—even intangible benefits—as almost more important than salary or wages. The Fifth Circuit Court of Appeals, for instance, said in a 1971 case, "The nuances and subtleties of discriminatory employment practices are no longer confined to bread and butter issues. As wages and hours of employment take subordinate roles in management-labor relationships, the modern employee makes ever-increasing demands in the nature of intangible fringe benefits. Recognizing the importance of these benefits, we should neither ignore their need for protection, nor blind ourselves to their potential misuse."[146]

Courts have held that an employer may not withhold a fringe benefit like severance pay once it has promised to pay it and that a company may not fire someone to avoid paying a bonus.

Whether fringe benefits are considered wages or not seems to depend on the circumstances, even though the employee may have a large stake in this seeming technicality. Courts include an employer's contribution to a pension fund when calculating lost "wages" (for purposes of calculating damages for an accident) but a controlling Supreme Court decision in 1959 said that fringe benefits are not part of wages when determining distribution of a bankrupt company's obligations. Whether "wages" or not, employee benefits are something that employees are not about to give up.

They have great advantages to employers as well. An increase in fringe benefits does not require an increase in payroll taxes paid to the government. Many commitments for increased fringes do not have to be met until far in the future—when the employee retires or gets hurt. If invested wisely, employee trust funds can appreciate in value so rapidly that an employer can promise all sorts of increased fringe benefits with little, if any, outlay of cash. As much as a way to attract and keep employees, fringe benefits are a way of giving employees increased "compensation" without direct, immediate expenditures from company revenues.

Sex Discrimination and Fringe Benefits

Fringe benefits are also a means for the new cadre of employees in the American workplace of the 1980s—many of them working mothers or working mothers-to-be—to establish complete equality on the job. Women strove in the 1970s to establish the principle under Title VII of the Civil Rights Act that a health insurance plan or a disability program that excluded pregnancy was discriminatory. They succeeded in getting the courts and the federal government to recognize this, until the U.S. Supreme Court in 1976 and 1977 temporarily halted the trend. And so, women successfully lobbied the legislative branch to enact the Pregnancy Disability Act of 1978. It amended Title VII, to require that women affected by pregnancy, childbirth, or related medical conditions be "treated the same for all employment related purposes . . . as other persons not so affected but similar in their ability or inability to work."[147] Twenty-five states have similar laws or regulations.

That means that if an employer requires or permits employees to take disability leave based on their ability to do the job, it must do the same for pregnant women. In other words, no more automatic pregnancy disqualification from working, if the individual woman can perform her job.

That means that pregnant employees unable to work must receive the same benefits in number of days and dollar amounts as other disabled employees.

That means that if an employer provides health insurance coverage for a full schedule of treatments, it must include pregnancy coverage.

That means that if an employer's leave policy is so short that it could not possibly cover a pregnancy and childbirth, it violates the law (even though the law does not require an employer to establish a disability leave program solely for pregnant women). Such a short leave policy would require a woman employee to choose between having a baby and getting fired.

That means that if an employer's insurance plan covers the medical expenses of the *spouses* of employees, the plan must equally cover the medical expenses of male *and* female spouses (including expenses arising out of pregnancy). That, anyway, is the position of the Equal Employment Opportunity Commission, which enforces Title VII. In a case involving Newport News Shipbuilding and Dry Dock Co. in Virginia, a federal appeals court upheld that interpretation, but the controversy is not fully resolved.

Leaves for pregnancy, also called maternity leaves, must be determined on the same basis as leaves for other temporarily disabled employees. And an employer cannot require a woman to exhaust vacation time before getting sick leave for pregnancy. Leaves for employees to care for their newborn children must be granted on a nondiscriminatory basis, on the same basis as leave without pay for travel or education that is not job-related. On this principle, some men are insisting upon "paternity leave," more properly called leave for child care. Presumably, the law does not permit them rights to leave-time equal to that of an employee who is actually carrying a child in pregnancy, but it does require that the father of a newborn be granted child-care leave-time on the same basis that a mother would.

Since 1974, Sweden has attempted to equalize parental time off from work with a system of parental insurance financed by contributions from employers and a 15 percent share from the national government. Both parents are entitled to share up to nine months of paid leave-time, six months immediately following the birth of their child and three months to be used anytime before the child is eight. A mother may take sixty days' leave-time before her anticipated due date; otherwise, parental insurance is applicable equally to fathers and mothers. Either parent may also take up to sixty days of sick pay to stay home with a sick child, or to stay home *when the babysitter is sick.* The Swedish policy attempts to lessen the conflict between the roles of parent and employee and "understands that sex equality is impossible in the marketplace unless fathers take their turn at home," according to Letty Cottin Pogrebin writing in *Ms.* magazine in April 1982.

Only 12 percent of working fathers in Sweden take advantage of the liberal leave policy, and some politicians are talking about making child-care leave compulsory for men. One cabinet minister supervising 63,000 postal workers set an example by taking a one-month leave to care for his infant son, during which time he brought the newborn baby to a ribbon-cutting ceremony.

Child Care Too

In the U.S. a more acute problem than equalizing parental leave may be making sure that there is someone to look after the children of the large numbers of single parents now in the work force—it is estimated that half of the mothers with children under six years of age will be working by the end of the decade. Companies have found themselves in the business of watching after children, as a means of satisfying the new corps of workers. Stride Rite Shoes in Boston runs one of the most highly regarded day-care centers in the nation. Polaroid Corp., Zale Corp., and American Can Co. have also established child care as an employee benefit. Some companies run their own day-care centers on the premises, encouraging employees to spend lunch hours with their kids. There are tax incentives under the Internal Revenue code and some state tax laws for capital expenditures on day-care sites. Expenses for employees' child care is recognized as a deductible business expense for companies. One large employer in Philadelphia operates a child-care center for its own employees and sells slots for children to other companies in the city.

Other companies give an employee a cash voucher, or salary increment, with which to purchase child care in the marketplace. A third method is for the employer to purchase child care in bulk or to contract with a provider of services. The Economic Recovery Tax Act of 1981 provides favorable treatment for industry-sponsored day care. Still other companies have subsidized their day-care operations with funds from federal or state programs for low-income workers.

These benefits do not exhaust the selection of fringes available to employees in the demanding 1980s. Many large corporations, like Hallmark Cards, Pitney Bowes, IBM Corp., and Xerox, provide cash payments for employees who adopt children. IBM has been doing this for a decade.

Bank of America offered an interesting deal to its employees. If an employee has no medical claims on his or her health insurance policy, the bank will pay a part of the insurance premium the next year.

With many husbands and wives both working, families often have duplicate fringe benefits available. Because of this trend and because of the diverse selection of fringes now available, some corporations are opting for the "cafeteria" approach. American Can Co. was one of the first to do this. Each employee is able to take advantage of the traditional core of benefits—vacations, health, disability and life insurance, and retirement benefits. To that core is added individualized benefits according to each employee's particular needs. These can include additional vacation times, dental or optical insurance coverage, preventive health programs, additional life or disability insurance, automobile insurance, cash bonuses, interest-free loans, legal or financial counseling, referrals to community services, stock options, mutual funds, investment opportunities, commuter van pools, reimbursement for tuition, seminars on job-related or personal topics, recreation facilities or subsidized membership dues at fitness centers, matching gifts to an employee's college, and release time for volunteer work.

The dollar amount to which an employee is entitled fluctuates according to his or her salary level or years with the company. The employee then selects the fringe benefits that serve his or her needs best.

16

Freedom of Due Process

In the 1980s, nothing is so crucial to a person's self-esteem and material security as his or her job. Yet, for two-thirds of employed Americans, the job can be taken away with a moment's notice—or less. Because of the system of "corporate Social Security" developed in the private sector, that means that a person's health insurance, life insurance, retirement benefits, and other necessities of modern life can be taken away just as abruptly.

This can happen because the individual said the wrong thing, was accused of impropriety, rebuffed the advances of a coworker, incurred a physical or mental disability on the job, was disliked by a supervisor, could not in good conscience do what the company demanded, was engaged in controversial politics, or simply chose not to contribute to the United Way campaign. It can happen because a company unilaterally decided to change its policy or its work force.

The approximately 22 percent of the work force who are protected by a collective bargaining agreement usually can resort to a formal grievance procedure or a hearing with an impartial arbitrator when confronted by an adverse action at work. The 15 percent of employees who work for government agencies (many employees are both unionized and government workers) usually have similar procedural safeguards guaranteed by law.

American courts have recognized in the past 100 years that the *government* may not take certain adverse action against individuals without following procedures that assure fairness. This stems from the language of the Fourteenth Amendment saying no state "shall deprive any person of life, liberty, or property, without *due process* of law." Here is the major question then: Is a job "property" that the government may not deprive a person of, without due process of law?

The Supreme Court in 1972 ruled in effect that it is not. It said that a state college teacher had no right to a hearing and no right to the reasons when his employer—a state agency—refused to renew his contract after one year. (In a companion case, however, the court said that a teacher with ten years' service in a state university who claimed he was let go because he criticized his supervisors *was* entitled to an opportunity to argue his case before his employer.) "To have a property interest in a benefit, a person clearly must have more than an abstract need or desire for it. He must have more than a unilateral expectation of it. He must, instead, have a legitimate claim of entitlement to it," the court said in the first case, and so the language of the Fourteenth Amendment wasn't applicable.[148]

In other cases, the court has said that the "due process" requirement does apply to the government's denial of welfare benefits, cutoff of electric service for nonpayment of bills, suspension of a driver's license, removal of a child from a parent's custody, and revocation of parole or probation. In at least three instances, the Supreme Court has recognized the right of an individual to have procedural fairness when victimized by private parties, not a state agency. This applies to disbarment from the practice of law, to the repossession of goods by a creditor, and to the garnishment of one's salary by a creditor. In the latter instance, the court in 1969 said the "interim freezing of wages [on the action of a debtor claiming an unpaid obligation] without a chance to be heard violates procedural due process." It emphasized, "We deal here with wages—a specialized type of property presenting distinct problems in our economic system."[149]

The Supreme Court opinions involving the teacher and the garnishment add up to this: Procedural due process must be followed when an outsider deprives an employee of part of his earnings, *but not when the employer itself deprives him of all of his earnings.*

This has not stopped aggrieved employees at private companies from asserting their rights to some kind of impartial and fair means for resolving disputes between employees and the company. In the 1970s, with so many disgruntled employees going to court—or taking to the streets—over failures to get promotions or unhappiness about how they had to wear their hair at work, it made sense for large companies to establish a mechanism for resolving these disputes "within the family."

Several prestigious companies did just that—IBM, Polaroid, and others. But most companies did not. Surveys by David W. Ewing of the Harvard Business School, author of *Freedom Inside the Organization,* showed the slow progress in developing due process in the private sector. Ewing surveyed nearly 2,000 companies of all sizes in 1971 and again in 1977. He found that 9 percent in 1971 reported having a grievance committee and only 14 percent in 1977. In 1971 an additional 8 percent had an "ombudsman" to handle complaints; in 1977, 11 percent had one. In 1971 only 6 percent had a formal hearing procedure with a neutral company official presiding and the employee entitled to legal representation; in 1977 the figure was 11 percent. Thus, at the beginning of the decade less than a quarter of the companies had a grievance procedure that Ewing would classify as likely to produce justice; toward the end of the decade 36 percent had such procedures.

In Ewing's survey nearly half the companies reported that they had somebody in personnel who investigated employee complaints and 63 percent said they had a senior executive whose "door is always open." Ewing was less impressed with these procedures, because such executives are preoccupied with other company duties and are often biased in their consideration of complaints from rank-and-file employees. But he noted a clear trend toward the tougher, fairer procedures.[150]

What American workers are seeking is apparently not the European prototype—a rigid hearing procedure established by law. For instance, the Industrial Relations Act in Great Britain requires a company to convene a three-person tribunal to determine claims of unfair dismissal by union or nonunion personnel. A labor representative, a management representative, and an attorney serving as chair conduct the hearing, with both sides represented by attorneys, if they wish. The burden is on the employer to show that the dismissal was, in the words of the act, for incompetence, misconduct, "redundancy," contravention of statute, or "other substantial reason." By law in other European countries, the employee simply holds on to the job until the dismissal is upheld by a tribunal.

Most Americans have shunned the idea that an employee is entitled by law to a full-dress tribunal whenever adverse action is taken. What they seem to want instead is an informal, but fair procedure that will permit disputes to be resolved in a manner that lessens the vast disparity between the power of the corporation and the power of the individual. The basic elements of such a procedure would include the following:

> A dispassionate hearing before an unbiased officer, even if the officer is employed by the company
>
> The right to legal or other representation, if necessary
>
> The right to call witnesses and to confront witnesses who testify

The right to advance written notice of the adverse
action and the reasons for it

The right to a prompt, fair, and clearly stated decision

As appropriate, a right of appeal within the organization

In hearing a case involving Enterprise Wire Co. in
1966, labor arbitrator Carroll R. Daughtery devised his own
test to determine whether a company was fair in disciplin-
ing an employee. His principles are applicable in a company's dealings with nonunion employees.

1) Did the company give to the employee forewarning
or foreknowledge of the possible or probable disciplinary
consequences of the employee's conduct? In other words,
were the policies and expectations of the company clear to
all employees? (Certain offenses are so serious "that any
employee in the industrial society may properly be expected to know already that such conduct is offensive and
heavily punishable.")

2) Was the company's rule related to the efficient and
safe operation of the business and did it require performance that a company might reasonably expect from an employee? If an employee believes that a rule or order is unreasonable, he must nevertheless obey it unless he
sincerely believes he would seriously and immediately
jeopardize his personal safety or integrity. The U.S. Supreme Court has recognized the right of an employee to
refuse work if he seriously thinks it will jeopardize his
safety.[151] And at least one court has recognized the right of
an employee to decline a task he believes is improper.

3) Did the company, before its discipline, demotion,
discharge, or other adverse action, try to discover whether
the employee in fact violated policy or did not meet standards? The investigation should be conducted before the
adverse action is taken. Many company officials figure that

a victimized employee will eventually get "his day in court," but by that time, even before an informal grievance committee, attitudes have hardened. The case of the worker standing idle on a ladder while the VIPs toured the plant is a good example of how a few simple questions could have resolved a misunderstanding before it magnified.

4) Was the company's investigation conducted fairly and objectively?

5) Did a detached company official obtain substantial evidence or proof that the employee was in the wrong? Proof "beyond a reasonable doubt" is not required but something more than hearsay and suppositions are. The investigating official ought not passively take the word of volunteer witnesses but instead actively pursue the truth himself.

6) Has the company applied its rules, orders, and penalties evenhandedly and without discrimination to all employees?

7) Is the degree of discipline proposed by the company reasonably related to the severity of the offense and the employee's record in his service with the company?

If a company can answer most of these questions affirmatively, and its "no" answers are minor in comparison, it should welcome the opportunity to confront the employee in a fair hearing within the company, at which each side has representation if it wishes, has notice of the complaint, and can confront the other and attempt to rebut opposing arguments.

For most Americans in the workplace a process like this is not a reality. Government employees and unionized employees do have grievance procedures, but often the current situation continues until the grievance is resolved. This means that the employee stays fired or disciplined unless and until the grievance procedure determines otherwise. This usually means that time is on the side of the company, not the employee. For employees represented by a union, there is the additional problem of assuring that the labor organization fairly, promptly, and competently represents the interests of the individual. Often the individual's interest conflicts with the union's. Under the National Labor Relations Act it is clear that a labor union is obligated to represent *all* members equally, without hostility or discrimination, and owes a duty of fair representation to the individual.[152] Some courts have said that a union breaches this duty not only when it is negligent but also when it is inept in handling a grievance.

For the majority of Americans not covered by a collective bargaining agreement or a civil-service law, due process in the workplace is an even more remote reality. The arbitrary power of the employer prevails, except in particularly egregious cases where the employee takes the matter to a court

17

Freedom from Abusive Firing

"Years ago the employee went away angry—maybe got drunk over the weekend—and on Monday started looking for a new job," says Howard Maier, who has handled his share of firings at McGraw-Hill Publishing Co. "Now he's just as likely to sue you."

Maier goes on to say, "Few things are handled worse in American business than the employee 'counseling' interview. The boss is full of so much baloney about how 'concerned management' should treat employees, says so many things about 'how much we've appreciated your efforts for the firm' that the poor employee leaves without the slightest inkling of what the boss really had in mind." In an interview with the Newsletter Association of America's newsletter, Maier recommended putting the reasons for an employee's discharge in writing. His three rules for handling terminations are:

1) Consider such actions only for "just cause."

2) Make sure you outline steps the employee can do to improve his or her situation.

3) Don't be intimidated by rules one and two.

Because as many as a third of all employees terminated may threaten legal action (and a high percentage have grounds to sue), employers are indeed intimidated by the firing process. This does not mean that they no longer fire persons. It means instead that they procrastinate, they give false reasons for the termination, they do it indirectly and impersonally, or they deliver the news in a flash, hoping the employee will simply disappear. Or, more commonly, they make life so miserable around the office or factory that the employee is forced to leave.

Courts have said that this latter tactic is "constructive discharge," and for all practical purposes amounts to an involuntary termination. "A constructive discharge occurs when an employee resigns in order to escape intolerable working conditions," said a court in a case involving sex harassment.

To be dismissed from a job and to have to dismiss someone from a job are not the end of the world. But employees and employers treat it as such, making the whole termination process stressful, traumatic, and distasteful. Instead of opening up an opportunity for the employee to find work more suitable—or to learn by his or her mistakes on the job—a termination generally creates bitterness and confusion. It has been turned into such a miserable occurrence that it has become the ultimate weapon for the employer.

A workplace where people are promptly let go for incompetence, insubordination, chronic absenteeism, failure to develop skills, unsuitability for the job, discourtesy to customers or coworkers, creating an unpleasant working environment, and other good reasons can be a vibrant place where employees stay on their toes. Instead, because the reasons for terminations are generally muffled and because firings usually become protracted messes, terminations (even of poor workers) often contribute to the demoralization of the American workplace.

A termination for unjust reasons can have an especially debilitating effect on the rest of the work force. It is as cancerous as keeping on an incompetent or unqualified employee, because it muddles whatever standards the employer might expect the whole work force to meet.

American courts have traditionally avoided second-guessing an employer's decision to terminate an employee. The "at-will" rule has prevailed for just about all of the country's history. The rule states that an employee without a contract may be terminated at the will of the employer. "The United States is the only industrialized country without some form of comprehensive protection against wrongful discharge," said the *Harvard Law Review* in an analysis in 1980.[153] "American common law continues to enforce the rule that the duration of employment is subject to the will of the employer when the parties have not explicitly stated otherwise. This at-will rule is based on outdated assumptions and leads to unnecessarily harsh results. Currently, in most states, at-will employees bear almost the entire risk of malicious or capricious firings by their employers."

The "at-will" doctrine is being challenged by many courts. The reason is that, since the passage of Title VII of the Civil Rights Act of 1964, more and more victims are bringing these "malicious or capricious firings" to the attention of judges. And what is a judge to do, for instance, when confronted with the ancient "at-will" rule and a waitress who came to him in 1975 with the following tale! The manager of the Ground Round Restaurant in Massachusetts called together all of the waitresses there and said that there was "some stealing going on." Until he discovered who was responsible, he would fire one waitress at a time, in alphabetical order. The first victim was named Agis. She sued for the emotional distress she suffered. In what was then an unusual step, the judge permitted her lawsuit, saying that an employee could sue on these grounds if the employer knew or should have known that his extreme and outrageous conduct would cause severe distress.[154]

What is a judge to do when confronted with a man named Frank Loeb who was let go at the age of 54 after four satisfactory years as an international sales manager at Speidel Co. in Rhode Island? In 1974 top managers decided that the company needed younger people. An executive vice president said at a meeting, "We have a greater proportion of our combined senior management over 55 than we do under 40. That's a warning." A year later, the man was shuffled in a reorganization and found himself working for new supervisors, one of them 37, the other 32. Shortly thereafter, Loeb was replaced by a 34-year-old man.

Loeb had a remedy in court because of the Age Discrimination in Employment Act of 1967, as did three long-time executives at I. Magnin in California. They were terminated after twenty-five, seventeen, and eighteen years with the department store company but they could not prove that age was the sole factor in their dismissals. Still, a jury found that age was at least a determining factor and awarded them more than half a million dollars each in back salaries.[155] These two cases show how the employer's former absolute power to hire and fire has been significantly curtailed by one of many laws on the books.

There have been many instances in the 1970s and continuing into the 1980s in which discharged employees have successfully challenged the traditional doctrine that an employer could terminate an employee at will if there were no employment contract to the contrary. These challenges have been based on different legal theories, sometimes on a breach of contract, sometimes on a theory that a tort (a wrong recognized in the law) has been committed by one person against another.

The tort of intentional infliction of emotional distress. This theory will not win a person back her job or get her back pay, but, if successful, will result in money damages being paid for the harm suffered. This is the theory used by the waitress in Massachusetts, and it has been used in many cases of sexual harassment that resulted in dismissal or "constructive discharge."

The tort of abusive discharge. A court in Ohio in 1953 recognized that an individual had a right to recover for an "abusive discharge" or "wrongful firing," and this theory has been revived during the 1970s and 1980s. "The trend seems fairly clear," said a federal district court in New York City in 1980, in ruling on Morton Savodnik's complaint, about getting terminated just before his pension rights were to be activated, mentioned in Chapter 15.

The tort of retaliatory discharge. This theory, which may be only a slight variation from the one previously mentioned, says that in certain circumstances an employer may not retaliate against an employee who is doing something proper, like filing a workers' compensation claim.

The employee-employer relationship implies a duty to terminate in good faith. This theory is alive and well in Massachusetts. An employee and employer can form an implied contract just by the week-to-week exchange of work for a paycheck. All contracts include an unspoken provision that both sides will deal in good faith, and some abusive firings clearly violate this provision. This was true of a New Hampshire woman who lost her job after rebuffing the sexual advances of her supervisor. It was true of a salesman in Massachusetts who said he was fired so that his company did not have to pay him commissions on a $5 million sale. And it was true of a fired American Airlines employee in California who could point to his eighteen years of service, the commendations and promotions he had received, the apparent lack of any criticism of his work, the assurances he was given, and the company's acknowledged practices, including a grievance procedure, that would lead employees to believe they would not be treated arbitrarily.[156]

Lawsuits based on a contractual relationship entitle the winner only to recover losses due to the breach in the contract (lost wages and fringe benefits usually), not consequential damages due to distress, loss of reputation, and the like. Under certain conditions, a court could order reinstatement of an individual who sues under this theory.

Not all contracts are written and not all are based on a

traditional, explicit agreement on both sides. A promise of employment by a company accompanied by some action by the individual in reliance upon that promise can create an unwritten employment contract. This would be true of an applicant who sells his house and moves to a new city in reliance upon a company's promise to hire him or of an employee who invests in new equipment or education in reliance upon an employer's promise to keep him around for a long time.

An employer's unilateral policies may create an employment contract that prevents firing without just cause. When Blue Cross & Blue Shield of Michigan issued a supervisory manual and guidelines to employees, the publication said that employment would be terminated only for *just cause.* Even though this was a nonlegal document distributed by Blue Cross, the employer was bound by it, according to the Michigan Supreme Court in 1980.[157] Other courts have said the same about faculty handbooks and employee brochures issued when an applicant is hired. There are court decisions going the other way, but generally an employee may point to the statements made in a company's manual or employee handbook as binding on the company. This was the successful argument of the McGraw-Hill employee mentioned in Chapter 4.

That flashy brochure entitled "Welcome to Our Company" is now more than a handout to get lost among a new employee's papers.

A law on the books may prohibit a termination. Companies are increasingly circumscribed by federal laws that flatly prohibit firings on certain grounds. Among them are:

Discrimination based on race, color, national origin, sex, or religion
Age (between the ages of 40 and 69)
Union organizing or collective bargaining efforts
Handicaps (if the company has federal contracts)

Filing a complaint regarding discrimination, un-
equal pay, job safety or health, pension
rights, or coal mine safety

Entering military service (or within a year after
return)

Pregnancy

Refusal to do a life-threatening or dangerous task

Wage garnishment for one indebtedness

Exercising a right under a pension plan (nor may a
firing be used to prevent a person from attain-
ing any right under the plan)

Refusing sexual advances

Not all of these federal laws give an individual a right
of redress; they are structured to punish the employer for
violations.

State laws and some municipal ordinances establish
additional grounds prohibiting discharges. For instance:

Marital status

Sexual preference (in about two dozen cities including Detroit, Minneapolis, Seattle, and
Washington, D.C., plus the State of Wisconsin)

Refusal to submit to a polygraph test (in nineteen
states)

Serving on a jury, engaging in outside political activities, voting, or filing a workers' compensation claim

By law in Maine and Missouri, *the reasons* for any
firing must be presented in writing to any employee.

*A firing by a private employer may violate the Con-
stitution.* Although there are cases prohibiting a *public* employer from terminating an employee who engages in certain constitutionally protected activities, like free speech,
no court has yet ruled that a private employer may not do

so (irrespective of the other theories mentioned earlier) But the time is not far off when this will come. There have been persuasive legal arguments that a court may not condone a private firing based on constitutionally protected activity without the court itself violating the Constitution, and somewhere, someday, a progressive court will find some termination sufficiently egregious to make this leap to a new legal theory.

An employer's arbitrary firing may undermine some important public policy. This has been the most popular theory in eroding the old "at-will" rule and is recognized in several states, including California, Massachusetts, Michigan, New Jersey, New York, Oregon, Pennsylvania, and West Virginia. It was developed in a case in which an employee was fired the day after he refused to commit perjury to protect his employer. Sound public policy encourages honest testimony, and so the California Court of Appeals ruled that an employer could not do this by firing the man, even if there was no employment contract giving him job security.[158]

Generally employees have been able to win damages under this theory if they have been fired simply because they refused to do something for their company that was illegal, because they properly reported improper conduct by the employer, because they did something they had a legal right to do (like express an opinion or file a workers' compensation claim), or because they refused to do something the law says they don't have to do (like submit to a lie detector test). To understand this theory, employers ought to imagine a situation in which a majority of a company's employees walked out simply because the company insisted upon withholding Social Security taxes from their paychecks or because the company insisted that employees not cheat customers. To permit these sorts of unilateral terminations of an implied employment contract because one party wouldn't do something improper undermines sound public policy.

This notion, now emerging among American courts, is best articulated by the West Virginia Supreme Court in a 1978 case:

> The rule that an employer has an absolute right to discharge an at-will employee must be tempered by the principle that where the employer's motivation for the discharge is to contravene some substantial public policy principle, then the employer may be liable to the employee for damages occasioned by this discharge.[159]

Like most language considered at first as a radical departure from previous rules of law, this statement is cautious ("must be tempered . . . substantial . . . may be liable") and it has directly benefited perhaps fewer than 500 employees. But it has alerted companies all over the United States that firings may no longer be arbitrary, malicious, capricious, and discriminatory. The beneficiaries of that awakening number in the millions.

PART III
SELF-DETERMINATION IN THE WORKPLACE

18

Alternative Work Patterns

It may seem that in the current malaise in the workplace, employees have done nothing but sue their bosses.

Legal developments are deceptive in a way. They merely reflect the more pronounced and the more prolonged disputes that arise when larger social forces are at work. And they generally lag behind these social changes by five to seven years. Going to court still involves a tremendous investment of time, energy, and money. Often in employment cases it involves exhausting, time-consuming administrative remedies before the issue is even framed as a legal dispute. Often also, in employment cases, an individual needs to find—or be found by—a public-spirited group or labor organization willing to underwrite and wage the battle to establish a new general principle of law. Even though the principles established eventually affect millions, the number of employees who actually go to court is miniscule compared to the total number in the work force. Then there are years of appeals to courts populated with judges who only belatedly become aware of new realities in the culture.

But, throughout the nation, salaried executives and wage employees are discovering in the 1980s that there are alternatives to accepting the arbitrary tyranny of the workplace and enduring a long court battle. They are using the realities of today's two-paycheck economy and today's social changes to work for their benefit. These changes were not originated as new bases for employee rights, but that has been their effect. This is a familiar trend. The Civil Rights Act of 1964 was intended to address the specific problem of race discrimination in employment; it was not intended to create a myriad of new policies and principles in nearly every aspect of the employment relationship, but that has been its effect. Reforms affecting women, mothers who work, the handicapped, retirees, workers in unsafe environments, persons in stressful jobs, and older executives all flowed from the 1964 law, even though that was not at all its intent.

The male head of household who leaves his wife and a child or two at home and heads to his 9-to-5 job is a vanishing breed. He now represents a minority of today's work force. His needs were relatively simple to meet. The pressure on him was to earn more money, even if it meant taking more time away from the family. Pregnancy did not prevent him from working; it probably prompted him to work even harder. Child care did not present a problem. He was willing to work from 9 to 5 because that is what he was used to, and that was when the wife didn't want him "under foot" at home and the children were in school anyway. The family knew very little about what went on at work, and if he had to accept indignity upon indignity at work, then the man of the house simply swallowed hard and accepted it. If he lived under a tyrant at work, then at least he was a man—perhaps even a tyrant himself—at home. If he lost his job, that was because he got too "uppity," forgot one of the rules, especially the unwritten ones, at work. It hardly mattered—to him or the family—whether he lived in the suburbs of Cleveland or the suburbs of Seattle or the American compound of Riyadh in Saudi Arabia. The company could transfer him at will.

Today's employee probably has a spouse who also works outside the home. They compare notes about their days at work. Better educated, they know their rights. Child care is a joint responsibility, because neither parent is home during the day. It is a prime consideration when comparing job possibilities. Pregnancy is an impediment to the work life of both spouses, not a motivation for the father to devote energy to earning more money. Leisure time is important; both spouses have hobbies or special interests important to them. Work patterns often have to be altered to accommodate those special interests. Transferring to a new community is a joint family decision now, for one spouse must carefully weigh the effect of the other's transfer on the *first's* career.

Employees who are single have similar concerns, especially those who are raising children—and an increasing number of employees are single parents. Whether or not parents, whether or not married, all workers have diverse interests now that compete with the workplace for their attention. According to the findings of Daniel Yankelovich—the same Yankelovich who alerted the nation to trends in the workplace a decade earlier—home life is more significant to today's workers. "In the 1980s, we're finding them staying home more, enjoying it more, finding they have to be home more because they don't have the money to run and travel and eat away and also they have found that there isn't as much satisfaction, necessarily, in being out there away from the family doing things by oneself," said Yankelovich's partner, Arthur H. White, in a 1982 speech. Yankelovich and White also found that Americans in the 1980s place great importance on consumer value, on making dollars buy worthwhile things. The way money is spent is as important in the 1980s as the way it is earned—and perhaps more important than the sacrifices one must make to earn it. At the same time, Americans continue to seek "diversity in life-styles, tastes, and preferences."

"One was supposed to go to school, save, work hard for the future, marry someone of the opposite sex, have two or three children, preferably of mixed sexes, etc.," White says. "Now there are really many, many more options available to everyone and the American people are taking them happily and seeking more." Clearly the rigidity of work must bend to accommodate these contemporary Americans' choice of options; even in hard times Americans will prefer to work where they can continue their diverse life-styles.

White also notes an emphasis on the future—perhaps it should have been anticipated in a generation that experienced the existential excitement of the 1960s and 1970s. This means that middle-aged and perhaps young workers take an interest in whatever pension might become available to them at retirement. After all, by law, the information is now available to them. Years ago most employees couldn't bother to consider retirement benefits until age 50 approached and even if they were interested they had no rights to know about their benefits.

Americans have choices. Even in the dislocating economy of the early 1980s, job applicants are not supplicants. Employees with special skills or scarce experience are in a position to use that as leverage to secure dignity at work. This is especially true in the "high-tech" specialties of computers and communications. Many of these companies are more desperate to find good people than skilled persons are to find work.

Employees in the 1980s are discovering that not all the bargaining chips are in the hands of the employer. The changes in life-style in recent decades have had the effect of providing employees with some bargaining chips of their own. Here are some of the major ones:

Flextime. Not all work need be performed during the traditional times between 9 in the morning and 5 in the afternoon. Besides, with so many workers having diverse interests and responsibilities, all work *can't* be performed during the traditional eight-hour shifts. The productive economies elsewhere in the world that Americans seem to admire—in Japan, Scandinavia, and Germany—accommodate different work schedules, and now a significant number of American companies are doing so.

Flextime actually includes different alternatives. The best known is flexible scheduling by a company that permits an individual employee to choose his or her working hours, often within a basic "window" of work between 6:30 A.M. and 8:30 P.M. During the core period, between 9:30 A.M. and 3 P.M. usually, all employees are on the job. Each employee arranges in advance to fulfill the requisite number of hours per pay period—with arrivals and departures that allow for peak traffic periods, child-care responsibilities, or perhaps simply individual tastes. If certain persons are "morning persons" who are peppy early in the day, it makes little sense to insist on their coming to work during their least effective hours.

These staggered hours not only increase worker satisfaction and therefore productivity, they also help the company become more effective—especially companies that do business by telephone across time zones or companies that must meet certain delivery deadlines at hours other than the end of the conventional business day. A by-product of this has been to relieve congestion at recreation, entertainment, and shopping facilities, allowing businesses in these fields to make better use of *their* work force.

Another kind of flextime, "work-sharing," permits more than one employee to take a standard shift, or work week. This has been used to accommodate the needs of working women, or to avoid layoffs. Suddenly American businesses discovered that no ancient rule says that a commercial artist or a mechanic must work a standard forty-hour week, or that two persons interested in reduced hours can't together make a more effective receptionist than one person dreading the 9-to-5 rigidity. A few states, beginning with Arizona and California, have accommodated this trend with "Shared Work Unemployment Compensation," which provides unemployment benefits when an employee goes on a reduced work schedule as well as when he or she is totally laid off.

Another new concept permits a full-time employee to reduce his or her hours for a chosen period, perhaps with a reduction in pay, perhaps not, to pursue outside studies, "rest and recreation," or volunteer work. These used to be called "leaves of absence" but companies were never overly generous in extending them, believing apparently that a full-time employee involuntarily bound to his job was better than a satisfied employee returning to work with "batteries recharged." Many employees, especially those in two-paycheck families, have sought jobs with summers off.

Another form of flextime that permits an employee to aggregate his or her requisite hours in four workdays a week, or eight days per two-week period, has the same effect. This "compressed work week" cuts down on costly clean-up or set-up time, and permits workers who perform better over a nine- or ten-hour day to do so. Employees enjoy the extended personal time, free of immediate pressure to prepare to return to work. Who hasn't envied the airline pilot's "three days on, three off," or the fire fighter's "twenty-four on, twenty-four off"?

Many companies have discovered this cuts down on absenteeism and impromptu time off for doctors' appointments or special family functions. Flextime often gives to employees a greater sense of responsibility, a greater sense that *work performed,* not hours devoted to being physically present, is what matters to the company. It certainly makes things flow better in the company parking lot. And it permits personnel officers greater latitude in hiring competent men and women who may have important family responsibilities to meet.

Flexible scheduling has reduced the trauma of immediate retirement as well. Many companies have gradually reduced the hours of retirement-age employees, drawing on their experience to train their replacements and permitting the retirees to adjust slowly to their new lives of retirement. These same companies, notably those in the insurance industry, have then drawn on their pool of retirees as a source of temporary part-time help who are already familiar with the routines of the company and can be called on during peak periods (without the expenses of an employment agency).

Careful scheduling and consideration of many diverse factors are necessary to make flextime work, and many companies are not able or willing to make the effort. Still, the idea seems to be catching on. Nearly a tenth of all workers are currently employed in one of the alternative flextime patterns. From 1974 to 1980 there was nearly a tripling of the number of workers involved in flextime.

The most prominent recommendation of the White House Conference on Families in 1980, and one supported by 93 percent of the delegates, was a call for "family-oriented" employment policies, including flexible schedules, leaves, shared and part-time jobs, and reasonable transfers. A prime way to lessen the conflict between home and work is to develop further the idea of flextime.

The federal government experimented with variations of flextime in 1981 and 1982. Legislation was passed in Congress in 1982 to authorize a three-year program of "alternative work schedules." The experiment allows more than half a million federal employees to arrange with their agency heads to work one of the following work schedules: Arrival and departure times each day set by the employee, as long as eight full hours are worked; credit for time off earned by employees working extra hours, in lieu of overtime pay; or a shift of nine hours a day for nine work days followed by a bonus day off (called "5–4/9"). It is important to remember that throughout the experiment the employees involved remain in jeopardy of having to return to conventional work hours. Flextime has not yet become a right that may be asserted by employees; it is a privilege extended by the federal government as employer until legislation is passed declaring it a permanent fixture. In a possible hint of the future, Pentagon employees took legal action to challenge the revocation of flextime once it had been instituted in their behalf.

In the private sector, about 2,000 office employees at Hercules, Inc., a chemical company in Delaware, suddenly discovered in April 1982 that their flextime could disappear about as fast as it had appeared. In what the company said was a move to save money in hard times, Hercules abruptly terminated a flexible schedule its employees had used for eight years. In 1977, three years into the program, a spokesman for the company had said that the results were favorable. By the first quarter of 1982, earnings were down severely (as they were at many other small companies that did not use flextime) and by the end of the second quarter flextime was gone. It is a concept that—like paid vacations at the turn of the century—management giveth and taketh away.

Gail S. Rosenberg, president of the National Council for Alternative Work Patterns, which monitors this trend, said that Hercules, Inc., did not adapt its flextime program to the changing needs of its employees, and that is why the program did not succeed. Reports on the effects of the idea at most other companies have been positive.

Flexplace. Commuting has become more expensive and time consuming. Both parents are taking on jobs. Office time is consumed by distractions. Our economy is now predominantly made up of services, not manufacturing (enterprises that usually require several workers gathering in the same place at the same time to assemble a product). More and more white-collar work is done over the telephone, at a word processor, or with a computer. One survey of executives' time in 1982 showed that no more than a quarter of the workday requires face-to-face contact with colleagues.

In short, there is less and less need to go to the office in order to hold a job.

Alvin Toffler predicted in *The Third Wave* a shift of work from both the office and factory to the home—what he called the electronic cottage.

Computer-oriented companies and individuals—not surprisingly—are leading the trend. Control Data Corp., fourth leading manufacturer of computers in the nation, is experimenting with "an alternative work station program." In 1979 the company began retraining disabled employees so that they could do computer-based work in their homes. Then the company involved a larger number of employees. Computer programming, design and editing of software, and educational consulting lend themselves to home computer work. Employees who work at home are given tasks with definite beginnings and endings. Periodically they are summoned to the office for consultation with supervisors and colleagues. Control Data found that productivity increased when commuting time was turned into computing time.

A professor of biochemistry in Dallas who finds driving to and from the office "totally nonproductive" spends many of his workdays at home before a computer linked to his place of work. "I'd either have to shuffle an awful bunch of papers at the office or I can shuffle video displays at home. I prefer to shuffle video displays at home," he says.

When Robert K. Wilmouth became president of the Chicago Board of Trade in the late 1970s, he shook up the traditional organization there. One thing he did was to have many employees install computer terminals at home. "When it snows," he says, "they don't come down to work.

They stay home and they work from home. Hopefully, I'm getting them to work harder and to be more productive. I'm going to tap that reservoir of the housewife who used to be a programmer." Still, according to *Infosystems* magazine, Wilmouth is accused of "coddling" his employees.

"Flexplace" has raised eyebrows among traditional managers. Control Data discovered that many supervisors felt nervous when their employees no longer had to report to work every day. Many employees felt nervous, too, feeling that they were "out of sight and out of mind" and that working away from the office would not enhance their careers. The employees missed the socialization of the office, too, and many returned to office hours. Others stayed at home but developed their own computer-stored collection of gossip, games, and commentary that functions like a gathering of employees in front of the bulletin board.

When "flexplace" is undertaken on a large scale, the company doesn't have to devote as many resources to the company parking lot, the company cafeteria, or the company infirmary. It does not have to get into the child-care business to the same extent. It can save money (and intraoffice squabbles) in the allocation of costly office square-footage. And it can radically lessen the bureaucratic hassles and interruptions that distract so many employees from their appointed tasks.

As jobs become more service oriented, more insular, we can expect a trend toward more work accomplished at home. Perhaps not all of a person's commitment to his or her occupation can be done at home, but in an age of computer networks and telecommunications, many of the extraneous agonies of the workplace can be eliminated with "flexplace."

A couple in Westchester County, N.Y., has developed the following arrangement since the birth of their daughter in 1981: The father takes the train the first day of the week to his job as a product marketing manager at New York Telephone Co. The mother, who holds down a similar position in the same department stays at home to work out sales plans on the couple's home computer. The next day, the mother catches the train to Manhattan and the father stays home, doing his work over a telephone and computer terminal. The sales manager at the telephone company finds the arrangement very productive for all involved. And the couple clearly has more leverage with their employer because they avoid many of the diversionary, nerve-racking complexities of the office itself. And they have more leverage because they take in two paychecks.

Two-paycheck families. Families in which there are two paychecks find they have more flexibility in bargaining for dignity at work. This is true, first, of workers who moonlight at a second job. These workers have the ability to press for change at one job while standing tight at the other. If he is fired or demoted for asserting his rights, the "moonlighter" can perhaps expand his hours at his second job, or at least the family can survive on one paycheck until he locates another job. An employee holding down two jobs often finds that he or she can play one boss off against the other. And the dual employee has the advantage of a continual comparison between two workplaces. Many employees have worked nowhere but their present place of employment; they have no way of comparing favorable and unfavorable conditions. Dual employees can do this daily.

The leverage is especially evident in families with two wage earners. In the 1980s both husband and wife work in 70 percent of all young families—the figure is 50 percent for families in all age groups. This has had a profound effect in the workplace. Most managers presume that the two-paycheck phenomenon has produced male and female employees highly motivated and highly beset by child-care concerns and unpaid bills. In fact, what American business has gotten are working duos who can more powerfully withstand the slings and arrows of outrageous terminations and layoffs than can the solitary worker. An employee whose spouse also works will be more willing to risk adverse action at work if his or her dignity is at stake. Besides, if one hears each night that the other employee in the family is not facing the same indignities from 9 to 5, one is motivated to change the situation.

Members of two-paycheck families will be less willing to accept out-of-town transfers. One mate will prefer to pass up the out-of-town opportunity, accept the termination if necessary, and use the cushion of the mate's paycheck for time to find another job. Members of two-paycheck families have different interests with regard to fringe benefits. Child care is very important, of course. But only one spouse needs to sign up for that particular benefit. Two-paycheck families may choose between plans offered by the husband's employer or the wife's. Members of such families may choose among alternative health-care pro-grams offered by two employers. For the spouse who is adequately covered by the other's health plan, the health insurance package at his or her place of employment has a diminished importance. His or her priority, by contrast, may be tuition subsidies, retirement, or leave time. That is why the cafeteria-style fringe benefit program offered by some employers (and mentioned in Chapter 15) is attractive to the majority of today's workers.

Amid the reductions in federal employment under the Reagan administration, it was not unusual in Washington for an unemployed middle-class federal worker to take a surprisingly unalarmed view of the job situation. Many viewed their terminations as leaves of absences. Many took time to explore their city, or to improve their homes, or to come to know their children. They could do this because another member of the family was still gainfully em-ployed—and just as important, the other member's con-tinued employment meant that crucial insurance benefits were not terminated. This softened the blow of unemploy-ment. In families with more than one job holder, the loss of fringe benefits that comes with termination is no longer the life-and-death matter that it used to be in single-job families. And the corporation's power to transfer out of town has lost much of its punch as well. The out-of-work spouse may even have the time and inclination for extensive litigation against his or her former boss.

In the 1980s, with a majority of families associated with more than one employer, a single company can no longer hold a Damocles sword of fear over the whole family, as the managers of the Lowell Mills were able to do in the 1830s or as Henry Ford was able to do in the early 1900s.

An employees' cabal. For two or more companies to get together to plot a common strategy would most likely violate the federal antitrust laws, which are intended to discourage anticompetitive trends. The same is not true of *employees.* In selected instances, groups of employees have banded together to perform certain tasks, or to devise sanctions against a particular company. They have literally "gone out and hired themselves a boss."

The best-known example of a "package deal" was conceived after World War II by a young Army Air Force colonel named Charles Thornton. "Tex" Thornton was impressed by the Air Force team he had assembled during wartime, and so he produced a handsome prospectus offering the managerial talents of the whole team. He mailed it to about twenty major companies. About half replied. But it was a telegram to Henry Ford II in Detroit that struck paydirt. To the team's amazement, Ford responded within seven hours, showing definite interest. Colonel Thornton dealt with Henry Ford much like the baron of an elite executive labor union. "How many of the Air Force managerial team can you use?" he asked. Ford responded, "That's up to you."[160]

Thornton's team decided to offer Ford ten men at salaries ranging from $9,000 to $14,000. It may not have been the best bargain Thornton ever made, but it was the Ford Motor Company's best deal in a long time. Although Thornton left Ford after two years (and later went on to buy Litton Industries, Inc., for $1 million and turn it into a multibillion dollar conglomerate), the team stayed together and soon became known around the Dearborn, Mich., headquarters as "the Whiz Kids."

In 1961 one of its prime members, Robert S. McNamara, was named Secretary of Defense by President John F. Kennedy. McNamara was at the time president of Ford Motor Co. McNamara left behind at Ford five of the original Thornton team in key executive positions. Another member of "the Whiz Kids," Arjay R. Miller, was later to become president as well.

Other teams of executives have followed the Whiz Kids' example and hired themselves out as a team. And sometimes they quit as a team. If an employer knows that a fired employee will take several talented colleagues with him or her, the employer generally does not abuse the employee.

A variation of this concept is the use of sanctions against employers by groups of professionals, usually in an association. Employees have banded together and refused to work for organizations that deprive employees of basic rights or that have policies that violate the group's standards. The American Association of University Professors has a long-standing program of this type. It processes complaints from 1,000 teachers each year, even from nonmembers. If the AAUP censures a university for intruding upon the academic independence of a professor, this can severely limit the ability of the university to recruit quality teachers in the future (although the AAUP leaves to the discretion of the individual whether to accept a position or not). It also has a legal defense fund for members victimized by unfair employment practices.

Other scientific and professional associations circulate lists of undesirable employers or get companies to agree to abide by an association's grievance procedure. Some associations have likewise established legal defense funds for aggrieved members.

A professional association can be influential in clearing

the name of an individual member unfairly fired or disciplined by a company because of the employee's legitimate activities. The association can "vouch" for the integrity of the member among other companies. Often a strong code of ethics developed by a professional association, like the American Bar Association or the American Medical Association, can serve as the means for an individual to resist improper demands placed on him or her by a company.

Whether or not an association has formal sanctions or even a code of ethics, the grapevine among members can be a powerful force. Through it, members avoid undesirable work environments and come to the rescue of colleagues victimized by companies. In the 1980s, the professional association often has a stronger pull on the loyalty of an individual than does the company for which the individual works. In fact, in the era of conventions and regional meetings, many individuals spend more working time with their professional colleagues around the country than they do with their coworkers at the company. Often, a person's prestige is determined more by his or her standing among professional colleagues than by treatment in the workplace. In the corridors of hotels where professional and trade associations are holding their meetings, there is a lot of talk about comparative working conditions. "We" now refers to one's professional colleagues around the country, not necessarily to one's company.

Today's corporate employees think of themselves more as "professionals" than businessmen. Making money is important and these corporate employees want to see their companies maximize profits, but they are more concerned about their standing among their professional colleagues at competing companies. They feel more comfortable among these colleagues than among their company coworkers, because there is less corporate infighting involved, and less risk in expressing oneself freely.

As this trend continues, groups of professionals—including those not employed by the company—will influence a company's treatment of an individual. A person's professional colleagues will claim a stronger loyalty than the individual owes to the source of his or her paycheck.

Self-employment. If your loyalty runs more to your profession than to your company, if you are spending most of your time on the road, if you are in a service industry, and if days spent at the company are a hassle, why in the world are you still working for the company? That is a question that apparently has occurred to many persons in the past decade. They have decided to work for themselves.

Once again, this trend was most evident in jobs involving computers. In Westchester County, N.Y., around Route 128 near Boston, in the Silicon Valley of northern California, and within the Beltway in Washington, longtime employees of computer-related companies suddenly became self-employed consultants. Many continued doing essentially what they had been doing before, but overnight they turned their employer into their customer. Instead of bargaining for salary and fringe benefits, they billed the company for the value of their services. There were drawbacks to be sure; individual rates for health insurance are higher than group rates; overhead costs for office space, clerical assistance, equipment, travel, and other necessities had to be faced; and the insecurity of next month's income exceeded even the insecurity of working for an employer "at will." But nearly 9 percent of the American work force was self-employed as the 1980s began.

The Bureau of Labor Statistics called the switch to self-employment "dramatic." Although the number of self-employed farmers decreased, other self-employment increased by 1.3 million from 1976 to 1979. At the end of the decade self-employment was growing by 17 percent, as compared to 11 percent for salaried employment during the same period. And these figures do not include more than 2 million owners of small incorporated businesses (because the government now counts these as salaried persons), nor more than 1.5 million persons self-employed in their *second* jobs, nor thousands of "casual" workers in the underground economy. For the first time, self-employment is attracting younger persons, who were traditionally thought not to have the capital and the experience to start businesses.

Not surprisingly, this self-employment is concentrated in service industries, like real estate, finance, insurance, consulting, editing, and data processing, according to the Bureau of Labor Statistics.[161]

The self-employed discover that nearly 100 percent of their workday is devoted to the substance of their work; by contrast when they worked for a large organization far too much of their time was devoted to bureaucratic infighting, office logistics, interruptions, extracurricular activities, personnel problems, settling disputes, unraveling misunderstandings, and fretting about ambitions of coworkers. The self-employed person no longer has to worry so much about what he or she wears to work each day. Arrival and departure times are not as crucial. There is more flexibility with family time and with work time. Self-employed persons say, "Let's have lunch," only when they mean it. And no one comes around demanding a contribution to the United Way campaign.

In the decade of the 1980s, self-employment, previously regarded as the preserve of the eccentric recluse or of the workaholic, became a viable alternative to working in the large corporation. The boss has come to think twice if he or she suspects that gifted employees will put their skills to work for themselves if hassled at work too much.

Describing himself as "your friendly neighborhood grocery store" in an age of supermarkets, Orson Welles, the independent film director and actor, once talked about the distinctions of self-employment. He did so when accepting an award from the American Film Institute. "There are a few of us in this conglomerated world of ours," Welles told the film moguls, "who still trudge stubbornly along the lonely, rocky road and this is, in fact, our contrariety.

"We don't move nearly as fast as our cousins on the freeway. We don't even get as much accomplished, just as the family-sized farm can't possibly raise as many crops or get as much profit as the agricultural factory of today.

"What we do come up with has no special right to call itself better. It's just different. No, if there's any excuse for us at all it's that we're simply following the old American tradition of the maverick.

"A maverick may go his own way but he doesn't think that it's the only way or ever claim that it's the best one—except maybe for himself. And don't imagine that *this* raggle-taggle gypsy is claiming to be free. It's just that some of the necessities to which I am a slave are different from yours."

Employee ownership. Or employees may buy the company. This is an alternative that has been tried sparingly in the United States and the results are not clear. It seems that when employees feel like owners of a company there are marked changes in productivity, efficiency, morale, job environment, and employment opportunities. Thus far, employee ownership has been invoked to save a failing company from demise, but there is no reason why it cannot turn around a company with unfair personnel policies.

One means for accomplishing this is an employee stock ownership plan, in which part of every employee's compensation is paid in the form of stock in the company. Foregoing short-term benefits, the employee gradually acquires more stock ownership in the company where he or she works. Through these plans, employees of a company can soon accumulate impressive leverage for effecting change.

There are federal tax advantages for companies to make these stock plans available to employees. Sen. Gary W. Hart of Colorado and others have proposed increasing the tax benefits, and he has encouraged use of cumulative employee stock ownership to avoid a hostile takeover of a company by a corporate giant.

For too long, managers have deferred employee attempts at reform with the excuse that the company's primary obligation to its stockholders requires it to maximize profits. This is said even though the company management hardly knows its stockholders or what they want and shows great contempt for stockholders who bother to show up at annual meetings. If a sizable number of stockholders are *in the office or factory itself,* the attitude of managers may change.

Many employees see this trend as a way to restore the person-to-person element of private enterprise that was present in the early nineteenth century in America when the capitalist entrepreneur was on the job himself. Increased employee ownership of companies could mean that by the end of the twentieth century America will return to the vitality of a workplace in which the owners work along with the workers.

19

Conclusion

In the 1960s, in the decade of upheaval in race relations, the schools bore the brunt of the legal pressure for social reform. Representatives of the schools cried out that they were not responsible for all of the nation's race problems and they were not adequate for the immense task expected of them—to guarantee racial equality for all in future generations. But the responsibility was thrust upon the school system anyway, until it was ultimately thrust in turn upon other institutions. Local governments, churches, families, the marketplace—any of them might have been more appropriate targets for the legal pressure to produce a desegregated society. But the original responsibility was placed, nonetheless, upon the schools. Courts are not always logical when the battlegrounds for social change are selected.

Ironically, changes from the civil rights decade were more lasting in institutions other than the schools—in the workplace, in politics, in government, in commerce; still, the *legal* responsibility assigned by the courts fell largely on the school system. One reason for this might have been that the most significant bulge in America's population in many generations—the "baby boom"—was at the time in the school system. Aside from civil rights, lots of attention was focused on improving the schools and lots of money was spent to do so. Now the "baby boom" has moved on. It is in the workplace. Perhaps coincidentally, perhaps not, the institution of the American workplace is being asked to bear the brunt of the current decade of social change. Now the issue is not racial equality, though that is part of it. Now the issue is human dignity. The quest for consumer goods, for more leisure time, and for more electronic entertainment has been found lacking. Americans are seeking meaning in their lives, individual dignity. And the workplace is the focal point of that quest. Americans find that they can discover their own dignity in their personal lives, in their separate communities. But they abruptly encounter degradation as soon as they arrive at the office or pass through the plant gate.

Like the schools, corporate America is saying, "We didn't create the problem, and we can't solve it." That may be an irrelevant complaint, as the school representatives discovered. But beyond that, there is evidence that the corporate workplace *is* responsible for much of the malaise in America. The social issues we are dealing with—women's demands for recognition, crime among young people, mental stress in all levels of society, arguments over appropriate child development, inefficient transportation systems, chronic inflation—ultimately come down to the workplace. Stress in the workplace clearly creates stress in the community, just as the reverse is true. One study at the University of California at Irvine has even suggested that teenagers might be better off not working, because of the bad habits and stress they pick up in the workplace. Indicators of stress, like drug and alcohol use and poor school performances, may be higher among kids who work than among those who do not.[162] What kind of a lesson is this for a nation that cherishes the Horatio Alger legend?

Corporate managers may respond accurately that the workplace is the inappropriate forum to resolve the "lifestyle" issues now being thrust upon it by American courts, but they cannot claim that the workplace as an institution had no role in creating the problem now being addressed by the "baby boom" reformers, now approaching middle age.

Institutions with pervasive influences over peoples' lives cannot choose when they will be the targets of social change.

The legal responsibility for desegregation was placed on the schools, even though they could rightfully assert that they did not create the racial problems that had to be resolved. In the 1980s, the rejoinder of corporate America to the courts is weaker; there *is* evidence that the workplace has contributed to stress in the society at large.

The main reason for that is that work, as it is conducted in the United States, too often conflicts with living. It forces us to choose between "making a living" and "making a life." Work doesn't complement our personal lives. It tears them apart. It often degrades us. It exhausts us. It consumes our attention. It moves us to strange communities at short notice. It makes us dependent on a huge profit-making organization for vital services like health care, pensions, child care, insurance, and professional education.

We look to work to give us our self-identity and our worth as individuals. Yet the providers of work in America have never been equipped or inclined to do that. The corporate aim is production and acquisition. Only to enhance those will corporate America adopt reforms. As a by-product these reforms also enhance the status and dignity of the individual. If vacations or dental plans proved to have no favorable impact on production, they would disappear.

Legislatures and courts, responding to human needs, have forced significant changes in the American workplace in the past five years, even though those changes have not yet filtered down to the majority of workplaces in the nation. The law is an inadequate tool for this sort of social change. Everybody agrees that changes in attitudes bring more lasting and meaningful reforms. But legal change, untidy as it is, does force eventual changes in attitudes. It happened with the legal pressure on the schools in the

1960s. It will happen with the legal pressure on the workplace in the 1980s.

This will be true regardless of the economic climate. Americans simply have seen too much and experienced too much to accept the degradation of most jobs much longer. In past years, the company has been able to keep working conditions degrading by offering higher compensation for the work. This permitted millions of employees to find gratification in their personal lives—a new home, a boat, perhaps a second car, a child in college, a nice yard. The company may no longer be able to do this, for at least three reasons. Americans have discovered that increased tax withholdings and inflation have neutralized many of the increases in compensation anyway. Americans use whatever raises they get "to stay ahead," not to splurge. Also, Americans have discovered that a higher paying job that may end tomorrow is no guarantee of the good life. They are insuring themselves against that risk by having more than one person in the family work, or by taking on second jobs. Beyond that, Americans have discovered that higher pay devoted to babysitters so that the parents can work or to psychiatrists so that they can cope with the pressures on the job does not represent an improvement at all. What good is it if a higher paycheck allows you to buy fancy consumer goods and the demands of the job hardly let you enjoy them? Because of the pressures of work, Americans hardly have time to raise their children. We are raising a generation of youngsters who see work not as an admired skill or a vocation of pride, but as a drudgery that takes both parents away and causes them to be spiritless when they return at night.

Corporate America will simply have to lessen the conflict between personal life and work life. In earlier times, a worker could tolerate the intolerable perhaps because the larger task was something significant—a railroad across the country, a skyscraper, a spacecraft, an innovative product. It is harder to accept indignity at work when you are sorting plastic parts, auditing identical insurance policies, entering millions of digits into a computer, or shuffling papers at a plant your neighbors feel pollutes the air around them.

So long as the broader rewards of work are not evident—and where in the world of American work are they evident today?—then individuals will seek their rewards in their individual lives. That is what is happening today. And that is why the quality of a company's day-care program matters more to an employee than the quality of its product.

Whereas a generation ago it was making the good life possible, corporate America is now finding itself *competing* with the good life. For corporate employers in the 1980s, it has been a losing battle.

Notes

1) Richard C. Edwards, *Contested Terrain: The Transformation of the Work Place in the 20th Century* (New York: Basic Books, 1979), p. 23.

2) Opinion Research Corp., "Strategic Planning for Human Resources: 1980 and Beyond," Princeton, New Jersey, 1981.

3) *Behavior Today*, March 16, 1981.

4) "Stress and the Work Environment," panel presentation by the Occupational Safety and Health Administration, Washington, D.C., December 1980; cited in *Warning: Health Hazards for Office Workers* (Cleveland: Working Women Education Fund, 1981), p. 7.

5) Barbara Garson, *All the Livelong Day* (Garden City, N.Y.: Doubleday, 1975).

6) *Adair v. United States,* 208 U.S. 161 (1908).

7) Quoted in *The Lowell Offering: Writings by New England Mill Women,* edited by Benita Eisler (Philadelphia: J. B. Lippincott, 1977).

8) *Ibid.*

9) Thomas Dublin, *Women at Work* (New York: Columbia University, 1979), p. 98.

10) Henry David Thoreau, *Walden* (New York: Rinehart Co., Inc., 1959), p. 112.

11) Edwards, *Contested Terrain,* p. 80.

12) Quoted in "Privacy: Employer-Employe Tug-of-War," by Lawrence Stessin, the *New York Times,* November 17, 1974.

13) "Criticizing Public Men," the *New York Times,* January 15, 1874, p. 4, quoted by David J. Seipp, "The Right to Privacy in American History" (Cambridge, Mass.: Program on Information Resources Policy, Harvard University, 1976).

14) M. C. Slough, *Privacy, Freedom and Responsibility* (Springfield, Ill.: C. C. Thomas, 1969), p. 22, quoted by Seipp.

15) Allan Nevins, *Ford: The Times, The Man, The Company* (New York: Scribner's, 1954), p. 554.

16) Edwards, *Contested Terrain,* p. 120.

17) Garson, *All the Livelong Day,* p. 150.

18) Edwards, *Contested Terrain,* p. 196.

19. *Ibid.*

20) Quoted by Donna Allen, *Fringe Benefits: Wages or Social Obligation?* (Ithaca, N.Y.: New York State School of Industrial and Labor Relations), p. 48.

21) Maurine Weiner Greenwald, *Women, War, and Work* (Westport, Conn.: Greenwood Press, 1980), p. 197.

22) Quoted in "Constitutional Validity of Employer Dress and Grooming Codes," 9 *University of San Francisco Law Review* 515 (Winter 1975).

23) John Kenneth Galbraith, *A Life in Our Times* (Boston, Mass.: Houghton Mifflin Co., 1981), p. 161.

24) Garson, *All the Livelong Day,* p. 90.

25) William H. Whyte, Jr., *The Organization Man* (Garden City, N.Y.: Doubleday & Co., 1957), p. 3–4.

26) Fall Industrial Engineering Conference, Washington, D.C., Dec. 6–9, 1981, Institute of Industrial Engineers.

27) Quoted in "Creating a New World of Work," *International Labour Review,* v. 115, January-February 1977, p. 1.

28) *U.S. v. Cruikshank,* 92 U.S. 542 (1875). The Fourteenth Amendment says, in part, "nor shall any State deprive any person of life, liberty, or property, without due process of law; nor deny to any person within its jurisdiction the equal protection of the laws."

29) *Civil Rights Cases,* 109 U.S. 3 (1883).

30) *Smith v. Allwright,* 321 U.S. 649 (1944), and *Steele v. Louisville & N.R.R.,* 323 U.S. 192 (1944).

31) *Marsh v. Alabama,* 326 U.S. 501 (1946).

32) *Lloyd Corp. v. Tanner,* 407 U.S. 551 (1972), and *Moose Lodge v. Irvis,* 407 U.S. 163, (1972).

33) Charles Morgan, Jr., *One Man, One Voice* (New York: Holt, Rinehart & Winston, 1979), p. 333.

34) "Constitutional Limitations on Corporate Activity—Protection of Personal Rights From Invasion Through Corporate Power," 100 *University of Pennsylvania Law Review* 943 (May 1952).

35. Julius G. Getman, "What Price Employment? Arbitration, the Constitution, and Personal Freedom," in *Arbitration 1976, Proceedings of the Twenty-Ninth Annual Meeting, National Academy of Arbitrators* (Washington, D.C.: Bureau of National Affairs, 1977).

36) Andrew Hacker, "Loyalty—and the Whistle-Blower," reprinted in *Individual Rights in the Corporation* edited by Alan F. Westin and Stephen Salisbury (New York: Pantheon, 1980), p. 88.

37) Quoted in *Datamation,* January 1982, p. 120.

38) *Spencer v. Toussaint,* 408 F. Supp. 1067 (E.D. Mich., 1976).

39) 42 U.S.C. 2000e.

40) 42 U.S.C. 2000e(k).

41) 29 U.S.C. 623.

42) *Gay Law Students Association v. Pacific Telephone and Telegraph Co.*, 595 P. 2d 592 (Cal. 1979).

43) 38 U.S.C. 2012.

44) 29 U.S.C. 793.

45) 15 U.S.C. 1681.

46) 29 U.S.C. 206.

47) 29 U.S.C. 206(d)(1).

48) *County of Washington, Oregon v. Gunther,* 452 U.S. 161 (1981).

49) *International Electrical, Radio and Machine Workers v. Westinghouse Electric Corp.,* 631 F. 2d 1904 (3rd Cir., 1980).

50) *Lemons v. City and County of Denver,* 620 F. 2d 228 (10th Cir., 1980), *cert. denied,* 449 U.S. 888 (1980).

51) *Weiner v. McGraw-Hill, Inc.,* 51 *Law Week* 2329 (Ct. App. NY 1982). There was a similar opinion in *Toussaint v. Blue Cross & Blue Shield of Michigan,* 408 Mich. 579, 292 N.W. 2d 880 (1980).

52) *Frye v. U.S.,* 293 F. 1013 (1923).

53) *State v. Community Distributors, Inc.,* 64 N.J. 479, 317 A. 2d 697 (1974).

54) Quoted by Edgar A. Jones, Jr., in " 'Truth' When the Polygraph Operator Sits as Arbitrator (or Judge): The Deception of 'Detection' in the 'Diagnosis of Truth and Deception'," in *Truth, Lie Detectors, and Other Problems in Labor Arbitration,* edited by James L. Stern and Barbara D. Dennis (Washington, D.C.: Bureau of National Affairs, 1979), p. 98.

55) H.R. Rep. 94-795, 93rd Cong., 2d Sess. "The Use of Polygraphs and Similar Devices by Federal Agencies," (1976), p. 46.

56) *Hearings on the Use of Polygraphs and Similar Devices by Federal Agencies, Before a Subcomm. of the House Comm. on Government Operations,* 93rd Cong., 1st Sess., at 414 (1974).

57) David Thoreson Lykken, *A Tremor in the Blood* (New York: McGraw-Hill, 1981), p. 61.

58) Ibid., p. 61.

59) *Personal Privacy in an Information Society,* the report of the Privacy Protection Study Commission (Washington, D.C.: U.S. Government Printing Office, 1977), p. 239.

60) "Business Buys the Lie Detector," *Business Week,* February 6, 1978, p. 104.

61) *Griggs v. Duke Power Co.,* 401 U.S. 424 (1971).

62) *Detroit Edison Co. v. NLRB,* 440 U.S. 301 (1979).

63) David W. Ewing, *Freedom Inside the Organization* (New York. McGraw-Hill, 1977), p. 18–19.

64) *Percival v. General Motors Corp.*, 539 F. 2d 1126 (88th Cir. 1976).

65) "What is 'Business Ethics'?" *Public Interest*, No. 63, Spring 1981, p. 18.

66) *Pickering v. Board of Education*, 391 U.S. 563 (1968). The First Amendment to the Constitution states, "Congress shall make no law . . . abridging the freedom of speech, or of the press; or the right of the people peaceably to assemble . . ." Courts have declared that this prohibition applies to the states as well as Congress.

67) *Rafferty v. Philadelphia Psychiatric Center*, 356 F. Supp. 500 (E.D. Pa. 1973); *Muller v. Conlisk*, 429 F. 2d 901 (7th Cir. 1970); *Downs v. Conway School District*, 328 F. Supp. 338 (D. Ark. 1975); *Tepedino v. Dumpson*, 249 N.E. 2d 751 (N.Y. Ct. App. 1969); *Dendor v. Board of Fire and Police Commissioners*, 297 N.E. 2d 316 (App. Ct. Ill. 1st Dist. 1975).

68) Thomas I. Emerson, *The System of Freedom of Expression* (New York: Vintage Books, 1970), p. 677.

69) *Harless v. First National Bank in Fairmont*, 246 S.E. 2d 270 (1978).

70) *Geary v. U.S. Steel Corp.*, 456 Pa. 171, 319 A. 2d 174 (1974).

71) *Kenneally v. Orgain*, 129 Mont. 80, 606 P. 2d 127 (1980).

72) *Fortune v. National Cash Register Co.*, 271 Mass. 96, 364 N.E. 2d 1251 (1977).

73) *Public Aviation Co. v. NLRB*, 324 U.S. 793 (1945).

74) Quoting Staughton Lynd, "Company Constitutionalism?" 87 *Yale L. J.* 4 (1978).

75) Title VII of the Civil Rights Act of 1964, 42 U.S.C. 2000e-3(a); Equal Pay Act of 1963, 29 U.S.C. 206(d)(1); Fair Labor Standards Act, 29 U.S.C. 206; Age Discrimination in Employment Act, 29 U.S.C. 630; Coal Mine Safety Act, 30 U.S.C. 815(c)(1); Occupational Safety and Health Act, 29 U.S.C. 651.

76) *Chin v. American Telephone & Telegraph Co.*, 410 N.Y.S. 2d 737, *aff'd.* 70 A.D. 2d 791 (1979).

77) Cal. Labor Code 1101.

78) *Black v. Kroger Co.*, 527 S.W. 2d 794 (Ct. of Civ. App. Tex. 1975).

79) *Bodewig v. K mart Inc.*, 635 P 2d 657 (Ct. App. Ore. 1981).

80) *General Motors Corp. v. Piskor*, 340 A. 2d 767 (Md. App. 1975).

81) Lawrence Stessin, "Employees Don't Take Anti-Theft Moves Lightly," the *New York Times*, March 4, 1979, p. F-3.

82) *Privacy Journal*, April 1977, p. 7.

83) *Privacy Journal*, Dec. 1979, p. 4.

84) *Burdeau v. McDowell*, 256 U.S. 464 (1921). The Fourth Amend-

ment to the Constitution states, "The right of the people to be secure in their persons, houses, papers, and effects, against unreasonable searches and seizures, shall not be violated . . ."

85) *Stapleton v. Superior Court,* 70 Cal., 2d 97, 447 P. 2d 967 (1969).

86) *5 Golden Gate L. Rev.* at 133 (1974).

87) M. Cherif Bassiouni, *Citizen's Arrest* (Chicago: De Paul University, 1977), p. 173.

88) *U.S. v. Francoer,* 547 F. 2d 891 (5th Cir., 1977), *cert. denied* 431 U.S. 932 (1977).

89) *U.S. v. Blok,* 188 F. 2d 1019 (D.C. Cir., 1951).

90) 18 U.S.C. 2510.

91) *Nader v. General Motors Corp.,* 255 N.E. 2d 765 (Ct. App. N.Y. 1970).

92) Louis Harris & Associates, Inc. and Alan F. Westin, *The Dimensions of Privacy,* Stevens Point, Wisc.: Sentry Insurance, 1979).

93) Quoted in Justice Thurgood Marshall's dissent in *Kelley v. Johnson,* 425 U.S. 238 (1976).

94) *Kent v. Dulles,* 357 U.S. 116 (1958).

95) *Kelley v. Johnson,* see note 93.

96) *Keys v. Continental National Bank and Trust Co. of Chicago,* 357 F. Supp. 376 (N.D., Ill., 1973).

97) John H. McGuckin, Jr., "Employee Hair Styles: Recent Judicial and Arbitral Decisions," *Labor Law Journal,* March 1975.

98) 29 U.S.C. 651.

99) *Atlantic and Gulf Stevedores v. OSHRC,* 534 F. 2d 541 (3rd Cir. 1976).

100) 29 Code of Federal Regulations 1910.20.

101) *General Motors Corp. v. Director, National Institute of Occupational Safety and Health,* 459 F. Supp. 235 (D. Ohio, 1976).

102) National Safety Council, *Accident Facts,* 1982 ed. (Chicago: National Safety Council, 1982), p. 32.

103) Bureau of Labor Statistics press release, November 17, 1982 (Washington, D.C.).

104) Quoted by Joel Makower, *Office Hazards* (Washington, D.C.: Tilden Press, 1981), p. x.

105) *Smith v. Western Electric Co.,* 51 *Law Week* 2200 (Ct. App. Mo. E. Dist. 1981). See also Morley Swingle, "The Legal Conflict Between Smokers and Nonsmokers: The Majestic Vice versus the Right to Clean Air," 45 *Missouri Law Review* 444 (1980).

106) *Work in America: Report of a Special Task Force to the Secretary of Health, Education and Welfare* (Cambridge, Mass.: M.I.T. Press, 1973).

107) From "Proceedings of Occupational Stress Conference," U.S.

Department of Health, Education and Welfare. Publication number 78-156, March 1978.

108) Quoted in *Mind as Healer, Mind as Slayer,* by Kenneth R. Pelletier (New York: Delacorte Press, 1977).

109) *Carter v. General Motors Corp.,* 361 Mich. 577 (1960).

110) *Albanese's Case,* 389 N.E. 2d 83 (Sup. Jud. Ct. of Mass., 1979).

111) Joseph W. Little, Wex S. Malone, and Marcus L. Plant, *Workers' Compensation and Employment Rights* (St. Paul, Minn.: West Publishing Co., 1980).

112) *Doyle v. Continental Airlines,* No. 75 C 2407 (N.D. Ill. Oct. 29, 1979).

113) *Beidler v. W.R. Grace, Inc.,* 461 F. Supp. 1013 (E.D. Pa. 1978), *aff'd mem.,* 609 F. 2d 500 (3rd Cir. 1979).

114) *Rogers v. Loews L'Enfant Plaza Hotel,* 526 F. (D.D.C. Supp. 523, 1981).

115) Frank Allen, "Executives' Wives View Marriages as Combining Rewards, Sacrifices," the *Wall Street Journal,* December 16, 1981, page 1, section 2.

116) Robert Seidenberg, *Corporate Wives—Corporate Casualties?* (New York: AMACOM, 1973), p. 14.

117) "IBM Loses Suit over Suitor's Ties With Staffer," *Computerworld,* February 8, 1982, p. 27.

118) *Monge v. Beebe Rubber Co.,* 114 N.H. 130, 316 A. 2d 549 (1974).

119) 15 U.S.C. 1674.

120) 29 Code of Federal Regulations 1605.

121) *Corne v. Bausch & Lomb, Inc.,* 390 F. Supp. 161 (D. Ariz. 1975). *vacated and remanded,* 562 F. 2d 55 (9th Cir. 1977).

122) *Bundy v. Jackson,* 24 F.E.P. Cases 1155 (D.C. Cir. 1981). The information in the text about this case comes from the court's opinion.

123) *Schomer v. Smidt,* 170 Cal. 662 (Ct. App. 4th Dist., 1980).

124) 29 Code of Federal Regulations 1604.11.

125) 6 *Women's Rights Law Reporter* 287 (Summer 1980).

126) New Jersey stenographer: *Tomkins v. Public Service Electric and Gas Co.,* 568 F. 2d 1044 (3rd Cir. 1977). Airline stewardess: See note 123. Minnesota woman: *Continental Can Co. v. State of Minnesota,* 22 F.E.P. Cases 1808 (Minn. Sup. Ct. 1980). Washington, D.C. woman: *Barnes v. Costle,* 561 F. 2d 983 (D.C. Civ. 1977). New Jersey industrial engineer: *Kyriazi v. Western Electric Co.,* 461 F. Supp. 894 (D.N.J. 1978). Restaurant assistant manager: *Rogers v. Loews L'Enfant Plaza Hotel,* See note 114. Washington woman harassed by company president: *Clark v. World Airways,* 24 F.E.P. Cases 305 (D.D.C. 1980).

127) Homosexual case: *Wright v. Methodist Youth Services, Inc.*, 511 F. 2d Supp. 307 (N. D. Ill., 1981). Heterosexual case: *Huebschen v. Rader*, 81-C-1004 (W.D.Wisc. 1982).

128) Russell B. Stevenson, Jr., *Corporations and Information* (Baltimore: The Johns Hopkins University Press, 1980), p. 67.

129) Greenwald, *Women, War, and Work*, p. 76.

130) *Campbell v. Ford Industries*, 274 Ore. 243 (1976).

131) *Personal Privacy in an Information Society*, p. 225, 233.

132) 26 Me. Rev. Stat. 631.

133) *Privacy Journal*, March 1982, p. 1.

134) *Drennen v. Westinghouse Electric Corp.*, 328 So. 2d 52 (Dist. Ct. App. Fla. 1976).

135) *Schomer v. Smidt*, see note 123.

136) *Lotspeich v. Chance Vought Aircraft*, 369 S.W. 2d (705 Civ. App. Tex. 1963).

137) *American Republic Insurance Co. v. Union Fidelity Life Insurance Co.*, 470 F. 2d 820 (9th Cir. 1972).

138) Phillip I. Blumberg, "Employee Participation in Corporate Decision Making," reprinted in *Individual Rights in the Corporation*, p. 348.

139) *Savodnik v. Korvettes*, 488 F. Supp. 822 (E.D. N.Y. 1980).

140) 29 U.S.C. 1001.

141) Michael J. Casey, "ERISA—The Exclusions and Limitations of its Protection," *Employee Benefits Journal*, Winter 1978, p. 8.

142) Allen, *Fringe Benefits*, p. xvi.

143) Quoted in *Retirement Income, A Report from the Pension Rights Center* (Washington, D.C., 1979), p. 7.

144) *Employee Benefits, 1981,* (Washington, D.C.: Chamber of Commerce of the United States, 1982).

145) Allen, *Fringe Benefits*, p. 258.

146) *Rogers v. Equal Employment Opportunity Commission*, 454 F. 2d 234 (5th Cir. 1971), *cert. denied*, 406 U.S. 957 (1972).

147) 42 U.S.C. 2000e(k).

148) *Board of Regents v. Roth*, 408 U.S. 564 (1972).

149) *Sniadach v. Family Finance Corp.*, 395 U.S. 337 (1969).

150) David W. Ewing, "What Business Thinks About Employee Rights," 55 *Harvard Business Review* 5 (1977).

151) *Whirlpool Corp. v. Marshall*, 445 U.S. 1 (1980).

152) *Vaca v. Sipes*, 386 U.S. 171 (1967).

153) "Protecting At Will Employees Against Wrongful Discharge: The Duty to Terminate Only in Good Faith," 93 *Harvard Law Review* at 1816 (June 1980).

154) *Agis v. Howard Johnson Co.*, 371 Mass. 140, 355 N.E. 2d 315 (1976).

155) *Cancellier v. Federated Department Stores*, 28 F.E.P. Cases 1152 (9th Cir. 1982).

156) *Monge v. Beebe Rubber Co.*, See note 118; *Fortune v. National Cash Register Co.*, 373 Mass. 96, 364 N.E. 2d 1251 (1977); *Cleary v. American Airlines Inc.*, 111 Cal. App. 3rd 443, 168 Cal. Rptr. 722 (1980).

157) *Toussaint v. Blue Cross & Blue Shield of Michigan*, 408 Mich. 579, 292 N.W. 2d 880 (1980).

158) *Petermann v. International Brotherhood of Teamsters*, 174 Cal. App. 2d 184, 344 P. 2d 95 (1959).

159) *Harless v. First National Bank, in Fairmont*, 246 S.E. 2d 270 (W.Va. 1978).

160) Elie Abel, "Robert McNamara," *The Kennedy Circle* (Washington, D.C.: Luce, 1961), p. 177.

161) T. Scott Fain, "Self-Employed Americans: Their Number Has Increased," *Monthly Labor Review*, November 1980, p. 3.

162) Ellen Greenberger, Laurence D. Steinberg, and Alan Vaux, "Adolescents Who Work: Health and Behavioral Consequences of Job Stress," 17 *Developmental Psychology* 691 (1981).

Acknowledgments

I have relied heavily on the research and writing of the following lawyers: Arthur P. Menard and Anne K. Morrill of Boston; L. Nicholas Counter III and Gordon Krischer of Los Angeles; Alan F. Westin of Columbia University in New York; Ann Fleisher Hoffman of New York City; Henry H. Perritt, Jr., of Villanova Law School, Philadelphia; Merton E. Marks of Phoenix; and Robert R. Belair, Gerald S. Hartman, and Terry R. Yellig of Washington, D.C.

The following representatives of public-interest organizations provided useful information: Terry Noble Foster of the American Bar Association National Institutes; Paul N. Pfeiffer of Action on Smoking and Health; Tim Sweeney of Lambda Legal Defense and Educational Fund Inc.; Timothy Saasta of the National Committee for Responsive Philanthropy; Gail Rosenberg of the National Council for Alternative Work Patterns; and Stephen Bruce of the Pension Rights Center. The bar association is in Chicago; the Lambda Fund is in New York City; the others are in Washington.

I have been assisted by Ralph Keyes, author of *Taking Risks;* Nelson Lichtenstein of the Department of History, Catholic University, Washington; Luree Miller, author of *Late Bloom: New Lives for Women;* and David J. Seipp of Harvard University.

I am especially grateful for the special contributions of Jerret Engle, editor at Dutton, and copy editors Randy Ladenheim and Rollin Stearns; Douglass Lea of Waterford, Va.; Ronald B. Lewis of Washington, D.C.; Kathleen

McCarthy, who assisted me with the research; J. Stanley Pottinger of New York City; Kathryn Ritter, who persuaded me of the need for this book; Raphael Sagalyn, my effective literary agent in Washington; Marc O. Smith and David E. Smith.

ROBERT ELLIS SMITH

Index

DATE DUE